Order, Crisis, and Redemption

Order, Crisis, and Redemption
Political Theology after Schmitt

PETER LANGFORD and SAUL NEWMAN

Cover image from WikiArt: *Mercury Passing Before the Sun* (1914 oil painting by Giacomo Balla).

Published by State University of New York Press, Albany

© 2023 State University of New York

All rights reserved

Printed in the United States of America

No part of this book may be used or reproduced in any manner whatsoever without written permission. No part of this book may be stored in a retrieval system or transmitted in any form or by any means including electronic, electrostatic, magnetic tape, mechanical, photocopying, recording, or otherwise without the prior permission in writing of the publisher.

For information, contact State University of New York Press, Albany, NY
www.sunypress.edu

Library of Congress Cataloging-in-Publication Data

Name: Langford, Peter, author. | Newman, Saul, author.
Title: Order, crisis, and redemption : political theology after Schmitt / Peter Langford and Saul Newman.
Description: Albany : State University of New York Press, [2023] | Includes bibliographical references and index.
Identifiers: ISBN 9781438493442 (hardcover : alk. paper) | ISBN 9781438493459 (ebook) | ISBN 9781438493435 (pbk. : alk. paper)
Further information is available at the Library of Congress.

10 9 8 7 6 5 4 3 2 1

Contents

Introduction		1
Chapter 1	From States of Emergency to Forms of the Political	17
Chapter 2	Who Is the Subject of Political Theology?	37
Chapter 3	Person, Identity, Transformation	57
Chapter 4	Political Theology and the Anthropocene	75
Chapter 5	Technology as Political Theology	97
Chapter 6	Political Theology and Democratic Constitutionalism	117
Chapter 7	Political Theology and Contemporary Challenges to Democratic Constitutionalism	137
Chapter 8	*Katechon* and the Problem of Order	161
Coda		185
Notes		191
References		211
Index		231

Introduction

Why add another text to the already vast corpus of literature on Carl Schmitt's political theology? It is exactly one hundred years ago that his influential work *Political Theology* (*Politische Theologie* [1922]) was published. Since then, it has served as a touchstone for subsequent inquiries into sovereignty and the secularization of theological into political concepts, producing no end of commentary. This has only grown in recent decades. Ever since the so-called "war on terror" and the unfolding state of emergency—the expansion of the security and surveillance state and the widespread deployment of extralegal measures to combat terrorism—Schmitt's theories of the sovereign state of exception and the crisis of liberal democracy have gained greater prominence, becoming the subject of numerous debates in political and legal theory, continental philosophy, and international relations (see for example Agamben, 2005a; Odysseos & Petito, 2007; Hooker, 2009; Galli, 2015; Vinx, 2015; Head, 2016; Meierhenrich & Simons, 2017; Scheuerman, 2020).

The ghost of Schmitt continues to loom large over contemporary political events. But why is this the case? What is it about this Weimar and Nazi era jurist and political theorist that seems to speak to us today? Why does this revenant appear every time the political order undergoes a crisis of legitimacy? What is there in Schmitt's political theology that makes it such a penetrating diagnostic tool for understanding moments of breakdown and rupture in the constitutional system, even if the political thrust of his analysis—that of revolutionary conservatism—ended up bringing about the destruction of the very system he purported to defend? Schmitt's eventual endorsement of National Socialism as a solution to a weakened and exhausted Weimar constitution, and his later participation in the Nazi regime, suggests that the desire for order and authority risks destroying the thing it is intended to protect. For Schmitt, living as he did through the instability of the Weimar period, the only solution was a strong, authoritarian, and decisive sovereign, a figure that, moreover, takes on a theological significance. This was, according to Schmitt, the only way of restoring order and legitimacy in a modernity characterized by liberal individualism, nihilistic consumerism, technological domination, godless atheism, and revolutionary agitation. Yet, the famous first line from *Political Theology*—"Sovereign is he who decides on the exception"—foreshadowed and essentially paved the way for the Nazi (counter)revolution that culminated in the total destruction of the German state, not to mention the extermination of European Jewry.[1]

Our impetus for writing this book was the COVID-19 pandemic, which also poses significant challenges to the current constitutional order. This is not, of course, to say that our time is equivalent to the prewar Weimar period. Nevertheless, the past two years have seen unprecedented emergency measures imposed by liberal democratic states to deal with a public health crisis, measures such as lockdowns and restrictions on public gatherings and social interactions, vaccine mandates, and new forms of surveillance that would be unthinkable at any other time and that entail a severe infringement of civil liberties. Many commentators, including, most controversially, Giorgio Agamben, invoked Schmitt's concept of the state of exception as a way of understanding these developments. Others (see Runciman, 2020, 2021) commented on the return of the strong Hobbesian state and on the way that crises such as pandemics reveal, as Schmitt himself maintained, absolute sovereignty as the hidden core of liberal democracies. However, the contemporary crisis of the liberal order is observed not only in the uncanny reappearance of the Schmittian sovereign state of exception but also in the broader tensions, fractures, and antagonisms, domestically and globally, that seem to have been accelerated by the pandemic. For instance, the social and economic inequalities revealed most sharply in: unequal access to vaccines and health care in different parts of the world; the return of the big state after a decade or more of neoliberal austerity; heightened geopolitical tensions and the fragmentation of the liberal international order into competing power blocs;[2] the rise of antiliberal populist forces in many parts of the world; new forms of authoritarian politics; the breakdown of trust in government and in the representative structures of democratic governance as seen in high levels of political disaffiliation and "post-truth" discourses; and the proliferation of wild conspiracy theories, anti-lockdown and anti-vaccine protests, as well as new forms of protest and dissent over issues like racial justice and the environment. Indeed, one of the most serious aspects of this crisis is the looming ecological catastrophe, which poses an absolute limit to our current way of life, and indeed to human existence itself, and yet which we have no idea—or at least not the will—to effectively deal with. We discuss many of these examples in the book—but they can all be seen as symptoms of the legitimation crisis of liberal democracies.

And what of the question of political theology itself? For Schmitt, political theology referred to the translation of theological concepts, like God and the miracle, into secular political and juridical concepts, like sovereignty and the legal exception. Schmitt thereby sought to confine theology to a narrow set of political and legal categories, and to mobilize it in support of an authoritarian sovereign state. For Schmitt, in the time of secularism, characterized by the collapse of theological authority, the political sovereign must become the new God. This harnessing of theology for the revalorization of political authority and legal order is the constant imperative in Schmitt, and it forms a continuum in his thinking from his early work on political theology and the Roman Catholic Church in the 1920s, to his postwar essay *The Nomos of the Earth* and his writing on the Christian figure of the *katechon*, right through to his last major published work, *Political Theology II*, in which he responded to critics such as Hans Blumenberg and Erik Peterson, defending his initial, and what Peterson considered entirely illegitimate,[3] politicization of theology. In engaging with political theology, Schmitt was responding to the modern condition of secularism and to the decline of theological sources of moral and political authority.

However, in more recent times, and in the context of what has come to be termed the "post-secular" condition (see Habermas, 2008), the line between the religious and the secular, the sacred and the profane has become increasingly blurred in ways both interesting and dangerous. Religious expression has become more prominent in public political life, taking both conservative and progressive forms, translating into modes of political engagement that are both authoritarian and emancipatory. This has forced renewed reflection on political theology and its current, contemporary meaning. One of the aims of this book is to extricate political theology from the sovereign-centric Schmittian paradigm it has largely been confined to. We want to think about the intersection of theology and politics beyond the sacralization of the sovereign state and thus to explore its radical and emancipatory potential. In other words, we want to think political theology *beyond* Schmitt. Certainly, we are not alone in this endeavor. Before, during, and after Schmitt's time, the relationship between the theological and the political had been configured in very different ways. Postwar theologians such as Karl Barth, J. B. Metz, Jürgen Moltmann, and many others recognized that "in the wake of Auschwitz" and the failures of the totalitarian state, Christian theology could no longer be legitimately recruited into the service of political sovereignty. Moreover, they sought to show how the church could accommodate itself to the conditions of secular liberal and democratic societies, and even play a role in supporting movements for social, racial, and environmental justice. We discuss a number of these alternative approaches to political theology. Our concern here is how political theology might be thought otherwise—not simply as a way of diagnosing the crisis of the current political order but also in thinking about alternatives informed by theological themes of justice and hope. Our point is that political theology has an important role to play in responding to some of the challenges we face today. For instance, coming to terms with the implications of the Anthropocene condition and the environmental crisis, or social injustice and the problem of state violence, or the legacy of slavery requires not only political investigation but also *theological reflection*. While we write as political and legal theorists rather than as theologians, we nonetheless believe that theology has something important to say about our current predicament.

As the title suggests, the three themes addressed in this book are *order*, *crisis*, and *redemption*. We develop a political theological framework to think about the nature of the current political order, how it falls into crisis, and how *we* (rather than the order itself) might be redeemed. So to be clear, the aim is not to find ways of preserving the liberal order in its current form, riven as it is with tensions and contradictions, such as that between the institutions of liberal democracy and the dynamics of the neoliberal capitalist economy. Rather, it is to show how the liberal order can be transformed in a more emancipatory way. We are fully aware of the seriousness of the situation and of the risks and dangers associated with the forces that are currently challenging this order. We find nothing redemptive or even vaguely appealing in communitarianism or in the return of strong national sovereignty as alternatives to globalization. Nor do we indulge in that easy radicalism and facile antiliberalism that welcomes the coming crisis as a path to salvation. As we argue in the book, Schmitt's antiliberalism and his authoritarian politics continue to have a strong affinity with the contemporary phenomenon of right-wing populism. His political theology has nothing redemptive about it and, in today's context, only perpetuates the coming disorder. The adoption of a critical distance to Schmitt also extends to, and is in contrast with, the presupposition by many thinkers on the left of the pertinence of Schmitt either for the critique of liberal internationalism or, as exemplified by Chantal Mouffe, in facilitating a renewal of the left-wing democratic project. Schmitt offers only authoritarian solutions to the problems of liberal democracy. Yet at the same time, we want to understand the ways in which the liberal political order—which is now in a process of decomposition—has engendered many of the problems it now faces. So by *redemption* we evoke the possibility at least of a different kind of order, a different kind of world: for instance, one organized around principles of social and environmental justice; cosmopolitan right; global solidarity; new, decentralized forms of democracy; and, above all, by the ethical principle of *care*—care for and conservation of the natural world and for nonhuman species with whose fate we are inevitably entangled. This requires a radically different approach to politics, and to political theology, to that which Schmitt affords us.

So the central argument we make in this book is that while Schmitt's political theology furnishes us with important insights into the nature of the current crisis, our situation at the same time demands a reflection on the limits of his paradigm. In other words, there are certain internal limitations to Schmitt's sovereign-centric model of political theology that prevent adequate comprehension of our current crisis. To give perhaps an obvious example, there is no room whatsoever in Schmitt's thought for any consideration of the Anthropocene and the ecological crisis—not simply because those concerns were not present in Schmitt's time, but more so because his understanding of political theology is entirely anthropocentric, deriving as it does from his, rather heterodox, interpretations of the Roman Catholic tradition. The sovereignty of God over the universe, and thus of the sovereign over society, finds its corollary in the absolute sovereignty of man over nature. Nature, for Schmitt, is essentially *human* nature, as this, rather than the natural world, is the exemplary domain of the theologico-political. It is this domain that is Schmitt's exclusive concern, and that is asserted against all attempts to present a different derivation of the (theologico-)political. The Schmittian insistence upon human nature—the relationship between humans—is entirely oriented by the rethinking of the theory of the state, constitution, and international law, from which the natural world is effectively absent. This is why we believe an alternative conception of political theology based on ecological awareness and entanglement, as we find, for instance, in thinkers like Catherine Keller and in process theologians like Alfred North Whitehead, to be necessary correctives to this lacuna in Schmitt's theory. So coming to terms with the parameters and implications of our current condition requires thinking both *with* and *beyond* Schmitt.

This book proceeds by an insistence upon the internal limitations and blind spots of Schmitt's political theology. The reflection upon these aspects of the Schmittian oeuvre ensures a more complex approach that resists the assumption of the direct, unproblematic applicability of Schmitt to contemporary phenomena. But why not simply bypass Schmitt altogether and turn to alternative approaches unencumbered by this Schmittian framework? Why summon up the ghost of Schmitt at all? There are a number of reasons why we consider Schmitt to still be important and to warrant renewed critical reflection. First, there are elements of his thinking that continue to be relevant today—such as his critique of technics and technological domination, which is perhaps even more pertinent in our technologically saturated age. We discuss this in chapter 5. Second, Schmitt's political theology shows how we might understand the recurring desire for sovereignty that haunts the political imagination. Sovereignty, in the era of a globalized economy, is more of a phantom than a coherent concept or institution, but the desire for it is no less real and intense for all that; indeed, perhaps it is more so. Recent political phenomena, such as the rise of populism, Brexit, the election of Trump and other far-right nationalist populist figures, can all be explained in terms of the projection of a fantasy image of sovereignty—expressed in terms of the restoration of national prestige ("Make America Great Again"), the repatriation of lawmaking powers and the control of borders ("Take Back Control"), and the idea of a strong executive state that can cut through the mire of bureaucratic complexity and act as a direct expression of the "will of the people" ("Get Brexit Done" or "Drain the Washington Swamp"). We address much of this in chapter 7. The renewed desire for sovereignty, which ensues from the democratic deficit—the sense of disempowerment and disaffiliation that many people feel today—is something that emerges whenever the political order experiences a crisis of legitimacy, when people feel that their elected governments no longer represent their interests, are unable to solve their problems, or cannot protect them from the buffeting winds of globalization. While the solution Schmitt offers to this democratic deficit is normatively deeply undesirable, and indeed unsustainable in the contemporary world, his politico-theological analysis nevertheless points to a real problem in actually existing liberal democracies. Finally, Schmitt's political theology, through its distinctive form of analysis, introduces a radical questioning of the foundations of political legitimacy, legal authority, subjectivity, ethics, technology, democracy, and the relationship between religious and nonreligious spheres of life, that contains within it the possibility of its own radical transformation. In other words, whether we like it or not, Schmitt's political theology is the challenge we cannot avoid, the test we must confront, in order to determine, *beyond and after* Schmitt, responses to our current predicament.

Methodology and Approach

This book focuses on Schmitt's political theology as *the* central thematic in his thought. The concern with the relationship between religious and political spheres of experience might be seen as the "red thread" that runs throughout Schmitt's intellectual career. Of course, Schmitt engages with this problematic in different ways and from multiple perspectives—whether through legal and sociological categories, the question of miracles, the "spirit" of technology, the mysterious figure of, or the historical significance and political role of, the Roman Catholic Church—but there can be little doubt that the relationship between theology and politics was his constant preoccupation. It is precisely because of the preeminence of this concept in Schmitt's oeuvre—not to mention the vast influence his thinking has had on subsequent debates in this area—that we have sought to consider his political theology anew with the aim of revealing its tensions, limitations, and aporias and to consider its relevance to the contemporary world. Doing so requires an engagement not only with his famous and seminal 1922 work but also with a series of lesser-known works from the same period (such as *Political Romanticism* [1919] and *Roman Catholicism and Political Form* [1923]), his prison writings after World War II (*Ex Captivitate Salus* [1945–1947]), and works from much later periods (such as *Political Theology II* [1970]). It also means unearthing subterranean dialogues with interlocutors like the philosopher Leo Strauss, the Dada artist Hugo Ball, revolutionary anarchists like Mikhail Bakunin, the rabbinical thinker Jacob Taubes, postwar German theologians like J. B. Metz and Jürgen Moltmann, and the legal scholar and justice of the Federal Constitutional Court, Ernst-Wolfgang Böckenförde. It is only by broadening out our investigations in this manner that we can form a more complete, variegated picture of Schmitt's political theology and gain a clearer sense of its contours.

Schmitt's political theology is oriented entirely around the problem of order and its preservation. The principle of authority—whether embodied in the form of the Roman Empire, or the medieval Christian European order, or the modern nation-state—had to be preserved at all costs. The Apocalypse—whether expressed as the moment of biblical revelation or the messianic promise of revolutionary redemption—must be deferred. As Taubes once put it: "[Schmitt] prays for the preservation of the state, since if, God forbid, it doesn't remain, chaos breaks loose, or even worse, the Kingdom of God!" (2003, pp. 69–70). To do so, politics has to draw on theological ideas, recruit into its service religious institutions, and inspire sentiments of faith, devotion, and sacrifice. Central to Schmitt's political theology is the veneration of sovereignty and the fear of anarchy. However, as we endeavor to show in this book, Schmitt's "radical conservatism" also meant the preparedness to invoke exceptional measures that risked destroying, in autoimmune fashion, the very order they are intended to preserve. In this way, sovereignty—unhinged from its normal constitutional constraints—starts to resemble the anarchy it seeks to prevent. We explore this autoimmune tendency in Schmitt's political theology in greater detail throughout the book.

In investigating the development of Schmitt's thinking—in exploring its tensions, limitations, and moments of fracture—we intend to advance the debate on political theology and to take it beyond the sovereign paradigm in which it has largely remained trapped. Of course, as we have already indicated, political theology as a broad field of inquiry has, since Schmitt's time, become much more diversified, engaging with different concerns, from economics (see Agamben, 2011) to the natural environment (see Keller, 2018b). It has embraced "secular" and emancipatory causes, from ecology and social justice (see Moltmann, 1985; Metz, 1969; Gutiérrez, 1998) to decolonization and black liberation (see Heinrichs, 2019; Cone, 2019). Where Schmitt sought to reunite church and state—or at least to mobilize religious authority in support of political authority—other political theologians have been much more attuned to the dangers of this ideological alliance, proposing instead that the church play a public role yet one that was independent and critical of state authority (see Moltmann, 1971; Graham, 2013). However, from a political theory perspective, political theology is still largely beholden to Schmitt's sovereign-centric way of thinking (see Kahn, 2011; Yelle, 2019; Rasch, 2019). In addressing

Schmittian themes of political order and legitimacy, but from a radically different position, we aim to transform the terms of this discussion. We hope to show that political theology can be taken in more radical directions; that it can be reoriented toward the goals of justice and human (and nonhuman) emancipation.

In identifying the limitations of Schmitt's approach, we must also acknowledge some of our own. Our focus is mostly on Christian political theology. The reason for this is obviously that Christianity, and particularly Roman Catholicism, is the tradition in which Schmitt was immersed, even if his Catholicism was somewhat heterodox and, even, according to Peterson, "pagan." However, there are important non-Christian traditions of political theology, particularly in Judaism, for instance, in the thought of Hermann Cohen (see Rashkover & Kavka, 2013), and in the more mystical tendencies of Weimar-era thinkers like Franz Rosenzweig and Gershom Scholem (see Jacobson, 2003). Indeed, there are many fruitful dialogues and critical exchanges that could have been opened up between Schmittian political theology and forms of Jewish political theology that go in radically different, post-sovereign directions: from Cohen's neo-Kantian cosmopolitanism to the anarchistic theopolitics of Martin Buber (see Brody, 2018).[4] While the question of Jewish political theology as a possible response to Schmitt has by no means been neglected in this book—see the debates with key interlocutors such as Strauss (discussed in chapter 2), Benjamin (discussed in chapter 7), and Taubes (discussed in chapter 8)—there is much more to be said on this subject. Moreover, political theology has in recent times become more diversified, with an interest in non-European religious contexts such as Islam (see Campanini & Di Donato, 2021), Buddhism (see Singh, 2012), and Hinduism (see Basu, 2020). For reasons of space, and in order to retain the focus on Schmitt, we have not engaged with these other traditions. However, bringing these into dialogue with Schmitt may well prove productive avenues for future research.

Structure of the Book

The theme of the crisis of the liberal democratic order is expanded upon in chapter 1. This chapter considers whether the state of emergency—which is central to Schmitt's political theology—is an adequate way of capturing the political *form* of contemporary society. Here we reflect on some recent debates about the pertinence and validity of Schmitt's concept of the sovereign state of exception for thinking about the state's response to the pandemic. In contextualizing this question, we then turn in detail to Schmitt himself and to his politico-theological defense of strong sovereignty. We explore three early works written around the same time: *Political Theology I* (1922), *Roman Catholicism and Political Form* (1923), and *The Crisis of Parliamentary Democracy* (1923). These key texts crystallize all the significant elements of Schmitt's conservative political theology: the sovereign state of exception as an extralegal dimension of state power; the translation of theological ideas into secular political and legal categories; the political role of the Catholic Church in representing and unifying society; and, lastly, Schmitt's rejection of liberal parliamentarianism as antithetical to authentic democratic identity. These ideas can be seen both as a response to the immediate and acute political crisis of the Weimar Republic in Germany, as well as to the deeper question of nihilism and the loss of firm moral and political coordinates that Schmitt detected in secular modernity. Our argument in this chapter is that, while certain parallels can be drawn with our situation today, Schmitt's antidote to secular modernity is normatively and politically untenable in the current crisis. Our critique extends here to certain contemporary thinkers who unproblematically adopt Schmitt's theories as a means of resisting (neo) liberal technocracy and as a way of renewing democracy today.

Our critical engagement with the limits of Schmitt's political theology is developed over subsequent chapters. In chapter 2, we ask the question, *Who is the subject of Schmitt's political theology?* In other words, what exactly is political theology engaged with, what is its field of operation, which political identities does it affirm, and who or what is it opposed to? The ambiguities of Schmitt's thinking are first revealed through the engagement of two central, early interlocutors: the founding member of Dada, and subsequent reaffirmed Catholic, Hugo Ball and the political philosopher Leo Strauss. The heterodox theological conservatism that orients Ball's essay on Schmitt's political theology seeks to proceed beyond the limits of the theological in Schmitt by according to the Roman Catholic Church the primary position in Schmitt's political theology, thereby absorbing the political into the theological. In contrast, Strauss approaches Schmitt with the presumption of the fundamental opposition of theology and political philosophy. Thus, Strauss considers the radical gesture of foundation—the friend/enemy opposition—in *The Concept of the Political* (1927) within the domain of political philosophy, emphasizing the limit of Schmitt's gesture due to its dependence upon the conceptual framework of liberalism for its articulation. This limit is to be overcome for Strauss by a return to Hobbes, which Schmitt can only intimate. Ball and Strauss represent the preliminary attempts to identify the limits of the subject of Schmittian political theology and seek to think beyond them, through their respective emphases upon theology and political philosophy. Yet, it is the limits of these critiques—a project of Catholic renewal (Ball) and the renewal of political philosophy as the perpetual re-presentation of the opposition of theology and philosophy (Strauss)—that, in turn, lead to a discussion of the contemporary subject of political theology. Here, we commence from an era where liberalism has largely been displaced by neoliberalism. In this displacement, neoliberalism is antipolitical in a sense diametrically opposed to Schmitt: it is a depoliticization and neutralization of the question of *justice*. In response, the subject of political theology, informed by Roberto Esposito's deconstruction of the duality of person and thing, becomes a different understanding of subjectivity as situated within a world that is not merely coextensive with a legal framework based on property and rights and opens onto a broader understanding of ethical responsibility and justice.

The theme of personhood and subjectivity is further developed in chapter 3, in which we seek to understand, from a theological perspective, how identity—of persons and communities—can be transformed in an emancipatory way. Here we engage in a close reading of Paul's Letter to Philemon, which is an intercession on behalf of a slave, Onesimus, to his former master, Philemon, in which Paul urges Philemon to treat Onesimus no longer as a slave but as a brother and spiritual equal—thus suggesting the possibility of the transformation of existing social and political relationships. While the letter leaves this possible transformation ambiguous and unconfirmed, especially within the broader context of the slave economy of the Roman Empire, we explore the emancipatory potential of Paul's gesture. This involves the letter's interpretation in relation to contemporary considerations of decolonization and the legacy of slavery. Despite its limitations and ambiguities, the letter expresses a sensitivity to injustice and the ethical responsibility to transform a situation of domination into noninjurious social relations. In exploring the radical potential of this idea, and how it might be more broadly applied, we develop a politics and ethics of fraternity through a discussion of Étienne Balibar, Roberto Esposito, and Jean-Luc Nancy. We consider fraternity or brotherhood to be a less restrictive and more emancipatory foundation for political theology than Schmitt's friend/enemy opposition.

Chapter 4 focuses on the Anthropocene and the looming ecological catastrophe as a major factor in the current crisis of the liberal political and economic order. The time in which man becomes the main geological actor, with disastrous consequences for the natural environment, not only poses urgent questions about human survival and the capacity of our economic and political systems to manage this crisis, but it also raises profound questions about what it actually means to be human, and the extent to which our fate is deeply entangled with natural ecosystems and nonhuman species—a fact that has been brought home to us in dramatic fashion in the age of zoonotic viruses like COVID-19. In this chapter, we argue that Schmitt's political theology is entirely anthropocentric, based as it is on a conception of human sovereignty derived from the Judeo-Christian tradition, and thus lacks the critical capacity for adequately thinking the Anthropocene. Furthermore, the foundation for law or *nomos*, in Schmitt's theory, is one of land appropriation and the domination of territory, thus mirroring the violent and extractive relationship humanity has established with the natural world. Here we develop an alternative orientation for political theology, one that accommodates a different kind of relationship with nature and nonhuman entities. We engage first with thinkers like Agamben, Deleuze and Guattari, and Felice Ciamatti in order to deconstruct the anthropomorphic dualism between man and animal. We then turn to new currents in ecopolitical theology, and to thinkers like Catherine Keller and Bruno Latour, in order to construct a different relationship to the natural world and to our ethical responsibilities to the environment—one that stresses ecological interdependence and entanglement, as well as *repoliticization*.

Chapter 5 focuses on the theme of technology and political theology—or technology *as* political theology. Here we explore Schmitt's critique of technicity or technological domination, as outlined in his early essay "The Age of Neutralizations and Depoliticizations" (1929)—a critique that is continually reemphasized throughout his later texts, including his final published work *Political Theology II*. Schmitt's ongoing concern with the depoliticizing and totalizing effects of a technologically saturated modernity can therefore be understood as a central theme of his political theology. In this chapter, we consider the continued pertinence of Schmitt's critique to the contemporary and unprecedented domination of digital technology, rather than to the industrial and analogue technologies to which the Schmittian critique is addressed. We interrogate Schmitt's conception of the relationship between technology and political theology through the comparative examination of the work of Peter Sloterdijk and Bernard Stiegler. Both Sloterdijk and Stiegler accord technology a central importance and respond to its further transformation into digital and biotechnological forms. This further transformation involves an acknowledgment of its profound alteration of the distinction between the human and the technological. We then proceed to examine the divergences between Sloterdijk and Stiegler. We show how Sloterdijk returns to Schmittian motifs of enmity and national homogeneity stripped of theological association. In contrast, in Stiegler, the theological is replaced with a notion of *spirit* that, as the insistence upon the primacy of conscience—the theoretical and practical basis of individual and collective consciousness—is the repository of a noninstrumental, ethical relationship between the human and the technological.

Chapter 6 examines the relationship between political theology and democratic constitutionalism. While most of the scholarship on Schmitt's constitutional theory focuses on his pre-war Weimar writings, we explore his complex relationship with the postwar German Federal Republic and with one of his key interlocutors, Ernst-Wolfgang Böckenförde. As someone deeply influenced by Schmitt, and part of his postwar intellectual circle, Böckenförde nevertheless elaborated an important critique of Schmitt— one that transforms the understanding and position of political theology in relation to constitutional social democracy. The transformation shifts political theology from the extrinsic Schmittian position to one *within* the framework of constitutional democracy. The internal critique, and the accompanying shift, are considered through Böckenförde's transformation of political theology—the Böckenförde-Diktum—into the historical process of an inherently problematic and fragile separation of state and religion, the explicit juridical integration and regulation of the state of exception within a democratic constitution, the deflation of the Schmittian opposition between democracy and liberalism (*Rechtstaat*), and the reduction of the Schmittian opposition between discussion and decision as the counterpart of the deintensification of the friend/enemy distinction. The difficulties of the Böckenfördian theory of constitutional social democracy, flowing from the internal critique of Schmitt, will then be revealed through the presence of continuing tensions underlying an apparently coherent, unified theory.

Chapter 7 continues this investigation of tensions inherent to democratic constitutionalism with a discussion of contemporary political mobilizations against the constitutional order in the form of right-wing populism as well as new protest movements for social, racial, and environmental justice. Both forms of politics call into question, albeit in radically different ways and to entirely different ends, the legitimacy of the liberal democratic system, and both can be seen as symptomatic of the failure of its representative functions. We show, first, how the key elements of Schmitt's political theology—the critique of liberal parliamentarianism, the identitarian, exclusionary, and authoritarian model of democracy based on the unmediated "will of the people" (articulated through the figure of the leader), strong sovereignty, and the friend/enemy opposition—all come into play in contemporary right-wing populism. We contrast this with extraparliamentary movements of the left today, which challenge the liberal democratic order in a different way, in the name of emancipation and greater justice for minorities or for the natural environment. These may be seen as a form of "post-secular" politics. Comprehension of this demands a different kind of political theology, one that can call into question state power and violence as well as social injustice and environmental destruction. Here we reconstruct religious themes of messianic hope and the promise of justice and redemption through a consideration of postwar Christian theology in J. B. Metz and Jürgen Moltmann, the utopian Marxism of Ernst Bloch, and the mystical anarchism of Gustav Landauer.

The final chapter, chapter 8, explores the key theme of the *katechon* as central to political theology. This enigmatic and obscure figure from Pauline theology, which restrains the coming of the Antichrist and yet, in so doing, also delays the Second Coming of Christ and the final triumph of good over evil, we take to be of central importance for thinking about politics today, particularly in our apocalyptic times. The *katechon*, we show, was also fundamental to Schmitt's counterrevolutionary politicization of Christian theology. In this chapter, we take full account of the ambiguities of the *katechon*, showing how it can be given reactionary or revolutionary meanings, how it can be used to maintain the status quo or to carve out an autonomous space for resistant and transformative politics. However, here we offer a reading of the *katechon* that is different from Agamben, who invests little value in it, seeing it as something that obscures the state of lawlessness (the reign of the Antichrist whose presence must instead be revealed). Rather, we argue that in the "end-times" of ecological catastrophe and political and economic crisis, the *katechon* enables an alternative theorization of radical politics—one that is based on caring for the world that exists and bringing a halt to the blind, nihilistic, and destructive drives of neoliberal capitalism. Our claim is that it is precisely the concept of national sovereignty itself that, so far from being a bulwark or restraint against the growing anomie of the world, actually hastens its arrival. Here we propose an alternative understanding of the *katechon* that we develop through the idea of planetary care and through a radical ethics and politics of cosmopolitanism. Thinking the *katechon* in this way allows an altogether different rendering of political theology.

1

From States of Emergency to Forms of the Political

In a series of interventions following the coronavirus lockdowns imposed by the Italian government in early 2020, philosopher Giorgio Agamben invoked Schmitt's notion of the sovereign state of exception to characterize the unprecedented restrictions on freedom and social life and the extraordinary powers accrued by governments: "The other thing, no less disturbing than the first, is that the epidemic is clearly showing that the state of exception, which governments began to accustom us to years ago, has become an authentically normal condition" (2020a). Such measures, he argued, were not only disproportionate but indicated a worrying tendency of governments to exploit emergency situations to extend their power. The state of exception was becoming the normal paradigm of governing.

Agamben's intervention sparked fierce controversy, with a number of interlocutors accusing him of downplaying the seriousness of the virus and even indulging in conspiracy theories about the way governments manipulate emergencies and deliberately provoke a state of fear (see Benvenuto, 2020; Berg, 2020; Nancy, 2020). Yet, there is much to agree with in Agamben's analysis. The measures and restrictions imposed by governments around the world were indeed unprecedented and seemed to blur the line between liberal democracies and authoritarian regimes. That governments were to consign their entire populations to a form of house arrest, to severely limit public gatherings (everything from funerals to protests), and to disrupt normal social life and interactions to the extent that they did, with very little public debate or accountability, is an extraordinary development and one that should give cause for concern.

The fact that this was largely accepted without complaint, aside from some isolated protests, shows the degree to which the biopolitical imperative is dominant. In the contemporary biopolitical era, in which biological life must be preserved at all costs, even at the cost of everything that makes life worth living, freedom is readily sacrificed to public health. As Agamben says, life in modern societies is increasingly reduced to bare life, that is, life stripped of any of the essential qualities that make a human life distinctive.

However, is Schmitt's theory of the state of exception—in which the sovereign suspends the constitutional order in times of emergency—really the most appropriate way of theorizing the problem of state power today? Certainly, as seen with the pandemic, governments use crises to justify emergency measures that would be otherwise unacceptable, bypassing constitutional constraints and parliamentary accountability and drastically limiting individual rights and freedoms. Such actions would seem to reveal the very core of sovereignty—the ultimate prerogative of the state to exert its authority over society without the legal constraints that would normally apply. At the same time, what is striking about the current situation is the way that governments have to constantly defer to medical and scientific authorities to justify their decisions. The scenes of government ministers holding news conferences flanked by their chief medical officers and deferring to the advice of scientists, health experts, and epidemiologists is indicative of the way that power in the modern biopolitical age is not unilaterally applied in the way that Schmitt had in mind, but is, rather, shared between the political sovereign and scientific authorities. Decision-making power, which Schmitt believed was the sole prerogative of the political sovereign, is today diffused and mediated through a variety of bodies, institutions, and discourses that derive their authority from scientific knowledge. To speak in Lacanian terms, the "Big Other" today, that which underpins and legitimizes the symbolic order, is not the exceptional authority of the sovereign but the epistemological authority of the scientist. That governments have to appeal to "expert opinion" and scientific guidance points to the way that in the modern age of biopolitics the purely political power of the sovereign has been displaced by other sites of power and knowledge, new sources of epistemological authority. As Agamben himself put it, "Science has become our time's religion, the thing that people believe that they believe in" (2021, p. 49). When governments are obliged to justify their decisions and policies by appeals to the technocratic expertise of scientists and doctors, there is very little of the genuine Schmittian sovereign decision in evidence.

For Schmitt, sovereignty is defined by the right to make the ultimate and final decision. Decision-making authority is at its very core. However, what is immediately apparent with contemporary sovereigns is their inability to make genuine decisions. Decisions that are made do not issue directly from themselves and from their own authority but, on the contrary, derive their legitimacy from external and more anonymous sources of authority and expertise. There is nothing of the *person* of the sovereign that Schmitt saw as being encapsulated in the moment of decision. Today's political leaders often appear incapable of acting decisively and taking responsibility for their decisions: decisions are endlessly deferred or reversed in a chaotic way, as we have seen in the often confused and incompetent response on the part of many governments to the pandemic. Today's sovereigns are rather more like the Baroque sovereign of Walter Benjamin's *The Origin of German Tragic Drama* (*Ursprung des deutschen Trauerspiels*). So far from the decisive, heroic sovereign imagined by Schmitt, Benjamin describes the absolutist sovereigns of the Baroque era as "being almost incapable of making a decision," as always changing their minds, subject to wild inconsistencies and volatile emotions that cause them to "sway about like torn and flapping banners" (Benjamin, 1998, p. 71). In the Baroque world described by Benjamin, no longer guided by firm theological coordinates—a world of contingency, insecurity, haunted by the ever-present specter of catastrophe, much like our experience of the world today—sovereigns must be able to effectively respond to emergencies and to act decisively. Yet they prove themselves utterly inadequate to the task. Sovereigns are impotent rulers who can neither reign *nor* govern. Much in the same way, sovereignty today comes across as highly dysfunctional and disordered. If the current situation can be described as a "state of exception," it is more like an *administrative* state of exception, and a chaotic, incompetent, and directionless one at that.

This chapter will explore the current crisis of legitimacy through Schmitt's political theology. Schmitt, writing as he was during the crises of the Weimar Republic in the 1920s and '30s—a situation not without parallels to ours today—was primarily concerned with the question of legitimacy and with the need, as he saw it, to reaffirm a strong form of state authority to defend the political order against forces of destabilization. However, it was precisely his attempt to reassert sovereignty through the idea of the state of exception that essentially foreshadowed and paved the way for the Nazi (counter)revolution that destroyed the constitutional order and, ultimately, the German state itself. This is illustrative of the autoimmune logic of the state of exception: just as a biological organism's immune system goes into overdrive in response to the threat of infection, and ends up destroying the body it was designed to protect, so a political order that tries to defend itself against various threats to its stability often ends up violating the very principles and institutions from which it derives its authority.[1] The sovereign state of exception, as Schmitt conceives it, is a response to the legitimation crisis of the political order—but it also hastens and intensifies this crisis, ultimately undermining the state's normative and institutional framework. Our aim in this chapter is to evaluate the pertinence today of Schmitt's sovereign-centric political theology as a way of responding to the current crisis of legitimacy. We will argue that due to the internal limitations of Schmitt's thought, his theory of the sovereign state of exception, while it has some diagnostic value, offers little in the way of a viable solution.

Schmitt and the Weimar Crisis

To consider the relevance and salience of Schmitt's theory of sovereignty, we must understand the context in which he was writing and the challenges to which he was responding. Schmitt was speaking to a similar crisis of political legitimacy, that of the postwar German Weimar Republic of the 1920s and early 1930s. This was a constitutional order threatened by economic and political instability, weakened by parliamentary dysfunction, and assailed on all sides by the radical left and the right. The instability of the Weimar Republic was emblematic of the broader trends of the modern period. Schmitt saw the world around him as characterized by the nihilistic drift and disorder brought on by the combined forces of technology, bourgeois individualism, philosophies of immanence, and revolutionary politics. He depicts a flattened-out world without meaning or substance, without any coherent image to unify it, lacking a transcendental point of order and authority that could stabilize it. Schmitt is essentially describing the modern condition of liberal secularism, where the metaphysical structure once provided by religion was absent. Without this sacred, transcendental dimension, there was nothing to guarantee the legitimacy and authority of the political order. Political authority was entirely subsumed by technological and economic imperatives. Rather than being genuinely sovereign and standing above society, bestowing upon it order and meaning, the modern state had become the servant of society, a mere technical instrument and an administrative machine, its authority reined in by rules, procedures, and constitutional constraints.

In an essay from 1929, "The Age of Neutralizations and Depoliticizations" (2007a, pp. 80–96), Schmitt describes the progressive displacement and neutralization of the political sphere. He outlines four successive historical stages of secularization, which he sees as intellectual and cultural domains from which concepts derive their distinct meaning. The transition from theology to metaphysics from the sixteenth to the seventeenth century was followed by the period of Enlightenment rationalism in the eighteenth century, which was in turn superseded by the age of industrial capitalism and bourgeois economics in the nineteenth century. The twentieth century experienced the most radical form of political neutralization with the reign of technology—what Schmitt calls *technicity* (p. 85). From each of these domains the state derives its historically specific meaning and legitimacy, yet with diminishing degrees of clarity. The theological age provided the strongest foundation for political legitimacy because in it the friend/enemy opposition could be distinguished most clearly. However, this opposition, central to Schmitt's understand of the political (see 2007b) becomes less discernible with each successive period. In the technical age, we had reached the final point of political dissolution and obscurity. Because technology appeals to everyone, because it presents itself as simply a neutral instrument that can used by everyone for whatever purpose, it "appears to be a domain of peace, understanding, and reconciliation" (p. 91). However—and here is the paradox—it is precisely *because* of its usefulness as an instrument that technology is not neutral, at least not in the usual sense, but rather a totalizing, *totalitarian* rationality: "But the neutrality of technology is something other than the neutrality of all former domains. Technology is always only an instrument and weapon; precisely because it serves all, it is not neutral. No single decision can be derived from the immanence of technology, least of all for neutrality" (p. 91). Schmitt describes technology as having a *spirit*, a kind of malevolent force: "The spirit of technicity, which has led to the mass belief in an anti-religious activism, is still spirit; perhaps an evil and demonic spirit, but not one which can be dismissed as mechanistic and attributed to technology. . . . Such a belief can be called fantastic and satanic, but not simply dead, spiritless, or mechanized soullessness" (p. 94).

Schmitt's diagnosis of the modern age of technicity speaks also to our experience today, when the domination of technology over our lives has reached unparalleled levels and has become our metaphysics, our belief system. We will have more to say about this in a later chapter (5). However, Schmitt's point here is that the reign of technics, because it is all-encompassing and because it claims to provide a rational, technical solution to every problem, it eclipses the political dimension, depriving it of its autonomous decision-making authority: "Neither a political question nor a political answer can be derived from purely technical principles and perspectives" (p. 92).

Schmitt's solution to the nihilism of modernity and the problem of political neutralization was to affirm the idea of strong sovereignty. It is only a strong, decisive sovereign that can give order and meaning to society and provide its legal and political institutions with legitimacy. The sovereign decision is what authorizes the law. It defines borders, boundaries, and limits, distinguishing inside from outside, friend from enemy. It imposes order on society and defines the contours of the political community. Just as for Hobbes, the sovereign must reside outside the law in order to guarantee its authority, the Schmittian sovereign must reserve for itself an exceptional space outside normal constitutional constraints in order to preserve the political order. Schmitt is, above all, a theorist of order. In a time of disorder and crisis, the only way to restore the legitimacy of the constitution was to invoke a moment of decision-making authority that was not bound by its rules. Yet, as we have said, Schmitt's authoritarian and decisionist understanding of sovereignty ended up undermining the very order it was intended to protect. The state of exception, based on various articles of the Weimar constitution (most notably Article 48, which allowed the chancellor to rule by decree), was exploited by the Nazis to declare a state of emergency and assume absolute power under the Enabling Act of 1933—a measure Schmitt approved of. In Schmitt's eyes, such a usurpation of an exhausted and weakened constitutional regime was the only way of preserving political order. To protect the political order, its constitutional baggage must therefore be cast off. Schmitt saw the Nazi state of exception as a legitimate (counter)revolution, and a genuine expression of the constituent or lawmaking power.

It should not surprise us that Schmitt's conservatism was perfectly reconcilable with his endorsement of the Nazi revolution and its wholesale destruction of the legal order. The notion of the "conservative revolution"—associated with figures like Schmitt, Jünger, Spengler—finds its expression today in the likes of Steve Bannon, Trump's former political adviser, who talked about tearing down the "administrative state," or Dominic Cummings, Boris Johnson's former political adviser, who spoke in similar tones. Far-right populist politicians—Hungary's Viktor Orbán would be a good example—routinely declare war on the rule of law and independent judiciaries, which they accuse of hampering executive power. *To destroy in order to conserve* is the mantra of today's conservative revolutionaries.

Schmitt's Political Theology

To understand this peculiar response to the legitimation crisis, we must come to terms with Schmitt's political theology and its preoccupation with the themes of order, authority, and representation. These themes are reflected in three closely interlinked texts that he wrote around the same time—*Political Theology I* (1922), *Roman Catholicism and Political Form* (1923), and *The Crisis of Parliamentary Democracy* (1923)—and that form a kind of triptych. They reveal a consistent core in his thinking, which is the idea that if order is to be preserved, a radical decision must be made.

The idea of the sovereign decision is central to *Political Theology I*. The text begins with the famous line: "Sovereign is he who decides on the exception" (2005, p. 1). For Schmitt, what really defines sovereignty, what is at its core as a political and juridical concept, is the right to decide unilaterally on exceptional situations—that is, to determine what actually constitutes an emergency of the state (*Ausnahmezustand*) and to decide what to do about it. In response to serious emergencies, the state must have the authority to suspend the constitutional order and rule by decree. The central claim here is that the sovereign state has to be able to act outside the normal constitutional rules and constraints if it is to protect the constitution from various threats. The very survival of the constitution depended on the sovereign right to suspend it. This was something that liberal political thinkers and positive law theorists, who insisted that political sovereignty be regulated by legal norms and constitutional constraints, simply did not grasp.

Schmitt's theory of the sovereign decision emerges on the basis of two earlier texts. In *Political Romanticism* (1919) Schmitt distinguished between genuine conservatives, who were able to make real decisions, and political romantics, who were not. Genuine conservatives—counterrevolutionary figures like Edmund Burke, Joseph de Maistre, and Louis de

Bonald—opposed the French Revolution, siding with the old order and seeking to preserve traditional institutions. They were prepared to take a side in this conflict. By contrast, those of a more romantic temperament, like Adam Müller, were "occasionalists" who lacked the capacity for action or genuine decision. Their inconstancy rendered them impotent and led to a romantic detachment from the affairs of the world. Romantics of this kind were also conservatives, but only in a half-hearted and politically inconsequential way (see Schmitt, 1986). Real conservatism, for Schmitt, involved choosing a side and taking responsibility for that decision, even resorting to authoritarian means to preserve the existing political order. A similar theme is pursed in *Dictatorship* (1921), in which the counter-revolutionary decision takes on the more distinctive shape of legal dictatorship. Here Schmitt addressed the infamous Article 48 of the Weimar constitution of 1919, which allowed the Reich president to suspend the constitution. Schmitt drew a distinction between *commissarial dictatorship*, in which the constitution was merely suspended for a limited period of time in a temporary state of emergency, and *sovereign dictatorship*, where the constitution was permanently abolished and a new one established. This really refers to the distinction between *constituted* and *constituting* power: that is, the power to defend and enforce the existing constitution, even if that means suspending it temporarily, and the power to overthrow and replace the constitution. Yet, this distinction is less significant than it seems. We have seen from the history of revolutions that the destruction of the old order always results in the construction of a new one, which in turn needs to be defended against new revolutionary enemies. Thus, there is a continual oscillation between constitution-making and constitution-preserving power. In a similar sense, the distinction that Schmitt sought to establish between commissarial and sovereign dictatorship ultimately collapses and becomes meaningless: just as commissarial dictators risk destroying the constitutional order they seek to defend, sovereign dictators, in abolishing the constitutional order, will only put a new one in its place. As Walter Benjamin (1986) showed in "Critique of Violence" from 1921—a text that Agamben maintains was the provocation for Schmitt's *Political Theology*—what remains intact in the constant oscillation between *lawmaking* and *law-preserving* violence, between revolutionary destruction and political-legal consolidation, is sovereign power itself, in all its potential and actual violence.

This idea of the sovereign state of exception is fully developed in *Political Theology I*. According to Schmitt, the sovereign decision on the exception is defined in law and derives authorization from it, but at the same time exceeds it. Sovereignty is, as he puts it, a "borderline concept" (p. 5). The sovereign exception cannot be wholly accounted for by the norm, nor does it derive from it. At the same time, the sovereign exception only has meaning in relation to the legal norm it transgresses. Sovereignty is a liminal concept—it inhabits a "gray zone," being inside and outside the law at the same time. This paradoxical logic emerges as part of a critique of liberal constitutionalism and, more specifically, of neo-Kantian positive law theorists like Hans Kelsen, who sought to identify the state with the law and developed a theory of positive law as wholly derived from a self-contained, self-referential series of norms. The problem with these theories, for Schmitt, was that, in trying to rule out the exception, they failed to acknowledge the way that legal norms and rules actually presuppose an exterior that grounds them, that constitutes their limit and has the authority to apply them to specific situations. In other words, sovereignty was the authority to decide when and how a norm is applied. It is the sovereign exception that therefore guarantees the totality of law (p. 13).[2] Moreover, unlike the norm, the exception embodies a certain contingency and vitality and should therefore be seen as prevailing over the rule. It has an existential quality that is lacking in the norm (see also Marder, 2010). As Schmitt says: "The exception is more interesting than the rule. The rule proves nothing; the exception proves everything. It confirms not only the rule but also its existence, which derives only from the exception. In the exception the power of real life breaks through the crust of a mechanism that has become torpid by repetition" (p. 15). In insisting on the supremacy of the exception over the norm, and in showing that the authority and efficacy of the legal order is reliant upon a sovereign decision that exceeds its limits, Schmitt is not only defining juridical and political concepts but actively defending the idea of strong, authoritarian sovereignty as a solution to the weakness of the existing constitutional order.

This is also reflected in the other major theme of the essay, which is that of political theology itself. In a secular world that lacks religious sources of authority, which no longer believes in God or recognizes the legitimacy of the church, new sources of order and authority must be found. However, if the political sovereign is to play this role, it must take on a kind of theological illumination. Schmitt is not advocating a theocracy or some kind of return to the old doctrine of divine right; such a return would be impossible. Yet, the political sovereign must fill the void, the place of the sacred left vacant by religion. It must have the transcendental properties of God. This is why Schmitt seeks to understand the modern state through theological categories: "All significant concepts of the modern theory of the state are secularized theological concepts not only because of their historical development—in which they were transferred from theology to the theory of the state, whereby, for example, the omnipotent God became the omnipotent lawgiver—but also because of their systematic structure, the recognition of which is necessary for a sociological consideration of these concepts. The exception in jurisprudence is analogous to the miracle in theology" (p. 36). There is a structural parallel between the God who transcends the universe and the sovereign state that transcends social relations. And just as God can suspend the laws of nature through the miracle, so the sovereign can suspend the constitutional order through the exception. In drawing these analogies between theological and political categories, Schmitt is doing more than simply proposing, as he puts it, a "sociology" of political and juridical concepts, following his "teacher" Max Weber. Weber, of course, was also concerned with the question of legitimacy in modern secular societies that were characterized by an experience of "disenchantment" and the breakdown of traditional sources of authority. Schmitt accepted Weber's secularization thesis but rejected its liberal conclusions. Rather, the sovereign state, if it is to provide a source of legitimacy and stability, must be invested with Godlike powers. As a radical Hobbesian, Schmitt wanted to create a modern Leviathan, a new mortal God that would tower over society and unilaterally determine law.[3] Central to Schmitt's political theology is a kind of secular political absolutism or even monotheism.[4]

Schmitt's radically conservative political commitments are further sharpened in the later parts of *Political Theology*. The final chapter stages a kind of polemic between reactionary Catholic legitimists like Donoso Cortés, whom Schmitt clearly admires, and revolutionary anarchists like Mikhail Bakunin and Pierre-Joseph Proudhon, whom he detests but also fears. Schmitt's somewhat oblique and subterranean dialogue with anarchism is not very much remarked upon; most commentators tend to focus on Schmitt's critique of liberalism. However, it is the debate with anarchism that can be seen as constituting the hidden core of his political theology. It is the revolutionary anarchist, rather than the liberal, who emerges as Schmitt's genuine political enemy and whom he regards as the greater threat to state sovereignty and political order. While Schmitt saw liberalism as a vapid philosophy, based on endless equivocation and deliberation—one that sought to neutralize the political domain by pretending it didn't exist or imagining that political conflicts could be resolved through rational dialogue—he saw in anarchism a political extremism that was implacably opposed to political authority. If liberalism occupied the middle ground in the ideological (and politico-theological) conflict, Schmitt's revolutionary conservatism, and Bakunin's materialist, atheist anarchism, were at the extreme opposite ends. Schmitt's hostility to anarchism is articulated through the figure of Donoso Cortés who was writing in the wake of the 1848 revolutions. Like Schmitt, Donoso Cortés saw the monarchical order as threatened on all sides by atheism and revolution; the only way to preserve moral authority and political legitimacy was through sovereign dictatorship. Moreover, unlike liberals, for whom he had nothing but contempt, Donoso Cortés regarded the anarchist as his true enemy, one for whom he at the same time had a certain sort of respect, even admiration, as if recognizing his own reverse mirror image (p. 63).

What the counterrevolutionary conservative and the revolutionary anarchist shared was a certain extremism and absolutism, particularly with regard to the sovereign state. The reactionary defended the principle of state absolutism *absolutely*, while the anarchist—who also regards the state as absolutist in principle—*absolutely* rejected it and sought to abolish it. In other words, for the reactionary, the sovereign state, which can only ever be absolutist, is an absolute good, or at least an absolute necessity; while for the anarchist, for whom it can also only ever be absolute, the sovereign state is an absolute evil and an unnecessary encumbrance upon otherwise freely formed social relations. Moreover, such was their hatred of the state and the church, and of the theological doctrine of original sin that led to man subordinating himself to authority, that led anarchists like Bakunin to appeal to Satan as a figure of emancipation. It was perhaps this employment of the Satanic trope that led Schmitt to conclude that anarchism could not escape its own politico-theological dilemma. According to Schmitt, the absolute hostility of the anarchist to both God and the state would lead him into another kind of absolutism; his materialism becomes another kind of antitheological theology: "and this results in an odd paradox whereby Bakunin, the greatest anarchist of the nineteenth century, had become in theory the theologian of the antitheological and in practice the dictator of the antidictatorship" (p. 66).

Schmitt's enmity toward anarchism is continued in his subsequent text, *Roman Catholicism and Political Form*, in which the figure of Bakunin looms up again. Bakunin is characterized here as the barbarian from the Russian steppes, representing the demonic forces of socialism and atheism, and posing an existential threat to political authority and to European Christian civilization (Schmitt, 1996c, p. 36). In the past, the Roman Catholic Church had played a counterrevolutionary role in the defense of the old order. Schmitt now calls upon the church to resume its role in this conflict, to take up the defense of Western European civilization against the forces of revolution. Again, a radical decision must be made: "There is, nevertheless, a type of decision the church cannot avoid—a type of decision that must be taken in the present day, in concrete situations, in every generation" (p. 38). Schmitt is describing a kind of "culture war" between the right and the left, one that bears some resemblance to our contemporary culture wars, even if the stakes were much higher for Schmitt. The terms of this conflict define a political role for the church in modern society, one that would fill the void left vacant by the collapse of the old theological order. The church is suited to this role because it is, as Schmitt puts it, a *complexio oppositorum*—a complex of opposites, which can adapt itself to different circumstances, incorporate opposing ideological and political positions, and even different and conflicting theological tendencies without losing its identity. Despite its ideological and theological promiscuity, the church has retained a coherent image of itself. In its internal consistency, Roman Catholicism has the capacity for *representation*; it can provide a unifying idea of the social order, once embodied in the person of Christ and in papal *auctoritas*, but now in the political form of the church itself: "From the standpoint of the political idea of Catholicism, the essence of the Roman-Catholic *complexio oppositorum* lies in a specific, formal superiority over the matter of human life such as no other imperium has ever known. It has succeeded in constituting a sustaining configuration of historical and social reality that, despite its formal characteristics, retains its concrete existence at once vital and yet rational to the *nth* degree" (p. 8). Therefore, like sovereignty itself, the church can have the function of representing society as a coherent whole, providing it with a point of stability and identity otherwise lacking in secular modernity. And it is only through decisive action in entering the fray of political conflict that it can once again fulfill its historical role.

However, can the church really play this role today? Even before Schmitt's time, the authority of the Roman Catholic Church had been severely diminished under a formally Protestant Prussian state and later under the secular order of Weimar. Following the Second World War and, later, the Second Vatican Council in the 1960s and its repudiation of the doctrine of papal infallibility, there was a further acknowledgment of the church's waning authority in secular modernity. In more recent times, however, and in a number of different political contexts, religious institutions have regained their political prominence—for instance, the increasing influence of the Catholic Church in Poland under the current socially conservative government, not to mention the excessive influence of Protestant evangelical churches in US politics and their growing power in Latin America. Right-wing populists often appeal to traditional religious beliefs and mobilize religiously conservative constituencies, in a way that is sometimes purely instrumental but nevertheless empowering to organized religion. While church attendance steadily declines, at least in many Western democracies, religious identity is increasingly politicized, co-opted into conservative and nationalist political agendas and weaponized in the current "culture wars." Nevertheless, there is little to suggest that organized religion can become once again a point of authority and legitimacy today, or that religious institutions can somehow provide a unifying image for our highly pluralized societies, as Schmitt imagined. The politicization of religion that we see today is much too disorganized and contested for that, contributing only to divisiveness and ideological polarization rather than to social order and unity.

If political legitimacy can no longer be grounded in religious institutions, can it be grounded in the sovereign will of the people? This is a question that Schmitt takes up in a subsequent text, *The Crisis of Parliamentary Democracy* (1923), in which he argues that constitutional authority derives ultimately from the sovereign lawmaking will of the people, rather than from parliamentary institutions. It was only the unified, singular will of the people, as an extraconstitutional, extraparliamentary force, that could bestow legitimacy on the constitutional order. By contrast, parliament, in Schmitt's eyes, was nothing more than a chamber of deliberation, a forum for political parties, factions, and sectional interests; in its pluralism it could not represent the singular will of the people. Here we see perhaps the most radical attack on liberal representative democracy. Not only were parliamentary mechanisms dysfunctional and unable to act decisively, particularly in emergency situations, but they were, for Schmitt, incompatible with democracy itself: "The belief in parliamentarism, in government by discussion, belongs to the intellectual world of liberalism. It does not belong to democracy" (1988, p. 8). Indeed, liberalism and democracy themselves were distinct and opposed concepts. Whereas liberalism was about the rule of law and the representation of a plurality of interests, democracy was always the expression of the unified will of the people. Moreover, while democracy was an egalitarian concept, it was an egalitarianism of a particular kind, one that presupposed a homogeneous identity, and which therefore excluded other identities and interests. Democratic equality, for Schmitt, was therefore premised on *inequality* and the privileging of one group over another (p. 9).

Schmitt's solution to this crisis of legitimacy was once again an authoritarian one. Because the people is a homogeneous identity, its will can only be represented in the singular person of the leader (the Führer). This was why Schmitt claimed that some form of plebiscitary dictatorship was compatible with democracy and, indeed, was a more meaningful and effective way of articulating the will of the people than parliamentary institutions and voting in elections:

> The will of the people can be expressed just as well and perhaps better through acclamation, through something taken for granted, an obvious and unchallenged presence, than through the statistical apparatus that has been constructed with such meticulousness in the last fifty years. The stronger the power of democratic feeling, the more certain is the awareness that democracy is something other than a registration system for secret ballots. Compared to a democracy that is direct, not only in the technical sense but also in a vital sense, parliament appears an artificial machinery, produced by liberal reasoning, while dictatorial and Caesaristic methods not only can produce the acclamation of the people but can also be a direct expression of democratic substance and power. (pp. 16–17)

It is tempting, perhaps, to see Schmitt's authoritarian, populist model of democracy in terms of *constituting power*—that is, the will of the people as a force of democratic renewal that is external to the constitutional order and as having the power to remake it. However, the democratic and revolutionary potential implicit in this notion of the "will of the people," which originates in Abbé Seiyès's theory of revolutionary constitution-making power (*pouvoir constituent*), is at the same time reined in within Schmitt's analysis and confined to a politico-theological framework in which the idea of constituting power originates from God (Schmitt, 2008b, p. 126).

The constituting power of the people is ultimately the constituting power of God; it is therefore a power and authority that cannot be exercised directly or democratically by the people, but rather through a sovereign representative. In other words, Schmitt's politico-theological conception of the constituting power of the people relies on a transcendental and hierarchical relationship between the people and the sovereign; it cannot be based on the equivalence between the government and the governed, as modern democratic theory would suggest (Schmitt, 2008b, p. 266).

Moreover, Schmitt has little interest in a broader conception of social democracy. Indeed, Schmitt's politics might be seen as a form of authoritarian liberalism, summed up in the formula of *strong state, free economy* (see Cristi, 1998; Heller, 2015 [1933]). In other words, Schmitt was hostile to *political* liberalism—the idea of public reason and constitutional government—but not necessarily to *market* liberalism. Like Hobbes, Schmitt's concern was for a strong political sovereign that would stand above society, being relatively indifferent to the private sphere of the market; indeed, a market economy presupposed an authoritative state that would secure the conditions in which it could operate. This is very close, of course, to the contemporary neoliberal model, in which the state is largely reduced to its security functions and the protection of property rights, and where authoritarian measures are sometimes required to enforce the discipline of the market and to crack down on dissent. Like Schmitt, neoliberals do not fear a strong state so much as the democratic public space and the extension of democratic controls over the economy. Given that the contemporary crisis of legitimacy is partly the result of the breakdown of the social welfare state and the excesses of a deregulated market economy, the formula of strong state, free economy would seem to only perpetuate the problem.

Evaluating Schmitt

In considering these early writings of Schmitt's in response to the Weimar crisis, we can conclude by saying that while they have a certain diagnostic value in understanding the terms of a legitimation crisis, they offer little in the way of a solution that is normatively compelling: an authoritarian sovereign unencumbered by constitutional constraints; a politically empowered church weighing in on the "culture wars"; and a highly reductionist, exclusionary, and authoritarian model of democracy based on a narrow form of identity politics, from which democratic deliberation and the extension of social democracy are largely ruled out.

Given this, it is perhaps surprising that Schmitt has over the last decades been taken up so enthusiastically by some thinkers on the left, not only as a way of critiquing the liberal global order and the "war on terror" but also as a way of renewing the idea of democracy. Andreas Kalyvas, for instance, draws on Schmitt's distinction between the *constituting* and *constituted* will of the people—the people *outside* the constitution with the authority to change it, and the people as constituted *by* this act of authorization—to highlight what he sees as the "extraordinary" side of democratic politics, an experience of direct political engagement, creativity, and participation where the people collectively determine the shape of the constitutional order. He says: "Democratic extraordinary politics dispenses with representation for the simple reason that, for Schmitt, the people should be physically present and publicly mobilized during the democratic creation of a new constitution, outside the mechanisms of state representation" (2008, p. 128). However, this would only apply if in Schmitt's theory of democracy the people were somehow immanent to itself and spoke for itself, in the manner of Rousseau's *volonté générale*. However, Schmitt makes it clear that the sovereign constitution-forming will of the people does not speak for itself but is *spoken for* and always represented in the figure of the leader. Rather than any genuine participation in democratic decision-making, the role of the people is simply reduced to acclaiming the leader in public gatherings, much like the acclamations of Mussolini in Italian fascism, and similar to the entirely hierarchical relationship of representation that we find in the contemporary phenomenon of populism.[5]

In a similar vein to Kalyvas, Gopal Balakrishnan has argued that Schmitt's theory of the constitutive power of the people offers a welcome antidote to the stifling politics of the liberal consensus and a way of radicalizing democracy in a manner that might be appealing to the left. This claim is unconvincing. As we have argued, not only are Schmitt's theories irretrievably oriented to the politics of the conservative right, and in a much more systematic way than Balakrishnan seems to think (see 2000, pp. 5–6), but his critique of liberal democracy is not in the interests of expanding the democratic project—and certainly not in the direction of social democracy or socialism—but, on the contrary, of reining it in through a sovereign dictatorship and in support of the market.

A similar point could be made in relation to Chantal Mouffe's attempt to incorporate Schmitt into a theory of political pluralism and "agonistic" democracy. Mouffe has drawn on Schmitt's critique of liberal parliamentarianism, as well as his friend/enemy opposition, to arrive at an understanding of the political based on contestation and antagonism, and on the acknowledgment of irreducible differences. As an alternative to rational deliberative models of public reason employed in liberal political theory, Mouffe has proposed a model of political engagement based on democratic "agonism" (see 1999, 2000, 2013). Here, Schmitt's figure of the enemy, the one with whom one is prepared to go to war, is transformed or sublimated into an adversary, a worthy opponent, one with whom one can have a respectful—if radical—disagreement. In utilizing Schmitt in this way, Mouffe is responding to the liberal consensus model of politics, à la Rawls and Habermas, in which it is supposed that disagreements can be resolved through a process of rational deliberation, an assumption that ended up marginalizing and suppressing ineluctable differences. There has to be a place for passionate disagreement in public debate, she argues. Indeed, the problem with the liberal response to populism is that it simply dismisses it as "irrational," thereby adding fuel to the fire (Mouffe, 2018, p. 17).

We do not necessarily disagree with her claim here. The response of the liberal center to the rise of populism has been largely ineffective and counterproductive. Moreover, there must certainly be room for the expression of passionate forms of discourse within the public sphere—and here we believe that political theology has a particular value in providing a language for passionate commitments and emotional affects not otherwise accommodated within the liberal discourse of secular reason. What we find unconvincing, however, is Mouffe's attempt to reconcile Schmitt with a theory of political pluralism. Schmitt is a thinker fundamentally hostile to pluralism—that is, to the idea of a diversity of viewpoints, interests, and perspectives that a democratic society should find ways of representing. Indeed, Schmitt's one-dimensional view of democracy—in which the sovereign will of the people is reduced to a narrow, authoritarian, homogeneous, and nationalist form of identity politics that deliberately and necessarily excludes other identities—is fundamentally inhospitable to difference, much more so than the liberal consensus model that Mouffe is critical of. Furthermore, we are somewhat skeptical of Mouffe's attempt to "gentrify" Schmitt's model of enmity and antagonism into the more polite form of "agonism." As Schmitt makes clear in his text *The Concept of the*

Political from 1932, the friend/enemy opposition—which is central to his understanding of the political relationship—cannot be mediated and always presupposes the real possibility of war, of killing one's enemy: "The friend, enemy, and combat concepts receive their real meaning precisely because they refer to the real possibility of physical killing" (see Schmitt, 2007b, p. 33). It is difficult to see how this kind of antagonistic disposition could be somehow tamed or safely integrated into the democratic public space in the manner that Mouffe proposes.

Our point in regard to these various left-wing appropriations of Schmitt is that they sanitize, in a wholly unconvincing way, a set of ideas and normative political commitments that remain hostile to any substantive notion of democracy—a notion that might, for example, also include respect for human rights and constitutional checks and balances—let alone being reconcilable with any left-wing emancipatory political project. No doubt, the existing liberal democratic model of politics is flawed and limited and has perhaps reached a point of exhaustion. However, the solution to its current crisis of legitimacy surely cannot be to turn to a decisionist account of sovereignty or an authoritarian populist model of democracy. The appeal of Schmitt in the eyes of some left-wing thinkers is that he offers an autonomous experience of the political as a domain of contestation irreducible to liberal normative commitments and constitutional frameworks. However, as we have shown, this "pure" concept of the political—which Schmitt wants to evoke in the moment of decision—is hinged to a theological framework from which it derives its energy and authority. Indeed, the recent and largely uncritical adoption of Schmitt by certain thinkers—who tend to downplay his authoritarian conservatism and his collusion with Nazism as merely historical details—is based on a neglect of the theological orientation of his political theory, an influence that, we suggest, continued to shape his thinking right up to his final work (*Political Theology II*) and that informed his antidemocratic and antiliberal conclusions.[6] Here it is hard not to agree with Habermas when he says: "Against Carl Schmitt, we might ask: why shouldn't the political find an impersonal embodiment in the normative dimension of a democratic constitution?" (2011, p. 21).[7] In other words, in the modern secular period, Schmitt's theologically charged conception of sovereignty is simply an inappropriate basis of political legitimacy, and other sources of legitimacy, such as the normative framework provided by a democratic constitution, might be more effective and binding, especially in a pluralized world.[8]

The crisis of political legitimacy is real. It was real in Schmitt's time, and it is real in ours. Schmitt provides a powerful diagnosis of the situation, and there are elements of his analysis of secular liberal modernity that we will take up in later chapters—particularly his critique of technological domination. There is a need to establish new sources of legitimacy in a world without a unifying principle, a world that is increasingly unstable and that seems to be fragmenting before our very eyes. There is no question that the liberal democratic political order—once pronounced to be the highest stage of rational human development, the "end of history" as Fukuyama put it—is in deep trouble. However, as we have argued in this chapter, Schmitt's political theology is limited in being able to offer any viable solution to this crisis of legitimacy. Today, the desire for sovereignty, hinged to an aggressive and authoritarian politics of ethnonationalist populism, appears more as an accelerator of the coming disorder, leading to increasing geopolitical tension, rather than being a force for stability. This does not mean that political theology no longer has any relevance. On the contrary, as we shall suggest, the nexus between theology and politics might be reconfigured in more radical and democratic ways. The possibility of an alternative and more emancipatory approach to political theology is something we will elaborate in the chapters that follow.

2

Who Is the Subject of Political Theology?

The instability and fragility of contemporary political forms traced in the previous chapter opens the basis, in this chapter, for further critical intervention in the Schmittian framework. The particular focus of this critical intervention involves the transformation of the "subject" of Schmittian political theology into the more open question of "who" or "what" comes *after* this Schmittian "subject." This is initiated through two central, early interlocutors: the former founding member of Dada and, subsequently, reaffirmed Catholic Hugo Ball and the political philosopher Leo Strauss. These early critical engagements indicate the limits of the Schmittian framework and emphasize either the primacy of the theological over the political (Ball) or that of the political over the theological (Strauss). These alternatives, while detaching critical reflection from the Schmittian parameters of *Vereinfachung* ("deliberate simplification," for Galli[1]), remain limited forms of questioning of the "subject" of Schmittian political theology.

In reflecting on these limitations, we commence from an era in which liberalism has largely been displaced by neoliberalism. Neoliberalism is antipolitical in a sense diametrically opposed to Schmitt: it is a depoliticization and neutralization of the question of justice. Our critical response to neoliberalism commences from an alternative thematization of the relationship between person and nature. In contrast to the initial Schmittian delimitation of this relationship, as one of human nature, underlain by an uncertain status accorded to evil, we understand nature as an environment that precedes and exceeds the human. This understanding is gained not through a process of reenchantment but through a sense of *responsibility*. Hence, it requires a thought of coexistence that is not simply fulfilled by the attribution of legal personality: the transition from thing (territory, property, etc.) to (legal) person. The broader understanding of nature is the counterpart of a reconsideration of the notion of the person and its connection to political form. Here, we draw on Roberto Esposito's deconstruction of the duality of person and thing as the basis to develop an alternative understanding of the relationship between person and body. This alternative understanding is derived by comprehending subjectivity as situated within a world that is not merely coextensive with a legal framework based on property and rights, opening up onto a broader understanding of ethical responsibility and justice.[2]

Ball contra Schmitt: The Limits of the Theological

The encounter between Ball and Schmitt is centered upon an extended review by Ball of Schmitt's work from *Political Romanticism* (1919) to *Roman Catholicism and Political Form* (1923) (Ball, 2013).[3] The review places a particular emphasis upon Schmittian political theology of the early 1920s. Ball attempts a reorientation of Schmittian political theology, which seeks to overcome the limits of the theological imposed by the political. This reorientation is animated by Ball's return to Catholicism in 1920, which is itself the preliminary stage for the subsequent reworking and significant shortening of the *Zur Kritik der deutschen Intelligenz* (1919) as the *Die Folgen der Reformation: Zur Kritik der deutschen Intelligenz* (1924).[4] The reworking, preceded, in 1923, by the publication of *Byzantinischer Christentum: Drei Heiligenleiben* (Byzantine Christianity: The Lives of Three Saints), is, through its newly amended title—*The Consequences of the Reformation*—a heterodox, Catholic critique, of the historical genesis and intellectual origins of the authoritarian destructiveness of the German state culminating in the disastrous defeat in World War I.

Ball's engagement with Schmitt, in the extended review in 1924, with its emphasis upon the theological in Schmitt's political theology, leaves the effect of a central aspect of the reworking unacknowledged: the rejection of the influence of Bakunin upon the critique contained in the original 1919 version.[5] From this perspective, the encounter with Schmitt—personal, epistolary, and textual—prior to the publication of the essay reinforces the rejection of Bakunin as part of the return to Catholicism.[6] For, from a textual perspective, both *Political Theology* (1922) and *Roman Catholicism and Political Form* (1923) consider Bakunin to represent the exemplary challenge to Schmittian political theology and the Roman Catholic Church.

Ball's 1924 review is also marked by another silence or elision in its selection and discussion of the corpus of Schmitt's works. The *Die geistesgeschichtliche Lage des heutigen Parlamentarismus* (1923) (Schmitt, 1988), which presents Schmitt's critical reflections upon the historical and intellectual situation of contemporary parliamentarianism, with its central opposition between liberalism and democracy, is excluded from consideration. This enables Ball to situate the selected works of the early 1920s as the further development of Schmitt's *Political Romanticism* (1919), and to designate *Dictatorship: From the Origin of the Modern Concept of Sovereignty to Proletarian Class Struggle* (1921) (Schmitt, 2013), as the work within the corpus that limits, rather than facilitates, this development. The limits of *Dictatorship*—the distinction between commissarial and sovereign dictatorship as the designation of a rational or irrational mode of exercise of exceptional authority—is overcome by the combination of *Political Theology* (1922) and *Roman Catholicism and Political Form* (1923).

The purpose of these selections, silences, and interpretations is to identify the underlying conceptual orientation of the works of the early 1920s as emphatically theological and, in this manner, to provide the basis for Ball to articulate, beyond and after Schmitt, a political theology in which the political has effectively been absorbed into the theological. The identification of this underlying orientation commences from its prefiguration in *Politische Romantik*: the critical separation, which, for Ball, is not yet explicitly theological (Ball, 2013, p. 68), from the impasse of the individualism of political romanticism and the parallel protection of Bonald, de Maistre, and Cortés from any association with political romanticism (Ball, pp. 72–73). It is *Political Theology* (1922) that then, in its distinctive Schmittian deployment of juridical categories, proceeds to overcome the impasse that *Political Romanticism* revealed through further recourse to Bonald, de Maistre, and Donoso Cortés. As Ball says: "The juridical definitions of his book [*Political Theology*] . . . serve to resolve the conflict whose contradictions led to Romanticism's collapse. The Catholic theologians of state . . . relate to the political Romantics as the practical example of an actualization does to a theoretical experiment that fails in spite of everything" (p. 73).

The actualization is the realization and preservation of the *metaphysical* reality that remains inaptly grasped by political Romanticism, through the notions of community and history, receiving its Schmittian articulation in the identity of "metaphysical freedom" and "metaphysical reality" (p. 76). It is here that Ball locates a fundamental opposition that animates Schmitt's approach: "spontaneous emergence of the divine into the chaos of history, the political miracle one might say, the transgression of the laws of nature by the sovereign person. This results in the opposition of *ratio* to the irrational" (p. 79).

In relation to this opposition, Ball introduces a further precision or double meaning of the irrational as the nonrational and the suprarational. This enables Ball to distinguish the state from the theological on the basis of their mutually exclusive relationship to one of these two senses of the irrational. The state, as the *ratio* represented by the classical philosophy of the state that, for Ball, commencing from Machiavelli,[7] encompassing Hobbes, and extending to de Maistre, Bonald, and Cortés, relates to the nonrational (p. 77): the population, as an unregulated mass traversed and directed by an impulsive will (p. 79). It is a philosophy whose *ratio* "justifies their estimation of the unorganized mass of men as a malignant material to be domineered, against which all means are authorized" (p. 79). For Ball, Schmitt retains only the question of human nature from this philosophy of the state and generalizes it to function as a descriptive category to characterize the particular doctrine of the state.

Schmittian political theology—Schmitt's path beyond the tradition of classical philosophers of the state—consists of the displacement of the nonrational with the suprarational. The passage beyond the tradition of the philosophy of the state utilizes the theological as the foundation for the concepts with which the tradition has sought to designate the state (p. 80). It is exactly this transition from the nonrational to the suprarational that Ball considers only to attain an explicit, coherent theological form in *Political Theology* and *Roman Catholicism and Political Form*.

Within this interpretative framework, Schmitt's *Dictatorship* can only assume the position of a confused or deficient analysis (p. 81). The confusion centers upon the text's distinction between commissarial and sovereign dictatorship and their designation as a rational or irrational mode of exercise of exceptional authority. The deficiency rests upon a preceding contraction of the subject matter, which confines the discussion of dictatorship to a comparison between its foundation in the papal authority of the Roman Catholic Church and its distinct exemplification in the Protestant dictatorship of Oliver Cromwell (pp. 81–83).[8] The medieval exercise of papal authority of the Roman Catholic Church institutes a dictatorship from an already existing source of authority that creates the model of a rational, executive, commissarial dictatorship (p. 81). In contrast, the Schmittian conception of an individual, exemplified by Cromwell, who institutes a dictatorship merely on the basis of being called by God—*homo a deo excitatus*—can only be an *irrational* and, for Ball, necessarily *heretical* usurpation of authority (pp. 81–82). The Schmittian heterodoxy is identified—the belief in sovereignty independent of the Roman Catholic Church—and admonished in the following terms:

> As a Roman Catholic one must adhere to the principle that nothing within the domain of politics can be founded on the irrational except a commissarial dictatorship, in which an instrument, under the command of an irrational power, establishes the higher intentions mandated into effect by rational means. The *homo a deo excitatus*, or the saint in the Puritan and German conception of the Reformation, is a rebel who believes not in the prince of peace but in the god of war, and how he exploits the wealth of the nation to confirm his political mission. So long as a universal faith does not prevail, the saint and the affairs of state exclude each other. That is the sense of the Church *qua* institution, and also of commissarial dictatorship. The sovereign dictator can only be legitimated within the Church. (p. 82)

According to Ball, the failure of *Dictatorship* is the overextended notion of personalism[9] that misrecognizes "an enemy of the Church" (p. 83) by designating this individual with both suprarational authority and sovereignty. The opposition between commissarial and sovereign dictatorship remains intelligible only *within* the Roman Catholic Church as an *internal*, institutional distinction between papal executive and principal.

For Ball, it is upon the confused and deficient analysis of *Dictatorship* that *Political Theology* (1922) imposes theological coherence by establishing the essential interconnection of sovereignty and the suprarational. In this interconnection, dictatorship, as suspension of the law, is absorbed within a wider conception of sovereignty as a decision that is an expression of the relationship to the suprarational (p. 83). For, sovereignty, in *Political Theology*, is now related to "the form of law [*Rechtsform*] in general, and rules out any individual solution of the kind the book on dictatorship held possible" (p. 84).

With this exclusion, Schmittian personalism returns to conformity with Roman Catholicism, as the decision on the exception expresses the intersection of the form of law and the theological. *Political Theology* demonstrates the essential identity of the Schmittian distinctions of *ratio* and the suprarational and the juridico-theological analogy (p. 87). For Ball, "the unity of Schmitt's work rests on his explication of the relations of reason [*Vernuftsbeziehungen*] to the suprarational, which is the principle that gives it form [*Formprinzip*]" (p. 87).

In this manner, Ball then introduces *Roman Catholicism and Political Form* as the foundational text, providing the retrospective unity for Schmitt's work of the early 1920s. *Political Theology* becomes the preliminary restoration of theological coherence for which *Roman Catholicism and Political Form* provides the theoretico-institutional foundation. Without explicit indication it purports to supply the answer to the question that Schmitt leaves open in the final pages of *Political Theology*: the tendency of decision, in de Maistre and Cortés, to dictatorship and the sense that can still be attributed to the notion of legitimacy. For Ball, the conjunction of the political and the theological is the conjunction of Roman Catholicism (theological) and political form (political): their transposition "to the sphere of the absolute" (p. 88).

The juridico-theological analogy of *Political Theology* is transformed and intensified into the singular power of the Roman Catholic Church to create form: "the Roman Catholic Church safeguards irrationality and is able to make its imprint on rational forms of the material state, which it apprehends and unifies according to norms" (pp. 88–89).

The sense of *ratio* is thereby itself transformed into the position of *ratio* within the Roman Catholic Church. The church is located between the higher revealed truth—revelation—of God and the state beneath it and, from this position, transposes this revealed truth into representation: the relationship between *ratio* and *representation* (p. 89). The Schmittian method of general juridico-theological analogy, in *Political Theology*, becomes the recognition of the singular origin of the "medieval supremacy of the Roman Church" (p. 89). The presence of this origin is its continued imprint in the later history traced by the juridico-theological analogy. These juridico-theological traces are of the Roman Catholic Church as the "rational formative power of the absolute" (p. 91).

For Ball, it is the absence of connection of the secular state, as the contemporaneous capitalist and socialist state, to the Roman Catholic Church, which renders each type of state without form or representation:

a reduction to a mere technical instrument for the realization of economic processes (p. 92). The secular state seeks an autonomous foundation that, in its separation from the religious, has relinquished a position as a "mediation of suprarational values" (p. 92). Thus, in this emphasis upon the foundation and coherence of Schmittian political theology in the Roman Catholic Church is the assertion, beyond and after Schmitt, of the primacy of the theological—the suprarational—over the political.

The assertion of the primacy of the theological—the Roman Catholic Church—as the foundation of Schmittian political theology elides the Schmittian conjunction of the theological and the political. Schmittian political theology arises as a response to the modern, which *Dictatorship* designates as the passage "from princely absolutism to the civil-legal state" (Schmitt 2013, p. 178) and which, in the 1923 work on parliamentarianism, passed over in silence by Ball, is the parliamentary form of the civil-legal state. It is the presence of this framework and its associated questioning in *Roman Catholicism and Political Form* that also disappears in Ball's characterization. For Schmitt of the early 1920s, the conjunction of the theological and the political is to be established "as much by the commitment of Rome as by the means of the given political state" (Doremus, 2004, p. 62).

The further path beyond Schmittian political theology is encapsulated in Ball's final essay, "Der Künstler Und Die Zeitkrankheit" (1926) (Ball, 1984), where the previous Schmittian corpus of political theology is no longer cited, and only a short discussion of Schmitt's *Political Romanticism* remains (p. 110). For Ball, within an investigation oriented by the general reorganization of the sciences, purposive causality has lost its value in the determination of state and society and has to be replaced with an artistic approach to *metaphysical* form (p. 102): aesthetics as the fundamental experience in relation to the realm of symbols. Thus, the relationship between the Schmittian juridical norm and the suprarational has been replaced with the realm of the symbolic in which there are no natural symbols, but only symbols created by God, from which the process of social formation arises through a process of purposeful identification (p. 147). It is the co-emergence of the Christian church and Christian society—the form of Christian *logos*—which has become Ball's exclusive concern.[10]

The importance of Ball's critique, as a theological critique of Schmitt's political theology of the 1920s, is that it preserves, rather than rejects, the possibility of political theology. The preservation of this possibility involves the adherence to a heterodox and unsystematized theology that also establishes its contrast with the absolute separation of theology and politics of Erik Peterson's theological critique of Schmitt.

Strauss contra Schmitt: The Limits of the Political

The effect of the critical encounter with Ball is a central, underlying orientation in Schmitt's subsequent work, *The Concept of the Political* (Schmitt, 1996b).[11] This implicit response to Ball is also the Schmittian text with which Leo Strauss engages in an extended critical review in 1932 (Strauss, 1996b). Thus, *The Concept of the Political*, in which an implicit conjunction of the theological and the political has replaced its explicit presentation in the works of early 1920s, is the text that Strauss considers to encapsulate, and to demarcate, a theory of the political.

The Straussian approach to Schmitt expresses a distinct position concerning the question of political theology. For Strauss's review of Schmitt occurs as part of a longer trajectory marked by a progressively critical distance toward the forms of response to the theologico-political within German Judaism (Meier, 2006a; Quélennec, 2018; Reinecke & Uhlaner, 1993; Strauss, 2002). The engagement with Schmitt arises at a stage in this trajectory in which there is a convergence with regard to a shared rejection of liberalism combined with the indication of the limitations of the Schmittian critique of liberalism.[12]

The Straussian comprehension of *The Concept of the Political* is of a conjunctural intervention—"not an eternal truth but only a present truth" (Strauss, 1996b, p. 83)—"entirely dependent upon the polemic against liberalism" (p. 84). The object of the polemic is the indication of the occlusive effect of liberalism:[13] "an antipolitical mode of discourse" (p. 84) that is itself the full realization of the historical process designated by Schmitt as that of neutralization and depoliticization. The purpose of the polemic is, through the indication of the failure of liberalism, to supplant it with "a system that does not negate the political but brings it to recognition" (p. 85).

In place of the misrecognition of the political, Strauss emphasizes the Schmittian recognition of the primacy of the political as one whose "radical foundation" (p. 83) determines the definition of the state. The radical foundation of the state, as the subject of the implicit political theology of the text, has, however, to have recourse "to elements of liberal thought in the presentation of his views. The tentativeness of Schmitt's statements results from that compulsion" (p. 85). At the center of this gesture of radical foundation is the constraint of its expression within the antipolitical lexicon of liberalism. The Schmittian presentation of the political has "to bring the autonomy of the political into recognition, in opposition to liberalism but nonetheless in continuation of liberal aspirations for autonomy" (p. 86).

The autonomy Schmitt seeks is the demarcation of a separate sphere or field that has a foundational position in relation to the existing set of values that liberalism (in the shared Schmittian and Straussian sense) recognizes. Thus, it is not the autonomy of an additional or complementary sphere of value that orients the Schmittian polemic, but that of the foundation obscured by the liberal framework of values. For Strauss, the Schmittian gesture of radical foundation, insofar as the liberal framework of the spheres of value can be categorized as the overarching domain of culture, reintroduces the early modern, and specifically Hobbesian, distinction between nature (*status naturalis*) and culture (*status civilis*) (pp. 88–89):[14]

> Hobbes understood the *status civilis* in the specifically modern sense of culture . . . as the *opposite* of the *status naturalis*; the *status civilis* is the presupposition of every culture in the narrow sense (i.e. every nurture of the arts and sciences) and is itself already based on a particular culture, namely, on a disciplining of the human will. We will here disregard Hobbes's view of the relationship between *status naturalis* and culture (in the broadest sense) as an opposition: here we only emphasize the fact that Hobbes describes the *status naturalis* as the *status belli*, simply, although it must be borne in mind that "the nature of war, consisteth not in actual fighting; but in the known disposition thereto" (*Leviathan* XIII). (pp. 89–90)

Schmitt's reintroduction of the Hobbesian opposition between nature and culture arises from "the insight into what is specific to the political" (p. 87)—the distinction between friend and enemy—in which there is always the possibility of its transformation into conflict and killing. For Strauss, rather than a simple return to Hobbes, the political, as the friend/enemy opposition, is situated as the ineradicable condition that remains an invariant at the basis of all politics (p. 90). Schmitt interrupts the Hobbesian logic of the state of nature—the fear of death—that contains the impulsion to enter the *status civilis*. The interruption transforms the state of nature into a fundamental ground—the political. In this transformation, the fundamental ground of the political has ceased to be the presupposition for the transition to the *status civilis* and, for Strauss, it has to demonstrate its continued and necessary reality.

The demonstration has to be of the impossibility of liberal thought to realize its distinctive domain of politics. Yet, insofar as Schmitt cannot exclude all possibility of its realization, the demonstration cannot be one of impossibility and therefore requires a further positive supplement: a human nature more fundamental and invariant than that present in the Hobbesian state of nature (p. 95). The recourse to this positive supplement transforms the demonstration from that of a *reality* to that of a *morality*. It is the supposition of an essential dangerousness and the requirement to govern: "the affirmation of power as power that forms states" (p. 97).

The supposition of this essential dangerousness raises the question of its further definition as a theory of human nature. In particular, for Strauss, it raises the question of the relationship between Schmittian dangerousness and the determination of evil. Here, it appears that Schmittian dangerousness is unable to be immediately and directly connected to either of the two senses of evil—human inferiority or animal power. The nonmoral sense of evil, as animal power, contains its possibility for transformation—socialization—the process of becoming human; but Schmittian dangerousness remains unconnected to a theory of socialization (p. 99). The alternative, moral sense of evil, human inferiority, is without explicit affirmation, as an affirmation of pure bellicosity, but is, rather, held in abeyance. For it is that which is itself subject to the erasure resulting from the realization of the political domain of liberalism. Schmitt, according to Strauss, "affirms the political because he sees in the threatened status of the political a threat to the seriousness of human life" (p. 101). Hence, beneath the stylistic method of *The Concept of the Political*, designated by Strauss as the concealment of the moral, is not the demonstration of a fundamental reality but "the affirmation of the moral" (p. 101).

It is this concealment of the moral, once revealed, that then affects the scope of the other central aspect of *The Concept of the Political*—the polemic against liberalism, as a polemic against the primacy of morality over politics (p. 104). For, if the Schmittian political is the affirmation of the moral, then the polemic against liberalism is a polemic against a particular morality—humanitarian-pacificism—and not against the concept of morality of which humanitarian-pacificism would be an instance.

The polemic would then remain within the framework and discourse of liberalism (p. 104).

For Strauss, this indicates the aporetic position of the Schmittian political, which is situated in an unstable position between that of subjective value and objective necessity. The assertion of the political against its suppression by liberalism is an assertion of value and, as such, confronts the Schmittian characterization of the political as that which exists objectively, beyond all assertions of value. The attribution of value, in contrast, can only derive from an entirely subjective position: the exercise of "arbitrary, private discretion" (p. 105). If the political is not to be—and for Schmitt it cannot be—derived from the realm of the subjective, then it has to derive from "an inescapable necessity" (p. 105), which presumes the primacy of the political over the moral.

The primacy of the political over the moral, the objective necessity of the political, as that which is not derived subjectively, can then only be the affirmation of the *generality* of conflict. It cannot concern itself with any further distinction or determination based upon the underlying aim or purpose of a party to the conflict: it cannot separate or distinguish means and ends. The affirmation of the generality of conflict is, therefore, to adopt, in place of means and ends, the distinction between values and validity, an objectivity of the political that can only result from a methodological *neutrality* toward values: the purely descriptive acknowledgment of the presence of the friend/enemy distinction and its particular expression in the existence of groups divided by this opposition (p. 105). This position of descriptive generality, as the objective necessity of the political, reveals an essential affinity with the methodological neutrality of liberalism. For it merely situates itself as the obverse of the conventional liberalism that accords descriptive recognition to all groups animated by peace (p. 105). Therefore, the objective necessity of the Schmittian political remains, due to its essentially methodological determination, "within the systematics of liberalism" (p. 105).

For Strauss, these difficulties entail the limit of the Schmittian political. The limit relates to Schmitt's simultaneous indication of the ground of the political, that which must be grasped by *The Concept of the Political*, and the incapacity to demonstrate it. The polemic against liberalism arises by confining the sense of all political concepts to the expression of concrete existence. This definition of political concepts confronts the other impetus of the text, which is to demonstrate a foundation of the political that is situated *beyond* concrete existence. It is the perpetual oscillation between these two senses of the political that confines the presentation of the Schmittian political to a merely *prefigurative* critique of liberalism.

The *prefigurative* character of the Schmittian political is traced back to the final part of *Political Theology*:

> The affirmation of the political as such can therefore be only Schmitt's first word against liberalism; that affirmation can only *prepare for* the radical critique of liberalism. In an earlier text Schmitt says of Donoso Cortés: he "despises the liberals, whereas he respects atheistic-anarchistic socialism as his mortal enemy . . ." (Schmitt, 2005, 63). The battle occurs only between mortal enemies: with total disdain—hurling crude insults or maintaining the rules of politeness, depending on temperament—they shove aside the "neutral" who seeks to mediate, to manoeuvre, between them. "Disdain" is to be taken literally; they do not deign to notice the neutral; each looks intently at his enemy; in order to gain a free line of fire, with a sweep to the hand they wave aside—without looking at—the neutral who lingers in the middle, interrupting the view of the enemy. The polemic against liberalism can therefore only signify a concomitant or preparatory action: it is meant to clear the field for the battle of decision between the "spirit of technicity," the "mass faith that inspires an antireligious, this-worldly activism" (Schmitt, 1985, 94), and the opposite spirit and faith, which, as it seems, still has no name. Ultimately, two completely opposed answers to the question of what is right confront each other, and these answers allow of no mediation and no neutrality (cf. the remark about "two-membered antitheses" and "three-membered diagrams" or "reconstructions" on [Schmitt, 2005, 74]). Thus, what *ultimately* matters to Schmitt is not the battle against liberalism. For that very reason the affirmation of the political as such is not his last word. His last word is "the order of human things" (Schmitt 1985, 96). (p. 106)

Thus, for Strauss, Schmitt's political theology of the earlier work of the 1920s, and the particular Schmittian conjunction of the theological and the political, continues to determine the limits of the Schmittian political in *The Concept of the Political*.

The extended review concludes with Strauss's indication that it is a return to Hobbes, reaching beyond that of Schmitt, that will enable the completion of the critique of liberalism prefigured by *The Concept of the Political* (p. 107). Hobbes is thereby to be situated as the origin of liberalism from which to achieve the critique of liberalism. However, this focus upon Hobbes, is itself displaced in the subsequent development of Strauss's thought, and the displacement represents the further interrogation of the relationship between the theological and the political.[15] The Hobbesian "origin" of liberalism is displaced by the concentration upon the medieval thought of Maimonides, which itself becomes the passage to Greek philosophy.[16]

These displacements reflect a continued reflection upon the parameters of the theologico-political problem.[17] The political, in the initial form of political philosophy, is to be distinguished from the theological by an active engagement with the theological. Thus, the possibility of political philosophy is demonstrated and, from this demonstration, the political can then be determined. It is the continued memory of the detachment from the theological that is the counterpart of the position accorded by Strauss to political philosophy with regard to the existing political regime in which it is undertaken: a double detachment represented by the establishment of a philosophical school (Meier, 2006a, pp. xvii–xx).

The Straussian position is, thus, the demonstration of political philosophy as the impossibility of the reassertion of the primacy of revelation over reason, and in the particular suprarational existence of the Roman Catholic Church, that Ball develops beyond the limits of Schmittian political theology. It is also, simultaneously, the rejection of the Schmittian conjunction of the theological and the political as the foundation for the political authority of the state (Strauss, 2007a, pp. 127–128) beyond liberalism: the separation of political philosophy from Schmittian political theology. This separation, as the demonstration of the limits of Schmittian political theology, is the renewal of political philosophy. Yet it is a renewal that is and remains in the mode of the interrogative: the perpetual re-presentation of the domain of political philosophy against its absorption by either theology or the existing political regime.

The Contemporary Subject of Political Theology after Schmitt

The conceptual and historical limits of the respective critiques of Ball and Strauss entail that neither has extinguished the question of the *subject* of political theology after Schmitt. Neither the primacy of the theological over the political of Ball nor the Straussian passage to the political through a renewed reflection on the theologico-political problem furnish pertinent conceptual resources that can be directly adopted. The limitations of the positions of Ball and Strauss, as positions beyond and after Schmitt, are reinforced by the transformation of the principal subject of the Schmittian critique of 1920s—liberalism—with its displacement by neoliberalism.[18]

Neoliberalism distinguishes itself from the presentation of liberalism in *The Concept of the Political* through the character of the displacement of the political by the economic.[19] The distinct character of this neoliberal displacement, in contrast to that of political liberalism, is marked by a greater internal differentiation in its conceptual and institutional composition. This reflects the resilience and enduring adaptability of neoliberalism in a context that has ceased to be accompanied by the dominant historical memory of the opposition to the specific regimes of absolutism and totalitarianism. Neoliberalism is determined by an end—a social order determined by market mechanisms—that has come to exist in a differentiated set of realizations: a tolerance of the range of means and regimes (Plehwe, Slobodian & Mirowski, 2020). This relates both to the types of contemporary political regimes within which market mechanisms are operative and, within democratic political regimes, to the degree to which the established, conventional parties together with more recent populist parties adhere to a market-determined social order.

The varied response of contemporary political regimes to the COVID pandemic reflects the continued persistence of neoliberalism.[20] In those regimes, while there is an apparent "return of the state" accompanied by significant forms of state intervention in the economy and in the wider regulation of social life, extending to the declaration and imposition of a "state of exception" in response to a natural emergency, the primary orientation remains the protection of a social order determined by market mechanisms. The cessation of the natural state of emergency and/or the gradual relaxation of the wider forms of regulation is predicated upon a return to the neoliberal social order. The inequalities revealed and exacerbated by the pandemic are simply not taken into consideration in these responses.

Neoliberalism is a depoliticization and neutralization that is to be understood in a sense that is diametrically opposed to Schmitt. In place of the occlusion of the friend/enemy distinction, it is a depoliticization and neutralization of the question of justice (Tarizzo, 2018). This is to be understood as a contraction of the parameters of the question of justice and, with this contraction, the concomitant diminution in the capacity to identify, acknowledge, and respond to injurious social relations. This effect of depoliticization and neutralization rests upon comprehending neoliberalism, from its inception, as predicated upon a level of reflection that is societal rather than confined to a particular, contingent economic or political problem (De Carolis, 2017, p. 143). The level of reflection is an expression of the extent and intensity of the societal problem to which neoliberalism responds, and involves a method that is consciously "transdisciplinary and inter-disciplinary" (Tarizzo, 2018, p. 446).

The societal problem for neoliberalism is that of reproducing order in conditions that are themselves perpetually open to change and transformation: the transition from "the domain of real and actual 'facts' to that of possibilities *in that they are* possibilities, before they are or are not fulfilled. . . . Collective life accentuated its character of possibility, virtuality or power to such an extent that it inevitably resulted in the *calculation and strategic management of possibilities, opportunities and risks* becoming the heart of all emerging forms of social life" (De Carolis, 2017, p. 145). The response of neoliberalism is to acknowledge the dynamism that inheres in this transition from actuality to possibility and to seek to orient it to create an entire social order that is itself dynamic. The level of consideration is that of the general behavior of populations, of which individuals are the particular components, and the specific capacity of market-directed behavior to reproduce social order. Neoliberalism is the conjunction of spontaneity and order—coordination—arising from the cumulative aggregation of individual market-directed behavior: the impersonal generalization of the population's "*strategic* calculation of possibilities" (p. 147). "This means that *living*, in the broader sense, must mean *being on the market*: being part of a *competitive* network of exchanges and transactions, working to acquire the highest market value and thereby, at the same time, *contributing*, through one's choices, in the constant updating of value listings that regulate the game and direct collective exchanges" (p. 141). The individual, as the particular instance of this general market-directed behavior, is presumed to be effectively oriented by this form of strategic calculation of possibilities, which is perpetually reinforced and reemphasized by market-directed interaction.

Within this framework, injustice is reduced to the dysfunction of market-directed behavior, and the question of justice is confined to its identification and regulation. The presence of dysfunction is located at the level of the state and its associated institutional apparatus insofar as its action ceases to assist the reproduction of a market-directed social order: ranging from the failure to uphold the background conditions of this social order to the active intervention in or assumption of the direction of this social order. Dysfunction is also located at the level of the individual and recognized as the "free-rider" problem—a form of noncooperative strategic calculation—with regard to the collective benefits of actions of other individuals (Spector, 2016, pp. 214–215). The occurrence of individual dysfunction provides a central, legitimate regulatory purpose of the neoliberal state: the expansion of law, beyond the form of contract, to prohibit behavior or to impose obligations to guarantee *cooperative* strategic calculation.

The contraction of the definition of justice entails that the domain of market-directed behavior requires a form of behavior that is one of adaptation and acceptance—a conformity with the strategic calculation of possibilities—in place of nonstrategic questioning and ethical interrogation. The primacy accorded to adaptation and acceptance indicates an underlying overlapping, rather than purported separation, of the neoliberal market-directed social order coordinated by strategic calculation and the state: the combination of force (coercion and command) and consent (agreement and acceptance) (De Carolis, 2017, p. 150). Adaptation to and acceptance of these market-directed dynamics express the distinctive neoliberal combination of force and consent: "*preventive control over other people's choices*" (p. 150), or the economy as a logic of the government of selective inclusion and exclusion (Bazzicalupo, 2016, 2018). The primacy accorded to adaptation and acceptance is reinforced by the inclusion and operation of categories from biology, with a predominantly (social) Darwinian origin, in which the strategic calculation of the individual and the particular market-directed social orders are oriented by a competitive evolution (Stiegler, 2019).

The subject of our approach arises against the neoliberal occlusion of justice. The notion of the subject contains a double sense encompassing both the domain or field upon which it focuses and develops its critique and the subjectivity that arises through this critique. The subject, in this double sense, commences from neoliberalism, as the domain of critique and, through this critique, the subjectivity of contemporary political theology is rendered apparent.

The neoliberal occlusion of justice is predicated upon a preceding reduction and internal division of the conception of nature. The natural world is subsumed by the market-directed sphere of strategic calculation, and this subsumption creates the distinctive neoliberal combination of biology and economics: a neoliberal biopolitics (Stiegler, 2019). It establishes a hierarchical relationship between the human—in the form of the physical person/group or legal personality of the corporation—and nature as the basic resources for strategic calculation and the reproduction of a social order of exchange and spontaneous coordination. It is the cumulative history of the effects of this subsumption that have created the contemporary condition of the Anthropocene[21]—the profound, permanent, and intensifying degradation of the natural and human world—which is unthematizable for neoliberalism. For the Anthropocene indicates the preconditions for the termination of the possibility of market-directed social order that remains unintelligible within the neoliberal notion of reparable market dysfunction. The critique, in relation to this aspect of neoliberal occlusion, reframes the conception of nature. The reframing involves the rejection of the subsumption of the natural world by market-directed calculation, which is *also* the rejection of the Schmittian response to liberalism centered upon the essentially antagonistic nature of the human. In place of the Schmittian retention of remnants of an early modern theory of the human passions, we conceive of nature as an environment that precedes and exceeds the human. This understanding is gained not through a process of reenchantment but through the sense of ethical responsibility—something that goes beyond and is entirely opposed to market-directed calculation and competitive social evolution.

This notion of responsibility is to be understood as something that is not simply and entirely to be transformed into the attribution of legal personality and its further expression within a framework of right and duties. The framework of legal normativity that emerges with liberalism is reinterpreted in neoliberalism in the later work of Hayek, in the 1970s (Hayek, 2019), in conformity with a market-directed social order. In opposition to this Hayekian mirage of social justice (2019, pp. 169–308)—which, we argue, actually occludes the real meaning of justice—we instead place emphasis upon the theme of *fraternity*, as that which is inseparable from freedom and equality.[22]

The essential supplement of fraternity to the conjunction of freedom and equality entails the dissolution of a neoliberal freedom confined to market-directed calculation. The surrounding legal framework of neoliberalism, which provides the background guarantee of the spontaneous coordination of the market-directed social order, overlays the internal distinction of human and nature with the legal distinction between person and thing. The retention of this legal distinction leads to a consideration of the convergence with Esposito's deconstruction, in *Persons and Things* (Esposito, 2015), of the dominant, organizing duality of the concept of person (as a relationship of sovereignty, property, and dominion over oneself and others) and concept of thing (all that which is not a person). The deconstruction reveals the body as the concept that, within this duality, is effectively deprived of significant expression.

The contemporary political consequences of this organizing duality, for Esposito, are evident in the concluding section entitled "Political Bodies" (pp. 138ff.) in which politics, in contrast to law and philosophy, is held to be the single sphere in which a notion of the body has been given expression. It is an expression, however, that has been structured by an internal hierarchy—the "binary division . . . between the personal element of sovereign control and the impersonal structure of bodily physiology" (p. 139)—which can be articulated as both unity and division. The contemporary situation is one that Esposito characterizes as the profound weakening of the continued reproduction and coordination of this combination of unity and division, and the assertion of the autonomy of the previously impersonal structure of the body:

> This part is made up of the living bodies of those who feel they are no longer represented by the institutions. . . . They seek to transform the systems into a form that cannot be reduced to the dichotomies that the political order has long produced. . . . Foreign to both the semantics of the person and to those of the thing . . . [it] demands a radical renewal of the vocabulary of politics, law and philosophy. (p. 147)

The critique then diverges from or qualifies Esposito's further development of the impersonal bodily structure insofar as it becomes a question of a radical renewal of its relationship with a theory of institutions (Esposito, 2021). The divergence relates to the presupposition that, in its detachment from existing institutions, the impersonal bodily structure can only exist as an absence of representation, and that it is this absence that then generates the necessity for a more radical institutionalization. For this presupposition is itself the result of a prior absence—the disappearance of the designations for a collective form of political existence arising *without* institutionalization. Thus, the term *masses*, which is utilized in the concluding section of *Persons and Things*, has become a category designating and describing this impersonality: an essentially deficient expression of collective political existence *because* of its absence of institutionalization. Thus, the impersonality of the bodily structure is established by this preceding withdrawal of categories of noninstitutionalized collective political existence, and, in this withdrawal, there is the substitution of a theory of institutions.

This divergence from Esposito is not then to revalorize these categories of collective political existence. It is not to replace a theory of institutions with these categories in which collective political existence becomes the further articulation of relationship between these categories (mass, crowd, multitude . . .). Rather, it is to indicate that removal of these categories involves a simplification, and, with this simplification, a theory of institutions becomes the exclusive focus. This then leads, in Esposito's subsequent reflection upon the relationship between types of instituting thought (2021, pp. 207–209), to the outlines of a general theory of institutions, informed by the Italian jurist Santi Romano. A general theory of institutions becomes the overarching descriptive framework for the identification and designation of all forms of organized collective existence and thereby subsumes the tentative conclusion of *Persons and Things*. In this subsumption, however, the question remains that of the character of its relationship to other existing and future institutions: the potential return of the Schmittian question of sovereignty and the attendant insistence upon the identification of an instance of absolute political authority.

In the effective disappearance of the impersonal bodily structure into a theory of institutions, combined with the limits of this theory of institutions, we return to the consideration of this structure in its relationship to a broader or more fundamental notion of a world. With this, we return to an enhanced notion of the environment from which the initial reframing of this final section commenced. In this return, the freedom of neoliberalism as strategic calculation, which imposes a responsibility of adaptation and acceptance, is replaced with a different dynamic of relational subjectivity. It is this rethinking of the representation of the impersonal bodily structure that provides the initial basis for the further consideration of relational subjectivity as fraternity. This will be explored in the following chapter.

3

Person, Identity, Transformation

The limits of the Schmittian framework revealed in the previous chapters lead our critical reflection to concentrate upon a sustained reconceptualization of the notion of the person. Here we seek to extricate the notion of the person, as an ethical and political subject, from its Schmittian limits: the combination of an inherently defective human nature and the imposition of a transcendent political order. This also involves a reconsideration of political theology. Here we do not propose a return to the personalism of Mournier and Maritain, in which the Schmittian limits are overcome by the purported connection between Christianity and democracy, as the background to the political subject of Christian democracy.[1] Rather, we proceed by displacing the Schmittian concentration upon the Pauline notion of the *katechon*,[2] and the textual primacy accorded to the Second Letter to the Thessalonians in which the notion of the *katechon* appears.[3] The displacement is undertaken by according central importance to another Pauline letter, the Letter to Philemon. Here, beyond the effect of relinquishing the interpretative division of the Pauline letters into major and minor (Badiou, 2003, p. 18) and/or public and private (Bornkamm, 1990, pp. 83–84), we seek to open the possibility of understanding the Letter to Philemon as centered upon the relationship between person, identity, and transformation.[4]

The Letter to Philemon, we show, contains both the indications of the wider transformative potential of this notion of the person and the limits that prevent its realization. The textual limits upon the transformative potential prevent the simple readoption of the notion of the person in this Pauline letter. For the letter represents an intersession—a speaking on behalf of the Christian slave, Onesimus, to his master and owner, Philemon—which is confined to the internal transformation of the social and spiritual relationships of an already existing and firmly delimited early Christian community. While this projected internal transformation reinforces the delimitation of the community from Roman law or Greek law, and the Roman Empire, it nevertheless leaves open the question of the wider transformative potential of the letter.[5] In order to think beyond these limits and uncertainties of the Pauline letter, the sensitivity to injustice and the responsibility to transform it into noninjurious social relations is recast by situating them within a world beyond the limits of predetermined community. This, in turn, will enable us to critically reflect on these intimations contained in the letter, through an engagement with the work of Étienne Balibar, Roberto Esposito, and Jean-Luc Nancy.

The Path to Reconceptualization:
The Pauline Interruption of Schmittian Political Theology

In *Political Theology* (1922), the Schmittian connection between sovereignty and political theology becomes explicit in chapter 3 through a theory of secularization—a sociology of legal concepts—as the analogical transfer of theological concepts into "all significant concepts of the modern theory of the state" (Schmitt, 2005, p. 36). The state of exception, introduced in the preceding chapters to unsettle and overturn the attempt of Kelsenian legal positivism to render this situation juridically unintelligible, is now designated as the analogical transfer of "the miracle in theology" (p. 36). The miracle functions as an example to enable a sociology of legal concepts to trace a history of the process of analogical transfer from theology to politics, and particularly into the idea of the sovereign state of exception, which suspends the constitutional order, just as the miracle is the suspension of the laws of the natural order.

The Schmittian presupposition of the centrality of the miracle to theology, as the preliminary condition for its subsequent analogical transformation into a concept of the modern theory of the state, involves recourse to a theology that has relinquished the Pauline deflation of the status of the miracle. The early modern theology to which Schmitt refers is a theology that confronts doubt—heresy and unbelief—and, in this confrontation, has to have recourse to a form of demonstrable proof as the essential supplement to faith as mere belief. Thus, Schmitt refers to an early modern theology in which miracles have assumed this integral position and the requirement for proof.[6]

The return and further delineation of the early modern philosophical-theological framework, in Schmitt, is centered upon Hobbes.[7] The *Leviathan* exemplifies the Hobbesian political resolution of the status of miracles through the distinction between an internal, private faith and an external, public confession. The distinction removes belief as the exclusive determinant of the truth of miracles and confers this upon the sovereign. The conferral renders the miracle "what the sovereign state authority commands its subjects to believe" and, in turn, "miracles cease when the state forbids them" (Schmitt, 2008a, p. 55). For Schmitt, Hobbesian political theology—"the unity of religion and politics" (p. 55)—rests upon the substitution of proof by sovereign command as the basis of the truth of miracles. The substitution installs the state "as the exemplar of public reason in contrast to the private reason of subjects" (p. 55). The Hobbesian resolution—"absorbing the right of private freedom of thought and belief into the political system"—while appearing to indicate a political theology emanating from the apex of sovereign power—is the origin of its internal dissolution: "the end of the mortal god" (p. 57).

The dissolution—the failure of the Hobbesian Leviathan—arises from the capacity for the reversibility of the Hobbesian primacy of the public over the private. For Schmitt, the Hobbesian acknowledgment of an inner, private realm renders the realm of the public, and with it, sovereign state authority, an *external* power:

> When the public power wants to be only public when the state and confession drive inner belief into the private domain, then the soul of the people betakes itself on the "secret road" that leads inward. Then grows the counterforce of silence and stillness. At precisely the moment that the distinction between inner and outer is recognized, the superiority of the inner over the outer and thereby that of the private over the public is resolved. Public power and force may be ever so completely and emphatically recognized and ever so loyally respected, but only as a public and only an external power, it is hollow and already dead from within. Such an earthly god has only the appearance and the simulacra of divinity on his side. Nothing divine lets itself be externally enforced. (p. 61)

It is the externality of sovereign state authority that enables the inner, private realm to constitute itself as a self-standing, independent domain and to initiate the further historical process of this reversal represented by the emergence of the state regulated by the rule of law (*Rechtstaat*) and liberalism: the European transition from the eighteenth-century absolutist states to the nineteenth-century bourgeois constitutional state. Liberalism becomes the repetition—the second death[8]—of the internal dissolution of the Leviathan, the secular state as a vast mechanism destroyed from within by the "duality of state and state-free society" (p. 73).

The Pauline reflection upon the status of miracles interrupts this Schmittian politico-theological history and provides a distinct position for the wider consideration of belief as a process of subjective transformation. The Pauline approach to miracles is one of acknowledgment, but detachment from their active utilization in the process of subjective transformation. The detachment, explicitly stated in 2 Corinthians 12, is presented through the example of an unnamed Christian individual who undergoes a miraculous, revelatory experience. While Paul is prepared to speak of this individual, and, thus of the possibility of this miracle, and, by extension, the existence of miracles in general, it is not by or through miraculous experiences that Paul seeks to communicate with the addressees of this Second Letter to the Corinthians. Paul explicitly states that he will refrain from this "so no one will think more of me than is warranted by what I do or say, or because of these surpassingly great revelations" (2 Cor. 12: 6–7). The exclusive designation, in the letter, of Paul's own speech and action as the chosen modes of address is the conscious embrace of "weakness" (2 Cor. 12: 9–10)—the prevention of individual "conceit" (2 Cor. 12: 7–8) and the conformity of the Pauline mode of address with God's mode of address to Paul: a gift of grace that itself confers no supplementary or positive power, but is, rather, a power "made perfect in weakness" (2 Cor. 12: 9). The Pauline mode of address "will have no other force than the one it declares and will not presume to convince through the apparel of prophetic reckoning, of the miraculous exception, or of the ineffable personal revelation. It is not the singularity of the subject that validates what the subject says; it is what he says which founds the singularity of the subject" (Badiou, 2003, p. 53). Thus, the Pauline position is not one of personification—a distinctive sovereignty or command—arising from recourse to the miraculous. The relinquishing of the miraculous expresses a conscious reserve or precaution in regard to a radically subjective experience: it can "only be experienced by the subject who has been visited by miracle" (p. 51). To include or found a mode of address on miracles is a discourse of subjective elevation—"a subjective discourse of glorification"—which can only interfere with "the discourse of conviction that bears a weakness within itself" (p. 51).

The setting to one side of the miraculous reflects the situation of Paul and the early Christian communities within the political form of the Roman Empire in which Christianity has yet to become the dominant religion of the Roman Empire. The early modern Hobbesian "resolution" of the status of miracles—the subsumption within the private/public division of the Leviathan—which Schmitt situates as the politico-theological origin of the subsequent development of a perpetually weakened state sovereignty—already presupposes the intertwining of Christianity and sovereignty.[9]

The initial disjunction between the early Christian communities and the Roman Empire establishes a different distinction between the private and the public that is incomparable to that of the early modern period and its Hobbesian conceptualization. The Roman Empire, and Roman law and the administrative and military apparatus through which it is governed, was unconcerned with establishing and maintaining a single "religion" within the territory of the empire. A plurality of cults or sects existed and endured to the extent that each of them was not considered a threat or challenge to the empire. The early Christian communities emerged, in distinction from the other religions and cults of the Roman Empire, as is explicit in the Pauline letters with particular reference to Judaism and Greek paganism,[10] and sought to maintain themselves in relation to both the political form of the Roman Empire and these other cults and religions.

The transformative potential of the Pauline letters has predominantly centered upon an analysis that itself has defined the letters as public (major) and private (minor) and, in this manner, relegated those deemed to be private to the margins of this analysis. The effect of maintaining this interpretative framework is to situate the transformative effect, and its subsequent analysis, as the process of becoming Christian through the particular form of cessation of adherence to another religion or cult of the Roman Empire. From this interpretative focus, the Pauline consideration of the internal, social structure and composition of early Christian communities ceases to be integral or important aspect of the Pauline letters. In contrast, if the predominant classification of the Pauline letters is held in abeyance and a renewed focus is devoted to the "private" Letter to Philemon, a distinct question of the transformative effect of the Pauline letters arises.

Letter to Philemon: The Preliminary Reconceptualization

Although the shortest of the Pauline letters, the Letter to Philemon concerns the Pauline consideration of slavery in the context of its presence within an early Christian community. The letter, as its title indicates, concerns Paul in the position of addresser and Philemon in the position of addressee. The central topic of the letter is the slave, Onesimus, who, at the time at which Paul composes the letter, is present with Paul but is to return to Philemon who is his master.

The presence of Onesimus with Paul is understood as either a result of Onesimus's flight from Philemon and refuge with Paul or a result of being "lent" to Paul by Philemon as part of the wider framework of relations and obligations created between Paul and this small, early Christian community, in Colossae. The focus of the letter is a discursive strategy to persuade Philemon, on the return of Onesimus, to transform the preceding relationship of master and slave.[11] Thus, the letter offers a distinct formulation of the relationship between person, identity, and transformation.

For, although addressed to a house church leader of a small, early Christian community in Colossae it also involves the potential transformation of Philemon's relationship to Roman law or, alternatively, a sphere of Greek law retained with the Roman Empire (Roth, 2014). For the letter, while never explicitly indicating that this specific decision should be made, speaks of the status and future treatment of Onesimus: "no longer as a slave, but more than a slave, a beloved brother . . . both in the flesh and in the Lord" (Phil. 1: 16). Hence, any subsequent decision to free Onesimus (manumission) involves the creation of both a spiritual and social equality, which has ceased to be directly regulated by the categories of Roman or Greek law. The letter indicates a potential and particular transformation of Onesimus from thing to person, and in this transformation, the assumption of an identity that is not directly determined by the range of subject positions of Roman or Greek law. It is a transformation that, through brotherhood, establishes an equal and enduring coexistence between Philemon and Onesimus,[12] and, thereby, in relation to any decision to free Onesimus relates that freedom to brotherhood, rather than the Roman or Greek understanding of a status as a freed slave.[13]

The distinctiveness of this Pauline position, and its transformative effect, is enhanced by elements of the recent perspectives upon the Pauline letters that have sought, from a postcolonial perspective, to reveal the letters as oppositional texts to the Roman Empire (Diehl, 2012). The preceding division of the Pauline letters between major and minor is replaced by tracing the presence of an increasing anti-Roman temper that is itself the reflection of Paul's treatment within the Roman Empire. The arrest and imprisonment of Paul then assumes a central determinative role, representing the fullest expression of this anti-Roman temper, and this, in turn, finds direct textual expression in those letters, which include the Letter to Philemon, composed during this final period of imprisonment (Callahan, 2007).[14] The cumulative radicalization of Paul would then shape the sense to be attributed to the entreaty to Philemon and the prediction of the conduct of Philemon and the community upon receipt of Paul's letter in relation to Onesimus.

Yet the lingering uncertainty as to whether Philemon and his community acted on Paul's entreaty points to the limits of this interpretation. The letter leaves open the possibility that there is a lack of correspondence in the understanding of brotherhood between Paul and Philemon or either a failure or reluctance to adhere to the Pauline understanding.[15] It is this enduring uncertainty that confines the interpretation of the distinctive transformative purpose of the letter to the prediction of historical human action.

The interpretation exists in parallel with an alternative interpretation in which the Pauline entreaty and the return of Onesimus to Philemon leave the social structure of the Christian community of Colossae essentially unaffected. Onesimus's position upon return to Philemon, despite the discourse of brotherhood, would remain and endure as that of a slave. Here, the letter encapsulates:

> Paul's construction of a Christian world that is different to the world around him, whilst relying on the latter's concepts and actualities. . . . The window opened in *Philemon* shows Paul's theology in action on a particular case (and identifiable individual): Onesimus, once converted, remains a slave under the rules of the "old" world (including his ownership by a fellow Christian, and by the apostle himself), whilst becoming an equal under the rules of the new world. There exists, however, no ultimate contradiction in Paul's thought because of the apostle's apocalyptic stance which transcends the "old" world: whilst in the latter there is Jew and Greek, slave and free, man and woman, it is through the act of active disregard (but not dismissal!) of such statuses and roles that Paul attempts to

> establish their fundamental unimportance. In Paul's theological construction, active *dismissal* of the worldly statuses and roles of slave and free would, in turn, function to (re)establish their importance. In practice, then, Onesimus' slave status has to *remain unquestioned* by Paul, *thereby* postulating its ultimate insignificance—through the creation of parallel universes. (Roth, 2014, p. 126)

The letter is the particular application of a broader reconfiguration of hierarchical relations—the inclusion and reconfiguration of existing master-slave relationships—whose character is simultaneously preserved and overlain by a set of hierarchical Christian relationships (pp. 126–127). From this perspective, the degree of internal transformation of the social and spiritual relationships of an already existing and firmly delimited community is limited and uncertain: "The ambiguity that we have seen was inherent in the practice of slavery—a 'social death' that nevertheless left the slave a part of society—and highlights the tension in Paul's own appeal for Onesimus" (Smith, 2012, p. 58).

The transformative potential or capacity of the letter circulates between these two forms of interpretation. A further interpretative effort is required in order to reveal a sensitivity to injustice and the responsibility to transform it into noninjurious social relations.

Excursus on Onesimus

The limitations of the Letter to Philemon indicate an unfinished or unrealized transformative potential that requires a further interpretative approach to the Pauline concept of a brother. The entreaty by Paul to the master, Philemon, to treat the slave, Onesimus, as a brother has to be considered as limited by both an ambiguity and its insertion within the broader linguistic framework of the letter. The ambiguity and limitation are equally applicable to the understanding of Onesimus's presence with Paul as resulting from an escape from Philemon or as an effective "lending" of Onesimus to Paul by Philemon as part of the wider relationship between Paul and this particular Christian community (Johnson, 2012, p. 95). The ambiguity results from the position of Onesimus in the letter where he remains silent: he is only spoken of—referred to—as the central topic of the letter, which is entirely structured as one between the addresser, Paul, and the addressee, Philemon (p. 94). Onesimus has no voice of his own.

The attentiveness to this ambiguity and the consequent limitation of the transformative potential contained in the Letter to Philemon arise from the historical encounter of Christianity and slavery in the United States of America. Here the Bible, which contains the letters of Paul, was placed in a central position in both the justification of (chattel) slavery and in the structure of the life of a slave on the plantations through the obligation to attend Christian church services shaped by the assumption of the fundamental biblical or scriptural compatibility of slavery and Christianity. The abolition of slavery, in the Thirteenth Amendment to the Constitution of the United States (1865), symbolizes the end of a structure in which only individual slaves can be freed—a decision entirely within the purview of their master—without affecting the system of slavery.[16] It is this sense of abolition that then severs the preceding intertwining of Christianity and slavery, and, in this severance, places reinforced emphasis upon overcoming the ambiguity and limitations of the Letter to Philemon.[17]

The memory and legacy of slavery and its abolition affect the interpretative sensibility in relation to the Letter to Philemon and, in particular, the position accorded to Onesimus in the letter. The particular position of Paul, an addresser who is speaking on behalf of Onesimus, can no longer remain uninterrogated. The speaking on behalf of Onesimus, the substitution of Paul for Onesimus, becomes the potential to supplant or occlude Onesimus. As Johnson says: "Paul, in speaking for and to the exclusion of Onesimus, operates as though he could exhaust the possibilities under the control and constraints he imposes upon the discourse, and thus contain the likelihood of more dangerous and disruptive elements shattering the neat rhetorical foreclosure on radical ethical alterity" (p. 96).

The limits created by the substitution of Paul for Onesimus therefore shape the character and content of the letter. The letter explicitly considers Paul's mode of address to Philemon, simultaneously indicating and relinquishing the capacity to order or prescribe to Philemon the course of conduct to be followed upon Onesimus's return (Phil. 1: 8–9). The mode of address is one of entreaty to Philemon, in which Paul attributes to himself the position of a "father" speaking on behalf of a "child," whose role is attributed to Onesimus (Phil. 1: 10). This is then the preparatory basis upon which Philemon is to "hear," identify with, and act upon Paul's message.

The adoption of this position by Paul on behalf of Onesimus continues to designate Onesimus—the shift from slave to fictional "child"—in an unequal position to both the addresser, Paul, and the addressee, Philemon. It is the shift in the character of the unequal position that is the preparatory stage for the subsequent entreaty that, upon Onesimus's return, Philemon treat Onesimus as a "brother" (Phil. 1: 16). The letter leaves the subsequent relationship between Onesimus and Philemon unresolved, and in this absence of resolution or clarity is contained both the limits, as well as the transformative and emancipatory potential, of the letter. The recasting of the central focus upon Onesimus emphasizes that these limits of the Pauline concept of brotherhood will be overcome by situating brotherhood beyond the limits of a predetermined community.

On Fraternity

The Pauline concept of a brother, as the central focus of the unrealized, transformative potential contained in the Letter to Philemon, reopens the question, *after* Schmitt, of its relationship to a notion of fraternity. The question concerns whether it is possible to retain the Schmittian approach, in *Political Theology* (1922), of an analogical transfer, and to inflect it in a direction that is no longer confined to one between theology and modern concepts of the state. The difficulty of this question relates not merely to the comprehension of fraternity as a secular brotherhood but also to whether the Pauline concept of a brother is itself an "origin" that obscures the essential, primordial enmity of brotherhood. These difficulties find their contemporary expression in the work of Jean-Luc Nancy and Roberto Esposito, and it is by considering their approaches that the possibility of a connection between Pauline brotherhood and fraternity emerges.

The primordial or originary enmity of brotherhood, which will always precede and disrupt the Pauline conception of brotherhood, arises, for Esposito, from the interweaving of Freud and Hobbes—which locates this enmity beyond the later Schmittian recourse, in *Ex Captivitate Salus*, to the Old Testament's exemplary origin of brotherly enmity in Cain and Abel (Schmitt, 2017a, p. 71).[18] The interweaving situates Freud prior to Hobbes "as the explicative key of the entire Hobbesian construction" (Esposito, 2010, p. 42). The Freudian presentation[19] of the dynamics of enmity is generated by the sons killing and supplanting the primal father, and the brothers then sublimating the mixture of guilt and competitive enmity, through prohibition (*Totem and Taboo*) or a form of association (*Moses and Monotheism*), into the symbolic substitute for the father: the prefiguration of an external order of constraint. The Hobbesian social contract, and the sovereign authority that it institutes, represents the response to "an originary guilt" (p. 42) that "always remains further behind with respect to where it is represented" (p. 37). The Hobbesian "origin" in the state of nature is already interwoven with the preceding Freudian presentation of the primordial origin. The interweaving reveals that the fear that traverses the Hobbesian state of nature is not merely the generalized fear of a violent death but rather of "its return as death to all those, namely, the brothers who once killed and then forever made this death one that belonged properly to them" (p. 36). It is a fear overlain by the originary guilt in which the Freudian "structural logic of the sacrificial paradigm" (p. 39) indicates that the passage from the state of nature to the social contract—"the sacrifice of basic instincts" (p. 34)—is preceded by the sacrifice of the father: "sacrifice is not only the result but also the presupposition of the *pactum societas*" (p. 39). Thus, Hobbes, as the exemplification of the parameters of early modern political theory and, in particular, of the central position it accords to the social contract as the creation of sovereign authority, remains shaped by the memory of a primordial enmity of brotherhood. It is a memory of double sacrifice: "first the sacrifice of the father and later the sacrifice of the same brothers to the sacrificed father" (p. 39). The social contract—the Hobbesian "formula of the authorization: personally taking on one's guilt" (p. 39)—is the relinquishing of individual political identity through identification with the Leviathan. This double sacrifice "responds to this origin, to the fear that the origin provokes: infinitely reactivating it in a circle from which we still have not emerged" (p. 14).

The further explicit invocation of fraternity in the French Revolution, as the passage from the early modern to the modern is, for Esposito, a reconfiguration of the essential enmity of brotherhood. The reconfiguration involves the transposition of this enmity into an "antinomy of nation and birth" (Esposito, 2008, p. 171). Fraternity, in the course of the French Revolution, assumes the predominant position, in relation to the liberty and equality of the 1789 Declaration of the Rights of Man and the Citizen, as the "invisible unity of the nation against its enemies" (p. 172). The primacy accorded to fraternity is to confine liberty and equality within a national and nationalistic framework: the expression of "a self-identification founded on consanguinity of belonging to the same nation. . . . It excludes all those who do not belong to the same blood as that of the common father" (p. 173). The underlying exclusionary logic is animated by "a conflictual, when not bellicose attitude" (p. 173) informed by the essential enmity of brotherhood.

The recourse to the Pauline concept of brotherhood would, therefore, appear to confront the irremediable enmity that Esposito considers inhering in any political articulation of brotherhood. The apparent intrinsic limitation of all political appropriations and rearticulations of the concept of brotherhood is qualified by the reconsideration that Nancy undertakes.[20] While acknowledging that to pose the question of fraternity anew requires the "exercise of a kind of reserve,"[21] it is a reserve that also operates against the presupposition that fraternity is confined to the expression of "the family understood as a patriarchal structure" (Nancy, 2013, p. 120).

In the space created by this reserve, fraternity is detached from the exclusive focus upon "the father and on transmission by males" and its necessary corollary, consanguinity as the sole definition of "generation and filiation" (p. 120). This enables, through the broadening of the definition of generation and filiation, the displacement of the exclusive determination of fraternity by blood—the lineage or brotherhood of "those who share the same bloodline" (p. 120)—with "the external, discontinuous and mediated gift of a nutritional substance" (p. 121). The family is now comprehended as "the minimal social group required to generate offspring and to take on what follows from that generation (that is, the care and supervision of children up to the point of their autonomy)" (p. 120). This returns consideration to the adulthood of the brothers and sisters as a process preceded by their birth,[22] in which infancy and adolescence are shaped by the original paradoxical connection to the mother: "the infant does not identify with, but *absorbs* the maternal substance into its own autonomous substance" (p. 121). It is this phenomenon of nourishment, not the identification with the father (which is always a secondary phenomenon in both time and importance) that establishes the form of connection between the brothers and sisters and, in turn, the content of fraternity: "autonomous subjects" whose connection is "founded on nothing other than the companionship of being nourished" (p. 121). The commonality of nourishment is a communality of "accident without community of origin or sense" (p. 121). Thus, " 'fraternity' does not carry with it *ipso facto* the values of the masculine and the paternal such as we hear them in the ordinary sense. Fraternity expresses coexistence without the necessity of 'nature' or 'destiny' or 'foundation' or 'origin'" (p. 121). Rather, it contains an essential contingency, "a relation that is erratic, and astray," reflected in *both* the "motif of the *enemy brothers*" and "memory of, as well as desire for, communal nourishment" (p. 121).

The motif of enemy brothers, and the enmity that it expresses, is therefore not the essence of fraternity—as Schmitt believed—but, rather, the obscuring of an essential contingency, through the reduction and simplification of the absence of a foundational relationship between the brothers. The essential contingency results from "the combination of chance (an encounter) and an embrace (a desire)" (p. 122), as the only prerequisites for the creation of the family—the minimal social group required to generate offspring and to guide them to an autonomous adulthood. The passage to autonomous adulthood is situated within the "sphere of nourishment" (p. 121) that is retained within the adult siblings as both memory and desire.

The essential contingency of the sphere of nourishment entails that fraternity is neither "manly brotherhood" nor a "masculine one-sidedness" (p. 121), but contains both a fraternal and a sororal element that are not predicated upon "making sisters equal to brothers." The two elements, as the coexistence of female and male siblings, express the "transmission and . . . sharing of nourishment." The sphere of nourishment exists "beyond or below the law" (p. 122), and thereby ceases to relate to an original parricide: the pacific regulation of the coexistence of the brothers through the installation of the symbolic replacement of the father in an instance of personified sovereignty. This extrinsic position in relation to the interweaving of Freudian and Hobbesian frameworks extends to the modern concepts of nationality and nationhood. For the sphere of nourishment presupposes a fraternal coexistence without fundamental determination or orientation by consanguinity.

It is the contingency of the sphere of nourishment—the combination of an encounter and a desire—that is the concern of law as formalization, standardization, and control of "chance or at least—and at the same time—of legitimizing the determinations" (p. 122).[23] This sphere and its contingency are subsumed beneath an overarching "socio-political organization" that, however, cannot eliminate fraternity, as modern sociopolitical organization is itself "founded upon the retreat of every foundational principle" (p. 122).[24]

For Nancy, and *after* Schmitt, fraternity is an essential, irreducible aspect of modern sociopolitical organization, which is "the lot of democracy: it must take on this vacuum without appealing to a mythology" (p. 122).[25] Thus,

> democracy aspires to open within itself and for itself—for that which, within it, exceeds the strict register of the law—a dimension that itself opens up access to desire or to affect, to what I am naming here in an awkward manner to designate this outside of the law and of power—vacant or not—within which being-together exceeds its proper sociality and its governmentality. If "liberty" and "equality" represent—on the condition of always being rethought—the minimal conditions of a civil association without given foundation, "fraternity" might be pointing to the horizon of this outside of the socio-political. If truth be told, it is not even a horizon: rather, it is an opening in every kind of horizon, in every kind of delimitation. This opening is that of sense: sense in so far as it always returns elsewhere, toward an elsewhere, and never forges a final meaning. (p. 122)

Fraternity is that which exists beyond liberty and equality, and in this existence holds open that which liberty and equality cannot express.[26]

The Universal

The continued pertinence of fraternity acknowledges its initial Pauline articulation, in the Letter to Philemon, but subjects it to renewed consideration. The limits of the Pauline concept of brotherhood are rethought and transformed into a concept of fraternity distinguished by an intrinsic openness. The concept of fraternity then facilitates an intervention in, and interruption of, the Schmittian suspicion of the universal. It leads from the Schmittian unmasking of the impossibility of the universal to a reconsideration of its possibility: a thought of the universal that arises from a reflection upon the difficulties of its articulation and realization.[27]

Schmitt's *Concept of the Political* represents the condensed expression of his suspicion of the universal.[28] The suspicion is the corollary of the Schmittian concept of the political predicated upon the ineradicable existence of the antagonistic relationship between friend and enemy. The antagonism is the exclusive determinant of the domain of the political and the impossibility of a concept of the political predicated upon a "political entity . . . embracing all of humanity and the entire world" (Schmitt, 2007b, p. 53). A political entity can only exist in a "pluriverse" demarcating the antagonistic "coexistence with another political entity" (p. 53). Universalism conceives the existence of political entities within a "universe," a coexistence founded upon an underlying unity that, for Schmitt, originates in the eighteenth century with the "nonpolitical term humanity" (p. 55). The concrete antagonism of friend and enemy renders the category of humanity, and the universalism it purports to articulate, an essentially abstract concept that facilitates either "the utopian ideal of total depoliticization and . . . the non-existence of states" (p. 55) or its particular, instrumental appropriation or usurpation by a state in its antagonistic coexistence with other states.

Our reconfiguration of the concept of fraternity allows the universal to be understood as other than an abstract universal, as it is without essential connection to, or dependence upon, the category of humanity. The absence of connection or dependence marks the lack of adherence to the underlying Schmittian opposition between abstract and concrete, which also excludes the recourse to fraternity as the assertion of a concrete category displacing or reorientating the friend/enemy relationship. Our alternative understanding of fraternity—as developed through Nancy—situates it outside the Schmittian demarcation of the reality of the political and its insistence upon the concomitant deflation and rejection of the universal.

Fraternity is an aspect of the relationship between the particular or singular and the universal. Both elements are components of a relationship that arises and proceeds through their essential interconnection. The interconnection entails that the character of their opposition is other than one in which the concrete, once revealed, demonstrates the empty, obfuscatory abstraction of the universal. For the universal is defined not by abstraction but by a more complex process of articulation between "three related but heterogeneous terms whose widespread use has prompted conflicting claims: the *universal* (if indeed it is singular), *universality* (which immediately calls for clarification and determination, for there is no universality 'in itself,' not even universality of the universal), and *universalisms* (which, decidedly plural, are thrown straightaway into a kind of 'performative contradiction')" (Balibar, 2020a, p. 96). The reflection upon this process of articulation is the comprehension of opposition as one that arises *within* these three terms. This provides a different orientation toward the liberalism and modern universalism that Schmitt holds to be inextricably intertwined with abstract universalism.[29] For the definition of the universal, as the articulation of these three terms, acknowledges that within modern universalism exist "certain differences at once *indissoluble and undefinable*" (p. 98), and that, in relation to these differences, modern universalism imposes stability through perpetually renewed delimitation (p. 100).

The perpetual renewal centers upon the determination of the coexistence of the notions of liberty and equality and, as a determination, can only be a particular or singular delimitation of the unconditional universality contained in these two notions.[30] Here, there is also violence, but a violence that expresses itself otherwise than within the confines of the friend/enemy distinction. The violence "lies *both* in the denegation of differences and in their absolutization, every revolt must face the difficulty of deciding whether it will emphasize the legitimacy of difference, the right to particularity, or the primacy of universality and the need for its reconfiguration on new grounds" (p. 100).

Fraternity is as an essential supplement to this idea of universality. Fraternity is that which exists beyond the particular delimitation of the coexistence of the notions of liberty and equality. It contains a sense of coexistence that belongs *with* but cannot be subsumed by liberty and equality. The supplement of fraternity enables a distinct response to the "sense of the connection between the differences that characterize *humans as humans* and the institutions of the universal, or the forms of institutional universality" (pp. 100–101). Fraternity qualifies and holds open both the delimitation of the human from the natural world and of the human from the human. Fraternity responds to the "insistent question regarding differences" (p. 104) differently from that resulting from the combined response of liberty and equality.

In its combined relationship with liberty and equality, fraternity is a thought and imperative for coexistence that arises without an immediate or necessary reference to an external or transcendent sovereign authority. Fraternity, as a subjectivity already related to others, is inconceivable within the Schmittian opposition between liberalism and the political. For this relatedness to others is neither that of liberalism nor "buried" beneath this, the Schmittian political of fundamental antagonism. The supplement of fraternity, resulting from a process of interpretative retrieval upon the Letter to Philemon, is a relatedness arising from injurious social relationships and their potential transformation. Fraternity insists that injurious social relationships create a relatedness, a transformative commonality, which persists in combination with liberty and equality. This commonality becomes the transformative horizon from which to respond to the problem of injustice and to prevent it from disappearing into the expression of a human nature with all its attendant "natural" inequalities and hierarchical distinctions. For this disappearance is the disqualification of fraternal coexistence and, with this disqualification, the contraction of the political to the external imposition of political authority.

4

Political Theology and the Anthropocene

The previous chapter explored a certain theological conception of social justice and emancipation embodied in the idea of fraternity and in the notion of a spiritual community of equals in which the escaped slave Onesimus was said to be included. While, as we argued, this is ultimately a limited gesture, being confined to a particular religious community and determined by an eschatological promise of future liberation—and, as such, having no power to effect a broader transformation of social and political relations in *this* world—it nevertheless indicates the potential for a less restrictive and more emancipatory approach to political theology.

Our aim throughout this book has been to develop an approach to political theology that is no longer bound to the sovereign-centric Schmittian model in which political and legal authority, crystallized in the "miraculous" decision within the moment of exception, is exercised in an absolute sense over the community. Schmitt's political theology is premised not only on the translation of monotheistic theological concepts—God and the miracle—into secularized political and juridical categories but also on the doctrine of original sin and the assumption of the fundamental evil of human nature (see Schmitt 2005, p. 56; 2007b, pp. 58–60; see also Meier, 1998). Mankind's dangerous passions can only be controlled through the imposition of a legal-political order founded on the sovereign decision. Moreover, it is this sovereign will that determines the contours and identity of the political community, differentiating friend from enemy, inside from outside, and constructing its unity around the principle of obedience to authority. In Schmitt's strictly hierarchical and monotheistic version of political theology, the subject is either one who authorizes and freely imposes his will, or one who obeys and sacrifices his freedom.

This idea of political subjectivity, moreover, is entirely anthropocentric. The monotheistic image of God as sovereign over the universe finds its counterpart in the secular human sovereign who governs over society and whose autonomous will exceeds and suspends the legal norms from which he derives his authority. Schmitt's political theology is based on the idea of *transcendence*: to be sovereign, in either a political or theological sense, is to transcend the external material conditions of the world, whether these be laws, economic relations, technology, and even natural forces and systems. Indeed, for Schmitt, it is the ability to transcend the immanence of the world and to act autonomously through a decisive will that actually confers meaning and form on the world, allowing it to be represented as a whole, as a coherent, unified concept. Schmitt's idea of sovereignty conveys the anthropocentric idea, derived from the Judeo-Christian tradition, of the central figure of man who acts upon the world and dominates it. For Schmitt, the problem with theories of immanence is that they eclipse this transcendent, singular, sovereign dimension of action and existence, subsuming what is properly human into a broader set of processes into networks of relations and forces that are beyond man's control and come to determine his existence.

Schmitt in the Age of the Anthropocene

However, our challenge to Schmitt is whether this anthropocentric model of relations is still thinkable today in the time of what has come to be known as the Anthropocene, referring to a geological period in which human activity comes to affect the natural environment, in often disastrous and irreversible ways. The implications of the Anthropocene age for political theology are what will be explored in this chapter. This will open up two key questions. First, if, as Schmitt argues, each epoch is defined by a certain conceptual principle—a "metaphysical" constellation of ideas that gives meaning to the world and shapes its political ideas and institutions—then how might we grasp the political consequences of the Anthropocene as the defining principle of *our* age? What problems does it pose for political legitimacy today? In *Political Theology I* Schmitt proposes a "sociology of concepts [that] transcends juridical conceptualization oriented to immediate practical interest. It aims to discover the basic, radically systematic structure and to compare this conceptual structure with the conceptually represented social structure of a certain epoch" (2005, p. 45). With the collapse of the theological world in the sixteenth century and the onset of the modern period, the unifying principle, once provided by religion, is displaced by a new "metaphysical" order defined in the nineteenth and early twentieth centuries by economics, individualism, bourgeois culture, and ultimately by technology, with its associated political form of liberalism.

We propose that the contemporary period is currently being determined by a new "metaphysical" concept of the Anthropocene that, like the earlier transformations that Schmitt surveys, will have, indeed is *already* having, dramatic political consequences, presenting the political and economic order with a new crisis of legitimacy. At the same time, the Anthropocene is radically different from the constellations that preceded it, in the sense that it imposes an absolute limit—one defined by the limits of nature—on the narrative of human progress, economic growth, technological hubris, and liberal individualism that defined the previous era. The ecological catastrophe not only poses major questions for the future of the capitalist economy and the capacity of our political institutions to effectively respond to and govern this crisis but also places in doubt the anthropocentric view of the world that has been dominant for centuries.

To some extent, the limits of anthropocentrism are foreshadowed in Schmitt's critique of Hans Blumenberg in the final pages of *Political Theology II*. In his reading of Blumenberg's *The Legitimacy of the Modern Age*, in which Blumenberg asserts the radical novelty and innovation of modernity as a sign of its legitimacy, Schmitt (2008c) characterizes Blumenberg's thesis as imbued with a kind of aggressive hubris borne of the idea of human and scientific progress:

> The new human being is aggressive in terms of the ongoing progress and continuous repositioning of himself. He rejects the concept of the enemy and any secularization or transposition of old conceptions of the enemy. He leaves behind the outmoded through what is scientifically, technically and industrially new. The old is not the enemy of the new. The old resolves itself, through itself, in the scientific, technical, industrial process-progress which either consumes the old— according to the measure of new utilities—or will be ignored as unusable or annihilated as invalid. (pp. 129–130)

Implied here is a critique not only of the narrative of scientific, industrial, and technological progress but also of the humanistic and anthropocentric image of the world central to modernity, which has displaced earlier theological representations. In Schmitt's eyes, Blumenberg's attempt to affirm the legitimacy of the modern age on its own terms, rather than seeing it as a secularization of theological ways of thinking (see Blumenberg, 1985), is an example of the new totalizing spirit of immanence in all its aggressivity. No doubt Schmitt is right to highlight the limits of this discourse of human and scientific progress—limits that are now being exposed by the Anthropocene. The Anthropocene signals the end of our anthropocentric modernity. However, our point is that Schmitt is just as beholden, in his own theologically inflected and antimodernist way, to an anthropocentric and anthropomorphic view of the world and of social relations.

The once dominant image of man—whether symbolized in Schmitt's terms as the transcendent figure of the sovereign, or in Blumenberg's terms as the immanent spirit of human progress—is no longer appropriate. We can no longer sustain an image of ourselves, derived from humanism and, ultimately, from monotheistic religions, of an autonomous sovereign agent who acts freely upon the external natural world, bends it to his will, exploits it for his enjoyment, and yet remains ontologically separated from it. The dramatic and damaging effects of human-induced climate change is, at the same time, a reminder of our entanglement with, and dependency upon, increasingly unstable ecosystems, which we share with natural and geological elements and nonhuman species. The contemporary age, on the contrary, is defined not by Promethean will or sovereign decisiveness but, rather, by human vulnerability and dependency—something that has been dramatically brought home to us by the pandemic crisis. Indeed, our sense of agency, autonomy, and exceptionality has been radically disturbed by a growing awareness of our embeddedness within complex systems and networks of relations with nonhuman natural entities, over which we have little control. This extends the meaning of the subject to the question of coexistence with natural ecosystems and with nonhuman species. Man has now to contend with Gaia.

Our claim, then, is that the Anthropocene exposes the limitations of Schmitt's model of political theology and demands a radical rethinking of the concept. There is no room for any kind of ecological awareness, let alone ecological politics, in Schmitt's political theology, because his thinking is largely beholden to an anthropocentric and anthropomorphic model of sovereignty and politics that is now no longer credible. The Anthropocene is not only an environmental crisis, but a crisis of all existing political forms, concepts, and discourses. It relates to major questions about human finitude, our survival as a species, and our relations with the natural world. It throws up new questions about what it means to be human and about how politics needs to be rethought in relation to our broader ecological and planetary entanglements. In this chapter, we explore the possibility of a new kind of political theology—immanent and "worldly" rather than transcendent—that can respond to the ethical, political, and, indeed, anthropological challenges of the Anthropocene.

The Anthropocene was identified by Paul J. Crutzen and Eugene F. Stoemer (2000), who pointed to factors such as the dramatic and unsustainable growth in human population, rapid urbanization—the fact that today, for the first time in human history, more people live in cities and urban rather than in rural areas—the growth in global cattle population, rising CO_2 levels in the atmosphere, the loss of tropical rainforests and coastal wetlands, and massive and unprecedented species extinction, among many other indicators of man's geological influence on the planet. While a contested term, the Anthropocene refers to the geological period—usually dated to the start of the industrial revolution in the eighteenth century—in which human activity begins to have a dramatic and irreversible impact on the planet. The Anthropocene was preceded by the Holocene, a period over the past ten to twelve thousand years or so in which the Earth's climate and ecosystems experienced relative stability. However, as it is argued, we have now entered into a new geological phase of climate and ecosystem instability, as a result of the accumulated and ongoing effects of human activity. A tipping point has been reached for the survival of the life systems of planet. Man, who once lived at the mercy of natural elements, struggling to survive and adapt himself to harsh environmental conditions, has now become the major geological actor, transforming the natural world around him and doing irreparable damage to it in the process. These developments have only accelerated to the point where the future of life on the planet—human and nonhuman—is now seriously at risk. Hardly a day goes by without the reporting of some sign of impending ecological collapse, whether it is record-breaking temperatures increasing year on year; more unstable weather patterns; melting sea ice and declining glacier density in the polar regions; rising sea levels and increased flooding of coastal areas; the pollution of rivers and oceans; the damage to marine life, ecosystems, and coral reefs due to rising sea temperatures as well as chemicals and pesticides; widespread deforestation; habitat loss; wildfires in the Artic; declining bee and other pollinating insect numbers; soil depletion; loss of biodiversity; and what scientists refer to as the Sixth

Great Extinction event. Such are the terrifying yet utterly mundane effects of human activity on the natural environment. The recent report by the Intergovernmental Panel on Climate Change (IPCC, 2021) reported an alarming increase in CO_2 emissions in the atmosphere and the rise of global temperatures, along with decreasing Artic sea ice and rising global sea levels, linking these unequivocally to human activity. Recent extreme weather events—such the heatwaves, wildfires, and flooding experienced in many parts of Europe in the summer of 2021—indicate that we are already living through the climate apocalypse. To limit global warming to 1.5–2°C in order to merely mitigate the effects of catastrophic climate change would mean completely ending the burning of fossil fuels within the next ten years—something that seems, in the current political climate, highly unlikely.[1]

The Anthropocene therefore poses acute political, social, technical, economic, and, indeed, philosophical and existential problems and questions for the entire human species. We now live in a condition marked, on the one hand, by human sovereignty and agency, and, on the other, by a sense vulnerability and finitude. The Anthropocene is at once an expression of human power and impotence as man, this most rapacious and relentless of animals, is confronted with the self-destructive consequences of his activity. Like the man of the Holocene, he once again inhabits a world he no longer controls; he is once again at the mercy of external natural forces, but these are forces he himself has unleashed. What better symbol is there of this than the COVID-19 pandemic? The viral contagion, which has so dramatically disrupted human life everywhere, serves as a powerful reminder of human limitation and of our vulnerability to biological organisms. That this virus apparently emerged from certain wildlife food markets in China is no accident. Like many previous epidemics and pandemics, whether Spanish influenza in 1918 or more recent outbreaks like "mad cow disease," bird flu, and earlier versions of SARs, COVID-19 also came about as a consequence of the commercial exploitation of animals, whether through large-scale industrial farming and animal processing or the trade in wildlife. The disruption of natural ecosystems resulting from these practices leads to the inevitable crossing of species barriers, with animal to human (and in some cases human to animal) transmission of viruses. Zoonotic viruses such as COVID-19 thus overturn the very hierarchy between human and animal established by humanism and ultimately by Judeo-Christian theology. Pandemics remind us of the permeability of our bodies to pathogens and of the susceptibility of societies to viral contagions that freely cross borders—physical, geographical, political—and from which we lack any effective immune response. Human agency is now seriously threatened by viral agency. Moreover, the ease of transmission, and the inability of governments to successfully contain the virus, despite the emergency measures employed, points to the limits of political sovereignty in fulfilling its most basic function of protecting its population. That the most powerful states in the world are powerless against a microscopic virus symbolizes in more ways than one the limits of a politico-theological paradigm based on the preeminence of the sovereign state of exception.

The Anthropocene, and the current pandemic of which it is a particular expression, presents political institutions—democratic and authoritarian alike—with major challenges to their legitimacy. Thus, it becomes, from its initial, natural scientific framework, a situation that remains to be considered in politico-theological terms. For, at present, there is simply no coherent or credible plan, short of the pronouncement of fairly modest targets for cutting CO_2 emissions, such as those set in the Paris Climate Agreement of 2015, for addressing the long-term problem of human-induced climate change and the impending environmental disaster. And yet, as the scientists have been warning us for decades, the effects of this on our societies in years to come will be severe—from food and water shortages, extreme weather events, heatwaves, crop failures, climate migration, and so on. These will no doubt result—indeed are *already* resulting—in serious antagonisms and conflicts, nationally and globally, that will have the capacity to render political systems inoperative, conjuring up a nightmarish Hobbesian vision of anarchy, scarcity, and civilizational collapse: a return to the "state of nature." Moreover, if there is to be any kind of genuine and coordinated response to the ecological question, this will require far-reaching changes to the way we live and consume, and to the shape of our economic systems. At the very least, the previously dominant neoliberal model of a relatively unregulated form of capitalism is no longer tenable.[2] In other words, responding in an adequate way to the Anthropocene will require radically new ways of governing the economy and protecting the global commons.

A sovereign-centric political theology such as Schmitt's lacks the conceptual resources to properly think the consequences of the Anthropocene. Not only is it anthropocentric, as we have argued, but it is entirely concerned with the question of the legitimacy of the nation-state. For Schmitt, the political community, whose identity he seeks to establish through the sovereign decision and through the friend/enemy distinction, is always the *national* community. Any vision of a global community, global governance, or even global collective action only exists in Schmitt's political imagination as a naïve, utopian, and dangerously totalizing vision to be opposed. Schmitt is a thinker of borders and boundaries, conceptual and political. This fetishization of boundaries recurs throughout Schmitt's corpus. In *Political Theology I*, the main concern is to establish the conceptual borders of the law—which is always *national* law—through the sovereign decision that exceeds them and, in doing so, authorizes them. The concept of the border is further radicalized by the friend/enemy opposition formulated in *The Concept of the Political* (1932). Here the relation of enmity is intended to establish the boundaries of the national community, whose homogeneous identity is differentiated from that of other potentially hostile national communities with whom one is prepared to go to war. While war can become internalized, given a sufficient intensification of antagonisms between different groups and identities within the community, Schmitt's concern is to push the possibility of conflict outside the boundaries of the nation-state into the international realm. The limited, bounded horizon of nation-state realpolitik that Schmitt seeks to preserve explains his hostility to international legal and political institutions and organizations, and indeed, to the ethical-political project of universal human rights and liberal internationalism. Not only are such devices and projects totalizing and therefore dangerous, in Schmitt's eyes they cannot be considered as proper sites of the political, precisely because they lack an outside and a stable, coherent figure of the enemy: "The political entity presupposes the real existence of an enemy and therefore coexistence with another political entity. As long as a state exists, there will thus always be in the world more than just one state. A world state which embraces the entire globe and all of humanity cannot exist. The political world is a pluriverse, not a universe" (2007b, p. 53). The same reservations about the international order are reflected in *The Nomos of the Earth*, in which Schmitt documents the breakdown of the old European telluric order of sovereign nation-states, based on land appropriation and clearly demarcated borders and boundaries, and the emergence, following the First World War, of a new international order based on bodies like the League of Nations.

Moreover, Schmitt's contention that all law (nomos) is based on the founding act of land appropriation, reveals the anthropocentric and extractive relationship between man and the natural world that his conception of law and politics is ultimately premised upon:[3]

> Appropriating land and founding cities always is associated with an initial measurement and distribution of usable soil, which produces a primary criterion embodying all subsequent criteria. . . . All subsequent legal relations to the soil, originally divided among the appropriating tribe or people, and all institutions of the walled city or of a new colony are determined by this primary criterion. Every ontonomous and ontological judgment derives from the land. For this reason, we will begin with land appropriation as the primeval act in founding law. (2006, p. 45)

Schmitt's political thinking is essentially tied to the bordered concept of the nation community, rooted in clearly defined territory, and to a hostility toward any notion of global entanglements and responsibilities.[4] Of course, Schmitt is right to point to the way that the idea of international law and justice and universal human rights norms have often been used as an ideological cover for imperialist projects, that, in the words he takes from the anarchist Proudhon, "whoever invokes humanity wants to cheat" (2007b, p. 54). However, what is foreclosed from Schmitt's political theology is the possibility of an alternative global ethical-political horizon beyond that of sovereign nation-states. And yet it is precisely this pluriverse of sovereign nation-states that is proving increasingly untenable in the context of problems of pandemics and ecological catastrophes, which are not confined to national borders and cannot be resolved unilaterally. These are problems that demand, in other words, unprecedented levels of global cooperation and governance.[5] The Anthropocene thus points to the need for a new nomos of the earth. In disturbing boundaries and borders of all kinds, it demands a new vision of a global political community and new concepts of global justice, even a new kind of cosmopolitan vision. We will return to this in a later chapter.

The limits of Schmitt's thought in contending with the Anthropocene have deeper theological roots, however. In his prison writings, *Ex Captivitate Salus*, Schmitt reflects on the expulsion of Adam and Eve from the Garden of Eden in Genesis, as well as on the killing of Abel by Cain, the act upon which the original condition of enmity, so central to Schmitt's political theology (see Meier 1998, p. 46), was founded:

> Whom in the world can I acknowledge as my enemy? Clearly only him who can call me into question. By recognizing him

> as enemy I acknowledge that he can call me into question. And who can really call me into question? Only I myself. Or my brother. The other proves to be my brother, and the brother proves to be my enemy. Adam and Eve had two sons, Cain and Abel. Thus begins the history of humankind. This is what the father of all things looks like. This is the dialectical tension that keeps world history moving, and world history has not yet ended. (2017a, p. 71)

This passage is revealing because it establishes as the foundation for political theology the initial expulsion of man from the Garden of Eden and the violent relations of enmity that ensued from it. In other words, Schmitt's political theology is precipitated by the event that symbolizes our detachment and alienation from nature. The "history of humankind" thus starts from the initial separation of man from the natural world, from the original Edenic state of oneness with nature. Moreover, it is the theological doctrine of "original sin," based on Adam and Eve's transgression at the tree of good and evil, that informs Schmitt's conception of human nature, serving as a justification for his authoritarian concept of sovereignty. Man's expulsion from paradise is, for Christian theology, the defining event of the human condition, as well as the basis for Christianity's promise of our future redemption and salvation in the coming Kingdom of God (see Agamben, 2020b). The initial rift between man and nature lies at the heart of Christian theology, and indeed the entire Judeo-Christian tradition. While, as we will show later, there is room within Christianity for a nonanthropocentric vision of the world, and even for a Christian political theology based around ecological awareness and environmental justice, the dominant position in this theological tradition has been an anthropocentric one in which man, divided from nature, seeks to objectify it and subordinate it to his will. The fact that Schmitt's political thinking essentially begins from man's original separation from his natural home reveals the anthropocentric orientation of his political theology.

Decentering the Human: God, Men, and Animals

As we have argued thus far, the Anthropocene radically displaces the dominant centrality of human experience, making us aware of our entanglement with natural ecosystems, actors, and forces that determine us as we determine them. The dualism between man and nature, between the human and nonhuman, thus breaks down. Central to this is the deconstruction of the binary division between man and animal upon which so many of our anthropocentric political categories depend (see Calarco, 2008; see also Derrida 2008).[6] Giorgio Agamben (2004) highlights the workings of an anthropological machine at the heart of Western political culture, in which the identity of the human is reproduced through the inclusion/exclusion of the nonhuman. In other words, the anthropocentric figure of man is defined through its binary opposition to the animal, which is at the same time presupposed by it. The nonhuman element is not merely excluded from human culture and identity but *included within it in the form of an exclusion*—a kind of "capture" that generates a zone of exception between man and animal. This authorizes not only the domination, brutalization, and exploitation of nonhuman animals but also the exclusion of certain categories of humans who are, at different times, reduced to the status of "animals."

Moreover, just as certain human beings are "reduced" to the level of the animal, certain types of animals are "raised" to the level of human beings. The anthropomorphic treatment of animals, whereby we attribute certain human traits and characteristics to other species, is merely the other side of this "anthropological machine." As Felice Cimatti (2017, 2020a, 2021)[7] argues, following Agamben's analysis, our "humanization" of certain animals, whether these be domestic pets or intelligent primates, leads to the same imposition of arbitrary exclusions, divisions, and hierarchies between animal species that we find in the human world. Once again, a certain arbitrary standard of the "human" is used to define, evaluate, and objectify animals, to identify and privilege those whom we regard as closer to us and as therefore worthy of a kind of personhood—granting them rights or legal recognition for instance—over those deemed further away from us and to whom we deny any kind of status or protection. Therefore, a more radical strategy is to acknowledge, in the words of Cimatti, that the animal *does not exist* (2020a, p. 2); that, in other words, the category of the "animal," a catch-all for a multitude of different beings, is a linguistic invention based on an arbitrary dualistic division. Rather, there are only *singular* living beings—something that would apply to both "humans" and "animals" (2020a, p. 25).[8]

All beings—humans and nonhumans—are in different states of *becoming*. We can understand this as the multiple connections that take place between different living forces, in which their identity changes and they become something else. Gilles Deleuze and Felix Guattari give the example of the assemblage that is formed when a wasp comes to procreate with an orchid, becoming part of the orchid's reproductive system: the wasp enters into a *becoming-orchid*. As Deleuze and Guattari put it: "Becoming is the movement by which the line frees itself from the point, and renders points indiscernible: the rhizome, the opposite of arborescence; breaks away from arborescence" (1987, p. 294). In other words, becoming refers to a threshold of intensity of connection that takes place *between* identities, such that the consistency of these identities is blurred and made indistinct. This produces what they call a "line of flight," an immanent field of haphazard and unpredictable connections that escapes the fixed, hierarchical, "arborescent" ordering of concepts and identities. As we can see, this idea of an intensity, produced through immanent, rhizomatic connections and multiple and contingent encounters, is very different from Schmitt's notion of the friend/enemy relation, in which intensity is understood as an increasing antagonism and *separation* between two parties, and through which their identities become more, rather than less, distinct (Schmitt 2007b, p. 26). In other words, the ontology of becoming, something that, according to Deleuze and Guattari, all living creatures take part in, proceeds in exactly the opposite direction to Schmitt's political theology, which is concerned with fixing concepts and identities, creating distance, defining borders and boundaries, and establishing a transcendent, hierarchical order. Rather, for theorists of immanence, identities break down on a horizontal plane characterized by multiple "rhizomatic" connections that form between them. The individual subject is not a fixed, essential identity but rather an infinite multiplicity.

Human beings can also engage in becoming-animal, as can be seen in totemic cultures. Indeed, as a way of breaking down the anthropocentric machine that fixes man and animal to established categories of meaning and existence, thus imprisoning both, we humans might, according to Cimatti, pursue the experimental strategy of "unbecoming" our humanity and identifying with animals, or with the animal dimension of ourselves. This does not translate easily into a distinct political strategy; politics, at least in its usual understanding, and in the tradition going back to Aristotle, is an exclusively human practice, involving human subjects, identities, and institutions. Nevertheless, as Cimatti suggests, becoming-animal can be understood in an ethical and aesthetic sense: in the same way that nonhuman animals inhabit the environment in which they live, *using* natural elements without exploiting them or establishing proprietary relations over them, human animals can adopt a similar nonproprietorial and nondominating relationship to the natural world and, indeed, to themselves (Cimatti, 2020a, pp. 203–204). To identify with the animal dimension of ourselves is a way of overcoming the anthropological—or as we would say *theological-anthropological*—machine that not only erects arbitrary divisions and hierarchies between man and animal but also alienates and divides man from himself.

Moreover, becoming-animal is associated with the formation of new kinds of groupings and collective assemblages. As Cimatti explains:

> "Becoming-animal" is a way to think of non-subjectivised individuality, single bodies that are not an "I" but "group individuals" (the challenge of animality lies within this oxymoron). But at the same time these bodies are extraordinarily more powerful than those trapped in the cage of subjective identity, and derive this power precisely from their not being stifled by the fear of losing their "I." New and previously unthought vital possibilities are thus disclosed, combinations that break the boundaries of the body, forming fluxes where distinguishing between who is active and who is passive, who is a subject and who is an object, who is human and who isn't, no longer has any meaning. (2020a, p. 161)

This new formation should not be taken to imply the domination of the collective over the individual, or the absorption of the subject into a totalizing community identity. Rather, it is a new composition of singularities defined by absence of essential identities or predetermined categories, whether of the individual or the collective.

It is therefore important to consider how the Anthropocene decenters human political experience and already evokes alternative understandings of community, subjectivity, and political engagement. Is it impossible, for instance, to imagine a form of politics no longer based around human exclusivity: new kinds of political communities and solidarities that we form with animals, or alliances that we make with nature?[9] Such conceptions of subjectivity and community are entirely different from the idea of a bounded national community and a unified, homogeneous demos central to Schmittian political theology. As we showed in a previous chapter, Schmitt's model of democracy leaves us with a populist and identitarian form of politics, defined by a hostility to pluralism and difference. Given the deeply confronting, existential challenges posed by the Anthropocene, in which the very idea of human agency and autonomy are thrown into doubt, it is perhaps not surprising that this sort of right-wing identity politics, based on the illusion of sovereignty and national identity, resurges today as a paranoid and defensive reaction to the growing realization of our vulnerability as a species and our complex interdependencies on natural ecosystems. Populism is a denial of complexity. It is an expression of the desire to not be encumbered by broader systems and relationships—whether these be global, technical, and especially ecological. We think of the contempt displayed by populist figures like Trump and Bolsonaro toward environmental concerns and the ethical and political obligations these impose upon us. Populism is, in other words, a politics of disavowal of the Anthropocene and its deterritorializing effects.

By contrast, the recognition of complexity and ecosystem entanglement involves alternative inventions of political community, subjectivity, and action—a new experimental "ecology of practices" as Isabelle Stengers puts it (2010)—in which solidarity with the natural world and with nonhuman species is the guiding ethical motivation. If this is a democratic politics, it is surely very different from the democratic model based on the sovereign, unified "will of the people" that is currently producing such disastrous and rancorous demagoguery. Rather, it would evoke a very different kind of democratic horizon, one that is decentralized and pluralistic, indeed cosmopolitan, and that would include, or at least acknowledge the interests of, nonhuman actors. This could involve a fuller extension of rights to nonhuman species and to the natural world.[10] Indeed, various organizations have called for legal recognition of the rights of nature alongside human rights, even drafting a "Universal Declaration for the Rights of Mother Earth" (see Cullinan, 2010). Or it could involve forms of activism aimed at disrupting industrial farming processes and emancipating animals from their mistreatment, servitude, and exploitation; or protecting and defending the natural commons from commercial enclosure and extraction; or experiments in autonomous and more ecologically sustainable ways of living. It will also involve complex interactions, of cooperation as well as contestation, with institutions and policymaking at regional, national, and global levels as part of a networked model combining both formal and grassroots organizations. Of course, there are already countless examples of such practices, movements, campaigns, communities, networks, and forms of direct action taking place everywhere throughout the world.

Central to this idea is the recognition that social and political domination and violence are intimately connected with the violence and domination we inflict upon nature, and therefore that the emancipation of human beings can no longer be treated as separate from the emancipation of nonhuman beings and the protection of the natural world. While, of course, this language of emancipation is itself part of the Enlightenment humanist discourse—and perhaps we lack an adequate terminology for what a post-anthropocentric, post-humanist experience of freedom might mean—the very possibility of including nonhuman species and wider natural ecosystems within practices and communities of emancipation already signals a shift toward an alternative conception of politics (see Cudworth and Hobden, 2018). At the very least, emancipation, understood in its post-humanist sense, must mean something more than individual autonomy—as in the idea of negative liberty—but, rather, a sense of ethical responsibility, not only for other human beings but also for nonhuman species and for the natural world.

A similar claim is also made by Bruno Latour and Timothy M. Lenton in their discussion of the political implications of James Lovelock's Gaia hypothesis. They argue that Gaia, and the conditions of the Anthropocene more generally, opens up new horizons of politics and indeed an expansion in the meaning of human freedom. On the one hand, ecological dependency, implicit in the notion of Gaia, imposes new limitations on human action, to the extent to which we can no longer think of ourselves as free, sovereign, and autonomous in the classical liberal sense. But on the other hand, ecological dependency leads to an extension of the notion of democracy and democratic freedom in so far as it poses a new relationship between the human and natural worlds: "It is for this reason that it is so important to define as precisely as possible the contribution made to this extended democracy by the discovery of Gaia; instead of replaying one more episode in the frustrating attempts at naturalizing human conduct, Gaia opens the possibility of extending the domain of freedom by sharing it more widely on both sides" (Latour & Lenton, 2019, p. 679).

The Political Challenge of Gaia and Ecopolitical Theology

The question we are left with is whether the Anthropocene should be understood as a wholly secular, detheologized condition to which we can only respond in the language of science, or whether theology still might have a role to play in coming to terms with the political and ethical challenges imposed by the ecological crisis. For the most part, the Judeo-Christian tradition is an anthropocentric one (see White, 1967) based, as we have argued, on an original ontological separation from nature. Certainly, this finds expression within Schmitt's later considerations on the relationship between theology and politics. However, there are divergent strands within the Christian tradition that evoke an alternative, nonanthropocentric worldview and a radically different relationship between man and nature.[11]

Our claim is that the challenges of the Anthropocene call for a new relationship between science, politics, and theology. This is apparently what Bruno Latour has in mind when he calls for a new political theology of Gaia. Writing in the context of the Anthropocene and the new climatic regime, Latour points to the deeply religious structure of secular modernity as a way of understanding our apparent indifference—or at least our incapacity to act—in the face of the impending ecological emergency with its connotations of the "end of times." This is because, he argues, we moderns live *as though the Apocalypse has already occurred*. In a sense, modernity has inherited from religion the apocalyptic narrative; but the peculiar attitude of many moderns—including climate skeptics and those who appear unperturbed by the warnings of ecological collapse[12]—is the idea that they inhabit a post-apocalyptic time at the end if history, where nothing further can happen to them: "It is thus completely useless to speak to them in apocalyptic terms announcing to them the end of their world! They will reply condescendingly that they have already crossed over to the other side, that they are already no longer of this world, that nothing more can happen to them, that they are resolutely, definitively, completely, and forever modernized!" (Latour, 2017, pp. 195–196). One detects this deeply nihilistic way of thinking in the contemporary politics of nationalist populism, which is closely associated with climate change denial and the abdication of ethical responsibilities beyond national borders. In the populist fantasy, people can carry on blissfully with their current way of life, consuming without limit while the world burns around them. Scientific knowledge and discourse about climate change cannot, on its own, dislodge this otherworldly belief system. Theology has a role to play here. So, for Latour, the only way this secularized religiosity can be countered is through another kind of (political) theology embodied in the figure of Gaia, the earth goddess derived from Greek mythology, deployed by James Lovelock and Lynn Margulis as a way of understanding earth as a complex, self-regulating system of living organisms and geological forces (see Lovelock, 2000). Yet, for Lovelock (2009), Gaia is just as indifferent to our survival as a human species as many of us are to it; human-induced climate change and environmental damage simply mean that Gaia will adjust to these changes while making the planet unliveable for us humans. This is why, for Latour, Gaia is a salutary figure of the real Apocalypse. It gives us a more worldly, earthbound experience of the contemporary world, one that is *pre-* rather than post-apocalyptic, and that therefore forces us to reflect on and take seriously the climate emergency:

> This is why it is so important, in my view, to try to face up to Gaia, which is no more a religious figure than a secular one . . . Gaia is a power of historicization. Still more simply, as its name indicates, Gaia is the signal telling us to come back to Earth. If one wanted to sum up its effect, one could say that, by requiring the Moderns to start taking the present seriously at last, Gaia offers the only way to make them tremble once again with uncertainty about what they are, as well as about the epoch in which they live and the ground on which they stand. (Latour, 2017, p. 219)

As a way of facing up to the challenge of Gaia, Latour calls for a politicization of the climate debate. The problem, as he sees it, is that the appeal to a pure, pristine idea of "nature," and to the scientific consensus around climate change, has led in the past to a kind of depoliticization of environmental questions. One appeals to science as the final, absolute arbiter to settle controversies over climate change. However, as Latour also recognizes, this situation has now changed: in the current era of populist politics and "post-truth" discourse, in which the legitimacy of established sources of knowledge and expertise are dismissed by many, especially populist leaders, as "fake news," it is no longer sufficient or effective to simply point to the scientific consensus. Politics once again enters the fray, as we engage in new and intense political disputes over existential questions.

Does this signify, after all, a return to Schmitt and his idea of politics as constituted by the existential opposition between friend and enemy? While we would agree with Latour that the Anthropocene question demands urgent politicization—and indeed a new kind of political theology—we have at the same time argued that Schmitt's model, based on sovereign exceptionalism, enmity, and nation-state geopolitics, is simply not up to the task at hand. While Latour cautions about taking Schmitt in appropriate doses, he nevertheless takes some value from Schmitt's skepticism about globalization, as expressed in *The Nomos of the Earth*, about the image of the globe as a new spatiotemporal ordering of the international system (see Latour, 2021). For Latour:

> It is precisely because Schmitt does not think for even a second about what will become of the ecological question that his way of talking about the Earth and its law, its nomos, as he says, can appear so useful to those who are trying to shed the weight that the concept of "nature" has imposed on the issues of the Earth, law, sovereignty, war, and peace that have become our questions with the intrusion of Gaia. It is because Schmitt doesn't give a single thought to the Globe that *The Nomos of the Earth* can be used to conceptualize the successor to the political, scientific, and theological notion of "nature." (2017, p. 230)

No doubt it is important to be critical about the discourse of globalization—a discourse that has, in any case, largely fallen out of favor in recent times. Indeed, liberal globalization, in its close association with global capitalism, enshrined in free trade agreements and the legal regulation of international commerce, has led to the overexploitation of natural resources and an acceleration of climate change. However, surely the solution to this problem is not a return to an old order of international politics defined by nation-state sovereignty and geopolitical competition, if such a return were even possible. This would be to affirm the populist fantasy of a self-sufficient, autonomous nation-state, aggressively pursuing its own national interests, extracting and exploiting its own natural resources without limit, and abandoning all responsibilities beyond its own borders. Therefore, to respond to the challenge of Gaia and the political demands of the Anthropocene, we need a different kind of political theology based on an alternative global image, a new nomos of the earth centered around a genuinely cosmopolitan vision of global justice and solidarity. We will return to this in a later chapter.

So while we acknowledge the diagnostic value of Schmitt's critique of globalization, he offers us no viable alternative. There is nothing redemptive in his largely reactionary geopolitical worldview and it offers no answers to our current predicament. It is here that we can agree with Catherine Keller in her critique of Schmitt (see 2018a): while Schmitt's notion of political theology is important for understanding global conflict, violence, racism, and neoliberal economic domination, its sovereign exceptionalism and anthropocentrism make it unsuitable as a model for a politics that recognizes planetary and ecological entanglements. In opposition to this, Keller proposes an idea of politics based on assemblages and interconnections that cut across lines of difference and antagonism. Indeed, Keller's aim—and our aim—is to blur, soften, and disrupt the hard lines between friend and enemy, and between man and nature, established on the basis of sovereign exceptionalism that seem only to be intensifying today.

We have suggested the need for a different way of thinking about political subjectivity, community, and engagement based on the recognition of our involvement with natural ecosystems and networks and on the affinities and solidarities that we form with nonhuman life-forms. In developing this alternative account of politics, we can draw some insights from Keller's ecopolitical theology. Her thinking is influenced by apophatic or negative theology—a form of Christian mystical theology in which God is essentially unknowable and unnamable, a mystery beyond signification. In engaging with this tradition, through theologians such as Nicholas of Cusa and Gregory of Nyssa, and by bringing it into dialogue with the process thought of Deleuze and Alfred North Whitehead, Keller develops a theological way of approaching the experience of entanglement, which she associates with nonknowing and nonseparability. The God envisioned here is a kind of pantheistic God, God as an infinite figure of becoming and immanence, of material processes and relations. With Whitehead, we can think of God as immanent within the world, and the world as immanent within God. At the same time, God transcends the world, and the world transcends God. In this conception of God as a creative process, the very distinction between transcendence and immanence is dissolved. As Keller puts it: "Process, not God, is the solvent that democratizes all processes as its instances. And therefore Whitehead's deity does not dissolve into the univocity of being but resolves into the solidarity of becoming: as the 'prime exemplification' rather than 'the exception' of creative flux. (Political theology of the sovereign exception will get no comfort from this God.)" (2015, p. 190). This sort of process thinking rejects the idea of *creatio ex nihilo*. Seeing the world in terms of an immanent set of processes and relations of complexity means that we cannot hold on to the idea of God as an "absolute controller" who creates something out of nothing (see Cobb & Griffin, 1979, p. 65); just as, politically speaking, we can no longer reduce meaning and action to the autonomous and exceptional sovereign decision that, on Schmitt's account, also comes out of nowhere. Instead, process theology embraces the idea of *complexity and interrelatedness*. Indeed, the more complexity and novelty there is in the world, the more enjoyment is stimulated. This is why process theology not only supports a more pluralistic experience of religion but also leads to a recognition of environmental interdependency: "An 'ecological attitude' would thereby be one that recognized the interrelations and hence interdependencies among things. However, 'ecology' has taken on an additional connotation, according to which one who has an 'ecological attitude' has respect or even reverence for, and perhaps a feeling of kinship with, the other creatures" (Cobb, 1975, 76). This attitude of respect, reverence, and kinship with other creatures is based, furthermore, on *enjoyment*, or what might be called enchantment, and it is this that impels us to treat nonhuman beings with equal ethical consideration. As Cobb and Griffin (1979, p. 77) say: "Accordingly, if all actualities, not simply human ones, are constituted by the enjoyment of experience, and hence are to some degree ends in themselves, then we should, to the appropriate degree, treat them as ends and not merely as means to our ends."

Keller also believes that an experience of affective attachment to the natural world can elicit a greater sense of responsibility toward the environment and can act as a supplement to climate science. The effects of the recognition of natural planetary entanglement are ambiguous, often producing as much uncertainty as certainty and, thus, at times giving impetus to climate change denial. How often do climate skeptics seize on the slightest shred of uncertainty within scientific discourse to affirm the view that human-induced climate change is not real or has been exaggerated? Despite the scientific consensus around climate change, facts and statistics alone will not convince everyone. There is thus a role for theology to play in the politics of the Anthropocene, not so much in increasing our stock of scientific knowledge about the natural world but, rather, in showing us how we might enjoy it, how we might become more aware, on an experiential, somatic level, of our entanglement with nature; how we might revel in the feeling of interconnectedness with natural ecosystems and nonhuman beings. As Keller puts it: "An apophatically canny ecotheology may, in other words, prove to be a useful ally of an activist cosmopolitics informed by environmental science. For it invites us to embrace, even to feel, the adaptive resilience of the planetary web of a living interconnectivity" (2015, p. 269).

Science is invaluable, of course, in making us aware of the damage we are inflicting on the natural environment and in proposing technical and policy measures that can mitigate its affects. But an ecotheology—or ecotheologies—can help us identify with and affirm the life forces and ecosystems that remain, thus motivating us to preserve them.

5

Technology as Political Theology

The prominence of technology, its ubiquitous presence in contemporary life, is a prominence involving the increasing capacity to shape and orient the character of contemporary life. This prominence relates both to the process of technological development—the continuing extension of that presence in contemporary life—and to the effect of that process upon the relationship between technology and existence. The depth and range of the process of technological development affects the individual and collective experience of existence and prompts further reflection upon the place and position of technology in contemporary social and political life. This reflection becomes critical reflection once it is acknowledged that technology has the capacity to affect social and political existence negatively. Contemporary existence is replete with instances of this negative effect, from the level of individual physical and mental well-being—the degradation of the relationship to self and others—to the collective level of social and political forms of life, in other words, the degradation of the relationship between state and society.

In exploring these negative effects, our chapter focuses upon the central position of technology in Schmitt's thought. This centrality is the counterpart of the absence, in Schmittian political theology, as seen in the previous chapter, of any fundamental consideration of nature and the natural world. The focus of Schmitt's critique of technology is not on its impact on the natural environment, but rather on the way it reshapes legal and political relationships between human beings. Technology, for Schmitt, becomes a logic of depoliticization or neutralization of the juridico-political domain. Technology, defined as a negative phenomenon, is one of the central aspects against which Schmittian political theology articulates itself.

Technology becomes a primary object of Schmittian political theology, in which it seeks to establish a position from which to interrupt technology's negative developmental logic. The adoption of this position is to acknowledge the enduring presence of technology—a world in which technology as absent is inconceivable—and to encompass it within a framework derived from a distinct and entirely nontechnological foundation. Technology as political theology is both the critique and the absorption of technology: the subordination of technology to the primacy of a distinctive Schmittian logic of the juridico-political. Yet, Schmitt's thinking, from his early to his later writings, is marked by an increasing recognition of the weakened potential of juridico-political forms to absorb the negative, neutralizing logic of technology. In Schmitt's final works, the recognition is expressed as a self-questioning of the possibility of a nontechnological foundation, and, thus, of the position from which to articulate a political theology (Galli, 2015, pp. 56–57; Schmitt, 2010b, 2018a).

From the initial tracing of the conceptual parameters of technology as political theology, we then proceed to the further interrogation of the Schmittian conception of the relationship between technology and political theology commencing from the explicit uncertainty of its final period. At the limit of this aspect of Schmittian thought, we turn to a comparative examination of the approach to technology in the work of Peter Sloterdijk and Bernard Stiegler. Both Sloterdijk and Stiegler accord technology a central importance and respond to its further transformation, beyond the industrial and analogue forms to which Schmitt's political theology relates, into digital and biotechnological forms.

This transformation of technology involves an acknowledgment of its profound alteration of the relationship between the human and the technological. The effects of this transformation are dealt with in different ways. In Sloterdijk, we find a return to the Schmittian motifs of enmity and national homogeneity stripped of theological association. In contrast, in Stiegler, the theological is replaced with a notion of *spirit* that, as the insistence upon the primacy of conscience—the theoretical and practical basis of individual and collective consciousness—is the repository of a noninstrumental, ethical relationship between the human and the technological.

The Schmittian Concept of Technology

The delineation of the Schmittian concept of technology is undertaken from an explicitly external position to that of technology and the natural sciences with which it is usually associated. The elaboration of the Schmittian concept is, from the outset, detached from the detailed conceptualization of technological objects and the accompanying conceptual framework of the relevant natural sciences. The detachment entails that the Schmittian concept is distinguished by its resolutely nontechnological and nonscientific character: it neither seeks to intervene in, nor is it oriented by, the theoretical and practical knowledge of technological objects and the associated natural sciences. The Schmittian understanding of technology is unconcerned with contributing to or being regulated by the internal coherence of this domain of theoretical and practical knowledge. The absence of concern is the conscious expression of a refusal—not mere indifference—to articulate a concept of technology that would be subsumed within or determined by this domain of theoretical and practical knowledge.

The refusal arises from the understanding of the general effect of technology as a form of human activity oriented by a particular rationality. The understanding develops from Schmitt's initial intellectual formation as a jurist (Schmitt, 2017b; Vinx & Zeitlin, 2021) that, during and immediately after World War I, is subsequently combined with, and modified by, the encounter with the poetry of Theodor Däubler (Schmitt, 2009),[1] the considerations on the visibility of the (Catholic) Church (Schmitt, 1996c), and the critique of political romanticism (Schmitt, 2010a). These elements are supplemented by a continued engagement with the work of Max Weber, which, with Weber's professorial appointment at Munich, included attendance at Weber's lectures, in Munich, 1918–1920, and participation "in Weber's special *Dozentenseminar* and several private conversations with Weber on politics and the state" (Ulmen, 1985 p. 5).[2] This constitutes the preliminary interpretative background upon which the Schmittian concept of technology is articulated.

The objects of technology, and the associated theoretical and practical knowledge of the natural sciences, are situated within a history of human activity that has become "economic" in the Weberian sense of an instrumental, means-ends, rationality.[3] The consequences of social action oriented by instrumental rationality extend beyond the economic sphere to determine the other spheres of social action. The Weberian conception of human activity, as instrumental social action, is, however, the reality against which Schmitt elaborates a position in which technology is conceived within political theology. The Schmittian emphasis is on the effect of instrumental rationality upon the sphere of the political and law, but this effect is considered to extend beyond the parameters of Weberian social science to place into question the possibility of politics and law. Schmittian political theology seeks a position from which to delineate and respond to the relationship with the technological.

Technology as Schmittian Political Theology

The combination of the conceptualization and absorption of technology—technology as political theology—receives its initial distinctive formulation in Schmitt's *Roman Catholicism and Political Form* (1923) (Schmitt, 1996d). The initial components of the Schmittian approach to technology are deployed within a framework that situates the distinctive institution of the Roman Catholic Church as an enduring juridical rationality unaffected by the instrumental rationality of economic action (Colliot-Thélène, 1999).

The explicitly theologically informed orientation is replaced with an exclusively juridico-political framework in *Constitutional Theory* (1928) in which the discussion of technology is broached in a short section devoted to the discussion of the right to freedom of expression under Article 118 of the Weimar Constitution (Schmitt, 2008b, pp. 206–207). Here, within the context of a discussion of special limitations upon this basic right, including censorship, Schmitt considers the emergence of film and cinema to represent a profound change in communication technology: "film technology does not signify a technology of expression of opinion in the same sense as writing and printing" (p. 206).[4] In this difference is contained film's extrinsic position with regard to writing and printing, as the medium for both "the dissemination of ideas" and "integration of a social unity" (p. 206). Film, as a "powerful psycho-technological apparatus," introduces the "political problem of influencing the masses." The Schmittian response toys with the juridical response of censorship, but, as the "the political is unavoidable," the state is encouraged to "place it in the service of the existing order" (p. 206).[5]

The broader Schmittian approach to technology is articulated in the 1929 essay, "The Age of Neutralizations and Depoliticizations" (Schmitt, 2007a), which we have already mentioned in a preceding chapter. Here the question of technology is situated within a wider sociohistorical account of the emergence of domains of neutrality. Technology represents the culmination or "end" of the sociohistorical process of "neutralization of various domains of cultural life" (p. 94), in which the purportedly "absolute and ultimate ground has been found" (p. 90). As we have seen, for Schmitt, technology is a depoliticizing rationality: it is "always only an instrument or weapon" (p. 91), and from its generalizable use and utility arise "purely technical principles and perspectives," which are incapable of deriving either a "political question" or "political answer" (p. 92). In 1929, Schmitt accords a provisional understanding of the twentieth century as the "century of technology" (p. 95) whose sense will be furnished not by technology itself, which "can do nothing more than intensify peace or war," but by the type of politics "strong enough to master the new technology and which genuine friend-enemy groupings can develop on this new ground" (p. 95). This, in turn, reconfigures the sense of "spiritual existence"—the "order of human things" (p. 96) arising from the struggle of spirit with spirit, life with life, and not its "renunciation" (p. 95).

The work of the early 1930s, prior to the end, or "suspension," of the Weimar Republic (Schmitt, 2001, 2003), reaffirms the concerns of *Constitutional Theory*, but with an acknowledgment of the fragility of the contemporary constitutional framework and the sense of the immanent closure of the tradition of constitutional thought of the late eighteenth and nineteenth centuries. In place of the hesitancy about formal regulation and/or censorship, there is now the acknowledgment that the state will necessarily explicitly adopt and utilize the new technologies and associated techniques of film and radio.

The installation of the National Socialist regime, in 1933, and the particular intertwining of the state and technology that it represented, is accompanied by Schmitt's joining of the National Socialist Party and the attempt to articulate a juridical framework within which to define and organize the new regime (Schmitt, 2021b; Caldwell, 1994; Scheuerman, 1996; Suuronen, 2021). In the later 1930s, Schmitt's theoretical focus detaches itself from direct juridical encapsulation[6] and is characterized by the rethematization of technology. The rethematization is oriented by the search for the origin of the technological framework of the modern state and the concentrated return to the field of international law involving the elaboration of the notion of *Großraum*. The technological origin—the state as mechanism—is situated in the work of Hobbes as the further development of the Cartesian philosophical break with the tradition of

Scholasticism (Schmitt, 2008b). The notion of *Großraum* is the attempt to reconceptualize the concept of space in international law as the interplay of power, technology, and law (Schmitt, 2014, 2021b).[7]

This theme is continued in Schmitt's 1942 work *Land and Sea: A World-Historical Meditation* (Schmitt, 2015). The spatial, as *Großraum*, is transformed into a geophilosophical reflection in which the categories of land and sea structure the presentation of the interplay of power, technology, and law. The geophilosophical framework is combined with the reappearance of a theological categorization in the form of Christian European peoples. The position articulated in *Land and Sea*, prior to its 1954 edition, is qualified by the 1944 lecture "The Plight of European Jurisprudence" (Schmitt, 1990), in which the geophilosophical reflection is replaced with a return to, and reaffirmation of, a source of European jurisprudence, for a reconstruction of legal science unaffected or untainted by the world war and law reduced to technicity (see Carrino, 1999).

The postwar volume *The Nomos of the Earth* (Schmitt, 2006) represents a form of integration of *Land and Sea* and the 1944 lecture, which is now overlain by a more overtly theological consideration, in which the Pauline figure of the *katechon*[8] is accorded a central position (pp. 59ff.) in the juridical history of spatial order. Technology remains situated in the interplay of power, technology, and law, but this is now presented within the emergence of spatial order predicated upon the concept of *nomos*. The juridical history of spatial order traces the emergence and decline of the *jus publicum Europaeum* and concludes with the intimation of the new nomos of the post–World War II international order.

The final major work of Schmitt, *Political Theology II* (Schmitt, 2010b), is the reiteration of the possibility of political theology in relation to the challenges of Erik Peterson's *Monotheism as a Political Problem* and Hans Blumenberg's *The Legitimacy of the Modern Age*. The reiteration, as a political theology of technology, arises in the purportedly "completely de-theologized and modern scientific closure of any political theology" (p. 128) and concentrates upon demonstrating that the figure of the enemy, as the human equivalent of theological stasiology—God's internal, conflictual division—is apparent in the aggressivity of the three interconnected freedoms of this modern scientific closure: "scientific neutrality, the technical and industrial freedom of production [and] the arbitrary nature of free human utilization" (Schmitt, 2010b, p. 130).

Schmitt returns, in one of his short, final works, in 1970, "On the TV Democracy: The Aggressiveness of Progress," to this question of technology. Here, the insistence upon the centrality of the friend/enemy distinction remains, particularly the "possibility of an enemy" (Schmitt, 2018a, p. 205), but technology is acknowledged to have developed to an extent that has encroached upon other elements. In this situation, the "possibility of an enemy" is to be sought as an internal division or divergence within the human use of technology, which indicates the continuing influence of the final section of Schmitt's *Political Theology II*. This is the analogy between a conception of God who alone is his own enemy and the human in receipt of technology, as this "terrible power over the earth and the environment. . . . would prove himself to be the true and authentic enemy of himself" (p. 205).

It is here that both *Political Theology II* and "On TV Democracy" point to the limit of Schmittian political theology. The limit is a final expression of political theology that, in its comparative tentativeness in relation to its preceding elaborations, indicates the fragility of this position as one from which to delineate and respond to the relationship with the technological.

Sloterdijk and Schmitt: From Distance to Affinity

The limit of Schmittian political theology explicitly present in *Political Theology II*—the sense of its difficulty or potential exhaustion—in the critical engagement with Blumenberg appears to be definitively confirmed in the first main work of Peter Sloterdijk. The *Critique of Cynical Reason* (Sloterdijk, 1988) represents an extended reflection upon modes of social critique within the Federal Republic that is without reference to Schmitt. This marginalization is reinforced by the historical interpretation of the Weimar period as the prefiguration of a general mode of social critique—the phenomenon of "reflective ideology" (p. 384)—which will find a weakened form of repetition in the later Federal Republic (pp. 89–90, 384ff.).[9] The development within this initial period of Sloterdijk's work involves the reworking of certain aspects of the *Critique of Cynical Reason*, and, in this reworking, a further distance is evident from the Schmittian framework. This is exemplified in *Eurotaoismus: Zur kritik des Politischen kinetik* (1989),[10] which holds that modernity originates in a form of human activity indissociable from a technological kinetics and its inevitably destructive dynamic, while adopting a mode of critique predicated upon the redundancy of theology (Sloterdijk, 2020a, p. 25) but not of a broader notion of religion.[11] In *Eurotaoismus*, as the title suggests, the mode of critique involves a recourse to a reflection upon non-Western religion in order to enable the extrication from the continued, contemporary attachment and mobilization by the dynamics of modern technological kinetics (pp. 59–86, 122ff.).

The anthropological connection to philosophy, which specifically distances itself from theology and the preceding German tradition of philosophical anthropology (pp. x, 69–70), is the aspect of this critique that is preserved in the subsequent development of Sloterdijk's work.[12] The conceptualization of technology, as anthropotechnics, detaches itself from the wider, preceding framework and constitutes an aspect of the three-volume *Spheres* project (Sloterdijk, 2011, 2014, 2016c). The essay "Regeln für den Menschenpark: Ein Antwortschreiben zu Heideggers Brief über den Humanismus" ("Rules for the Human Park: A Response to the Letter on Humanism," 2016a), situated chronologically between the publication of the first and second volumes of *Spheres*, represents a condensed exposition of Sloterdijkian anthropotechnics.

The notion of anthropotechnics, as the essential interrelationship between humans and technology, arises from a historical account of the technological marginalization of the humanist forms of cultural formation and coexistence—"books and letters"—by "a telecommunicative bond between members of a modern mass society" (Sloterdijk, 2016a, p. 14). For Sloterdijk,

> because of the formation of mass culture through the media—radio in the First World War and television after 1945, and even more through the contemporary web revolution—the coexistence of people in the present societies has been established on new foundations. These are, as it can uncontrovertibly be shown, clearly postliterary, postepistolary, and thus posthumanistic. Anyone who thinks the prefix "post" in this formulation is too dramatic can replace it with the adverb "marginal." Thus our thesis: modern societies can produce their political and cultural synthesis only marginally through literary, letter-writing, humanistic media. Of course, that does not mean that literature has come to an end, but it has split itself off and become a sui generis subculture, and the days of its value as bearer of the national spirit have passed. The social synthesis is no longer—and is no longer seen to be—primarily

a matter of books and letters. New means of political-cultural telecommunication have come into prominence, which have restricted the pattern of script-born friendship to a limited number of people. The period when modern humanism was the model for schooling and education has passed, because it is no longer possible to retain the illusion that political and economic structures could be organized on the amiable model of literary societies. (p. 14)

For Sloterdijk, the essence of humanism, within a situation of general technological marginalization, is revealed as a process of socialization: "the constant battle for humanity that reveals itself as a contest between bestializing and taming tendencies" (p. 15). Humanism, through its particular forms and means of dissemination and instruction, is, therefore, a set of determinate techniques of intervention in the moral-cultural formation of an individual—individuation—as the basis for human coexistence.[13]

This sense of humanism, disclosed by its technological marginalization, is the preparatory standpoint from which to proceed to reinterpret Heidegger's *Letter on Humanism* (1946). For Sloterdijk, the *Letter*'s radical interrogation of the limits of humanism is both acknowledged and provided with an inflection. The inflection consists in insisting, in contrast to Heidegger, that "there is a history, resolutely ignored by Heidegger, of the entrance into the Clearing of being—a social history of the openness of man to the *Seinsfrage* [question of being], and a historical progression in the clarification of ontological difference" (p. 20). In this inflection, a human history of anthropogenesis is introduced and situated as the social history that remains unthematized in the *Letter*.

The process of anthropogenesis—a transition in which the "thinking animal became the thinking man"—is composed of two aspects: a "natural history" indicating how "man becomes capable of worlds" and a "social history of taming, through which man became the being who could pull himself together in order to speak the totality of Being" (p. 20). The comparative anthropological deficiencies of the human (animal), at the moment of birth and infantile development, result in "an indeterminate being," whose indeterminacy detaches it from a definitive animal environment and furnishes the capacity "to develop a world in an ontological sense" (p. 20). The evolutionary process of human being-in-the-world is then rendered into one of a social history of coexistence: "For, as soon as speaking men gather into larger groups and not only connect themselves to linguistic houses but also build physical houses, they enter the arena of domestication. They are now not only sheltered by their language but also tamed by their accommodations" (p. 21).

The arena of domestication—the space of anthropotechnics—emerges as a concrete, spatial order from the territorial fixity of the house. From the house there then arise "decisions about who shall live in them" that, in turn, designate "which type of community dwellers will be dominant" (p. 21). The dominance of a particular type of community is indissociable from conflict and antagonism "as soon as men emerge as beings who form societies and erect social hierarchies" (p. 21). The conflict, rather than recapitulating that of the Schmittian friend/enemy distinction, is one that concerns the character of "the domestication of humanity." The Sloterdijkian focus is upon "the unavoidable battle over the direction of man-breeding" (p. 22) determined by the mode of "breeding, taming and raising"—the form of anthropotechnics—that is adopted (p. 23). The conflict centers upon the opposed orientation of these modes, "between the civilizing and bestializing impulses and their associated media" (p. 24) and the extent to which the course of the contemporary conflict involves an increasingly active, biotechnological intervention in the domestication of humanity.

The exposition of anthropotechnics, which appears within the period of the first and second volumes of *Spheres*, is then further extended and integrated into the third and final volume, *Foams* (Sloterdijk, 2016c). Here, anthropotechnics has ceased to be confined to the question of the self-domestication of the human and has become incorporated into a broader theory of the existence and coexistence of "anthropogenic islands" (p. 338). The anthropogenesis of these islands—their origin and development—rests upon the creation of an "anthroposphere," a "nine-dimensional space" resulting from nine "indispensable world-forming functions" (p. 338).[14] The earlier anthropological reconfiguration of Heideggerian thought, initiated in "Rules for the Human Park" as part of an extensive reworking of certain Heideggerian motifs,[15] is transformed, in *Foams*, into an autonomous and distinct anthropological theory.

The transformation is accompanied by the brief, but explicit, reference to, and critique of, the Schmittian state of exception or emergency and its overarching political theology. This critique is part of the presentation of the sixth world-forming function—the erotope—the "space in which the burdens of tasks are cooperatively distributed" (p. 384). The distribution of the burdens of tasks of a group requires a social synthesis in which social cohesion is maintained through the "capacity not to fall apart under maximum strain" (p. 389). The conception of social cohesion, guided by the work of Heiner Mühlmann (2003, 2005), rests upon the ability of the group "to synchronize its efforts in all-or-nothing situations, also known as 'emergencies'" (Sloterdijk, 2016c, p. 390). These situations of maximal stress cooperation redefine the states of emergency or exception as

> the politicized form of a standard biological situation to which primate bodies, and hence human bodies too, respond with an innate, endocrinologically controlled program of extreme energy release and syntonic solidarization. Its existence is ascertained through a cognitive schema: the emergency assessment. . . . In keeping with the evolutionary varieties of animal and early human intelligence, present danger is assessed in emergency-ontological terms: one interprets the situation as an interruption of prolonged calm by a now acute threat. The deep biological rootedness of the major stress reaction proves that the utmost is evolutionarily commonplace. (pp. 390–391)

Thus, Sloterdijk's theoretical project understands itself as situated definitively *after* Schmitt, as the interconnection between politics and theology is only to be conceived anthropologically.[16] The situation of emergency is thereby rendered anthropologically unexceptional and, in this manner, the Sloterdijkian project considers itself to have broken definitively with the history of the transfer of theological categories into juridical and political categories elaborated in *Political Theology* (1922). This, in turn, is a preparatory element for the subsequent anthropological presentation of the expansion of the political form of the socially cohesive group.

The presence of "Rules for the Human Park" reemerges in the description of the political form and dynamics of the socially cohesive group. In this description, Mühlmann's analysis is overlaid by Sloterdijk's nine-dimensional space, in order to provide for an account of the developmental dimension of the erotope. Here, the pre-stress, stress, and post-stress stages of Mühlmann's analysis are presented as the dynamics determining the continued existence of the expanded political form of a socially cohesive group. The essentially conflictual foundation of this analysis is explicitly acknowledged and the culture of the expanded political form of a socially cohesive group becomes the "rules of collective stress handling" (p. 391) that simultaneously contain the "civilizatory initiative to tame cultures" (p. 393). Within the dimension of the erotope, Sloterdijk's inflection of the

Mühlmannian analysis is to indicate that, at the conclusion of the twentieth century, the historical differentiation of the expanded political form into victor and loser cultures has ceased to have the capacity to maintain enduring rules of collective stress handling. The civilizatory initiative rests upon that which is "beyond victory and defeat" and, thereby, displaces or interrupts the underlying dynamics of stress and emergency "with the theorem of the ruled-out emergency: an interest in the non-occurrence of the emergency in the global political culture" (p. 397).

This civilizatory initiative with which Sloterdijk concludes the discussion of the erotope remains an outline whose further realization has initially to be sought in the subsequent dimensions of the nine world-forming dimensions. These suggest that it is in the appropriation and anthropological reinterpretation of a notion of immunity that the potential for the displacement of stress and emergency rests. The dimensions of the thanatotope/theotope (pp. 411–436) and the nomotope (pp. 436–456), which are those of religion and a constitution, contain an anthropological history centered upon revealing their essentially immunological function: the protection of the social cohesion of the expanded political form of the social group. The distinct anthropological history of religion and the constitution results in the presentation of a comparative decline of the immunological function of religion in comparison to that of a constitution. The importance of this presentation is that it acknowledges the continued presence or trace of the archaic in the historical process that it describes within each of the dimensions of religion and the constitution: religion as the outside and constitution as the shaping of behavior within the expanded form of the social group that it encompasses.

The reference to the presence or trace of the archaic effectively ceases in the subsequent structure and development of *Foams*. The cessation flows from the exclusive concentration in the final parts upon the "affluent society" and the emphasis upon the centrality of the concepts of boredom and frivolity (pp. 627ff.). The analysis, derived from the underlying architectural technology of the affluent society and its different aspects, presents a form of expanded social coexistence in which the notions of order, crisis, and redemption have ceased to have pertinence.

The archaic and protective immunological aspects, and their technological expression and support, gradually return to prominence with Sloterdijk's subsequent work. The return finds its initial, most concentrated expression in, *In the World Interior of Capital: For a Philosophical Theory of Globalization* (Sloterdijk, 2013b), and appears, in particular, in the second part, entitled "The Grand Interior." The anthropological history now considers that, as a result of its reflections upon globalization, the underlying technological architecture of the "affluent society" is traversed by difficulties that it can no longer resolve. The immunological effectiveness of the "affluent society" has ceased to be capable of displacing stress with a generalized frivolity and boredom: the "unthinking expectation of security without struggle" (p. 217). The decline of immunological effectiveness, accompanied by "a climate of irrefutable demands for a constant increase of relief," leads to "the periodically recurring imperative of re-burdening" (p. 221)—the active reintroduction of the necessity to struggle for security. The Sloterdijkian notion of pampering—an inherent civilizational process of (immunological) relief through the "psychosocial and semantic reflexes of the relieving process" (p. 212)—thereby reaches both its full visibility and limit. This involves the emphasis upon the reproduction of "sharply asymmetrical" (p. 261) distinctions within the "affluent society" that establish the strict external and internal boundaries of a particular national space. The external boundary is established through the attribution of citizenship—the division into members and nonmembers of a nation. The internal boundary concerns the attribution of entitlement to benefits of the social-welfare state and involves the combination of a division into "contributors and non-contributors and to limit its subversion by 'social parasites'" (p. 261). The technologically assisted reproduction of these divisions determines the capacity to maintain the particular national space. The ambivalence of this emphasis, which is an aspect of the "chronic unease in culture" (p. 222) in these affluent societies, indicates the inchoate presence of notions of order and crisis.

This, in turn, finds a parallel in the relationship between the particular territorial and immunological national space of an "affluent society" and the universal. An invariant anthropological primacy is accorded to the local as those attributes that "inhere in the infrastructure of becoming in real human spheres. They belong to the attributes of finite, concrete, embedded and transmittable existence . . . [and] being extended in one's own place is the good habit of being" (p. 263). The universal is anthropologically redefined as a "meta-life": a conscious relinquishing of the "relation to the world" determined by these local attributes.[17] The universal, in this anthropological redefinition, is dependent upon the particular. It can only find inherence through its improbable emergence within the particular.

The further transition to the explicit presence of notions of order and crisis is marked by the distinctly different treatment of the quotation from Carl Schmitt's *The Concept of the Political*[18] on the final page of *In the World Interior of Capital* and in the final pages of the later *You Must Change Your Life* (Sloterdijk, 2013c): "Whoever invokes humanity wants to cheat [deceive]" (Schmitt, 1996b, p. 54).[19] The interpretative position of *In the World Interior of Capital* is to cite the Schmittian phrase as an exemplification of a wider position with regard to "abstract universalism," and to leave open the possibility of universalism by qualifying its definitive definition and rejection as "devious nonsense" (Sloterdijk, 2013b, p. 264). In contrast, *You Must Change Your Life* adopts an entirely unqualified interpretation in which the Schmittian phrase encapsulates the absence of any current inherence of an instance of universality in the contemporary world order (Sloterdijk, 2013c, p. 450). The absent universal, now designated anthropologically as "an efficient co-immunity structure for the members of the 'global society'" (p. 450), requires, to become present in an anthropological history of "immune system battles," the interruption and displacement of "all previous distinctions between own and foreign"; thus, to actively "transcend" the Schmittian antagonistic distinction between "friend and foe" (p. 451).

The active transcendence of the Schmittian framework of *The Concept of the Political* is, however, confined to the intimations of the "concrete universal" in the concluding paragraphs of *You Must Change Your Life* (pp. 451–452). For the subsequent work of Sloterdijk is marked by a reemphasis of internal and external division. The internal division arises from the substitution of a critique of the social-welfare state for the preceding conceptual framework of the "affluent society" (Sloterdijk, 2009c, 2010; Honneth, 2009). The external division emerges with Sloterdijk's critique of refugee policy (Hesse, 2016; Münkler, 2016; Sloterdijk, 2016d, 2016e) and extends to a wider discussion of the intractable divisions of global migration and demographics (Sloterdijk, 2017).

This increasing affinity with, rather than divergence from, the Schmittian conceptual framework, is particularly evident in Sloterdijk's analysis of refugee policy in which the refugee, rather than the sovereign, is held to decide upon the state of emergency (Sloterdijk, 2016d). The recourse to this appropriation of *Political Theology* (1922) overturns the anthropological critique and dissolution of the state of emergency in *Foams* and reactivates the centrality of the question of sovereignty and decision. The figure of the refugee, as the new sovereign, dramatizes the separation of the nation-state and sovereignty, and, in this separation, the weakness of the immuno-technological architecture is revealed. Thus, the return to Schmitt seeks, through the figure of the sovereign refugee, to define the relationship between immigration, borders, and national identity as an existential threat to political authority: a state of emergency that will destroy rather than reconstitute the conventional political order. It is a definition that also reappropriates the Schmittian technique of unmasking in order to reveal in the duty of assistance the purported logic of national self-destruction.

Sloterdijk's analysis has become oriented by the notions of order and crisis, and, in this orientation, the understanding of its position *after* Schmitt is now one that suggests an interpretative affinity. The affinity, which from its anthropological approach to religion cannot be a simple resumption of Schmittian political theology, involves the presumption of an enduring "archaic" homogeneity. This presumption, following Mühlmann, assumes that social relations of companionship and belonging remain shaped by "tribal parameters" (Sloterdijk, 2017). This "tribal constant" provides the "archaic" basis for the contemporary immuno-technological framework that functions to ensure a sufficient degree of internal homogeneity. The immunological architecture, which functions to guarantee internal homogeneity, is simultaneously the necessity to identify and respond to that which exists outside the territorially delimited immunological space of a nation-state.[20] In this manner, Sloterdijk returns to the limit of technology as political theology in *Political Theology II*, the local and the global become the *internal* markers of a Sloterdijkian "archaic" stasiology that traverses the immunological architecture.

Stiegler: the Implicit Critique of Technology as Schmittian Political Theology

The insistent presence and reflection upon the question of technology in the work of Bernard Stiegler is distinguished by its absence of reference to Schmitt. This absence, in contrast to the explicit presence of, and increasing affinity with, the Schmittian framework in Sloterdijk, extends beyond mere lack of acknowledgment to encompass an implicit critique of Schmitt. The critique becomes evident by commencing from the Schmittian distinction, in *Constitutional Theory*, between the technology of writing and printing and the technology of film (Schmitt 2008b, pp. 206–207). The technology of writing and printing, as an integral medium for individual expression and the formation of public opinion (the liberal conception of "the means of integration of a social unity"), is distinguished from film technology that, "insofar as it is not simply posted writing, is only image and mimetic portrayal" (p. 206). This distinction, and the further Schmittian question of the determination of its constitutional regulation, is founded upon the presupposition of a nontechnological formation of human thought and speech—the foundation for public discussion—to which writing and printing are means of dissemination (p. 206).

Stiegler's critique arises from the Schmittian presupposition of the nontechnological origin of human thought and speech. The presupposition would obscure the initial technological shaping of language, which Stiegler, following Auroux (1995), designates as the process of grammatization (Stiegler, 2011a, 2014).[21] The process describes the effect upon language of the introduction of the linguistic technology of an alphabet and of alphabetic writing. The effect of this technology is to enable "a *becoming-letter* of sound and word," and this process "precedes all logic and all grammar, all science of language and all science in general, and which is the *techno-logical condition* (in the sense that it is always already both technical and logical) of all knowledge, which begins with exteriorization" (Stiegler, 2014, p. 54).

The exteriorization, in the form of an alphabet and of alphabetic writing, is the reconfiguration of language through its separation into "a finite number of components forming a system" (p. 54). In this reconfiguration, the "pre-individual milieu" of a language, as idiom, becomes structurally open to interpretation and, by virtue of its *"literalization,"* inserts itself "*as the inheritance and interpretation of a pre-individual past*" (p. 56). Grammatization as a linguistic technology is, for Stiegler, an integral element of both the development of language and of the process of individual and collective individuation.[22]

Schmitt's differentiation of human thought and speech from writing is, thereby, overturned, and they are combined as aspects of the first stage of grammatization. The invention and development of printing is then separated, and designated, by Stiegler, following Auroux, as the second stage of grammatization. Printing has, therefore, ceased to occupy the Schmittian position of the original medium of dissemination and has become the further development initiated by the first stage of grammatization (p. 54). Stiegler then proceeds beyond Auroux to establish a third stage of grammatization represented by the "generalization of information technologies and the resulting redefinition of knowledge" (p. 54). The outset of the third stage would, thus, encompass film technology and, in this manner, dissolve its purported Schmittian characterization as a form of technology without relation to a nontechnological thought and speech.[23] The third stage of grammatization is then the central focus of Stiegler's critique of technology as a critique of its affect upon the process of individual and collective individuation (Stiegler, 2008, 2011a, 2011b, 2014, 2015, 2019).

The third stage of grammatization is the inauguration of a third stage of industrialization—hyper-industrialization[24]—in which the techniques and technologies of grammatization profoundly interrupt the character of, and interrelationship between, individual and collective individuation. The presentation and critique of this interruption enables the third stage of grammatization to be situated within and against the final Schmittian attempt, in the postscript to *Political Theology II* (Schmitt, 2010b), to grasp technology as political theology. Stiegler's critique of hyper-industrialization, as the critique of the third stage of industrialization and grammatization, extends the implicit critique of Schmitt to encompass *Political Theology II*. The focus returns to, and situates itself at, the limit of the Schmittian thought of technology.

Stiegler's critique transforms the negativity that Schmitt's final political theology—"the reality of an enemy whose concrete possibility I can still see in its detheologized counter-image" (pp. 127–128)—considers inhering in "a completely detheologized and modern scientific closure of any political theology" (p. 128). For, the modern science that Schmitt considers instituting this closure has itself been subject to the further transformation into technoscience (Stiegler, 2011a). In this transformation, the negativity, as the aggressivity of the three freedoms that Schmitt identifies as "scientific neutrality, the technical and industrial freedom of production [and] the arbitrary nature of free human utilization" (Schmitt, 2010b, p. 130), is reconfigured. The aggressivity that Schmitt delineates rests upon the distinction between stability (science) and change (technology), in which technology, as that which creates the possibility for change, is attributed with the capacity to assert its primacy over the stability of scientific "description of the real" (Stiegler, 2011a, p. 204). The assertion of primacy is, in turn, the potential for the detachment of technology from the application of the scientific description of the real, and the constitution of the real as "a provisional (i.e., current) perspective on the possible" (p. 204). In this potential is contained the aggressivity and nihilism that Schmitt delineates in the form of the three Schmittian freedoms.

Political Theology II is, therefore, at the limit, in the sense of the point of transition from modern science to technoscience, and it is this transition that Schmitt, situated at the limit, cannot conceive, that Stiegler considers. Technoscience, is the "*com-position* of science and technology, meaning that science submits to the constraints involved in becoming the technology that formulates the systematic conditions of its evolution" (p. 203).[25] The "new rapport" between science and technology, as technoscience, places "science in the service of the development of technology, but whose conception is at the same time reversible" (p. 202). The essential reversibility—*com-position*—of science and technology has overcome the internal conflict between science and technology, which exemplifies modern science. The overcoming is simultaneously the generalization of a "science of becoming" (p. 191), as a generalization of the notion of possibility, and the relocation of the locus of negativity.

In contrast to the Schmittian effort to identify the negative in the presence of the enemy, within the aggressivity of the three freedoms, Stiegler's position considers the negative to inhere in "two linked criteriological possibles" (p. 192) of the "new reality" of technoscience. These center upon efficiency and making:

> Efficiency conceived as the probability of a beneficial outcome, the question being to know what its *"bene"* might be:
>
>> —is it "the good" of *We*, "our good"?; i.e., the series of events infinitely integrating the absolutizable future of this *We*,
>
>> —or is it "the good" in the sense of industrial production, consumer *good(s)* with a *bene*-fit conceived in terms of profits on investment, profits that are amortizable over a "reasonable time"?
>
> *Making* one of the following choices, each using a different sense of "make":
>
>> —one is feasibility, calculation of cost/benefit connections, but that must ask what it is to be called "cost" and "benefit,"
>
>> —the other is making a *difference that must be made*, and the other meaning of "to make," that knows nothing of being conditioned by efficiency or profitability since this difference, *which is a fiction*, can only appeal to a radical improbability and a default of reason. (p. 192)

These criteriological possibles are further reinforced by the passage, within technoscience, from the analog to the digital, which reveals another aspect of the limit of Schmittian *Political Theology II* in its concentration upon the technological object of analog television. For Stiegler, the passage to the digital is the passage to the generalization of reproduction—"hyper-reproducibility" (p. 215)—in which "the challenge to industry is always to render a phenomenon reproducible (as a prototype), then to stabilize and optimize the conditions of that reproduction, and finally to produce it serially, producing economies of scale that become mass markets" (p. 223).

In the transition to the predominance of hyper-reproducibility, the presence of the negative arises from its effect upon the process of individual and collective individuation. The expansion of the domain of hyper-reproducibility facilitates the potential for control—the rendering reproducible—of the central determinants of the process of individual and collective individuation.[26] Stiegler's response is to insist upon "the question of invention" (Stiegler, 2015, p. 79) as an invention of the possible—a making—that is other than the performative efficiency that animates the digital stage of hyper-industrialism.

The question of invention involves a return to the "theologico-political" (Stiegler, 2015, p. 89) in a manner that passes beyond the limit of *Political Theology II* of an internally divided God from which, in turn, to pass analogically to the secular internal division within man. The stasiology that Schmitt ascribes to God is already a heterodox theology, which suggests, in the antagonistic, internal division of the notion of God, a difficulty, through this diremption, in maintaining a consistent notion of God. In this inconsistency, is the intimation of the nullification of God, and, thus, of the underlying fragility or exhaustion—the limit—of Schmittian political theology. For Stiegler, situated on the other side of the Schmittian limit—after the "death of God"—the question of consistency has to be preserved: "the revelation of his inexistence, is not inevitably the nullification of the question of consistence" (p. 91). It requires a

> Return to that which was suppressed through the death of God. . . . This is the question of *consistence*, insofar as that which does not exist *cannot* become an object of calculation—the question of consistence insofar as it means that which distinguishes, but does not oppose, motive and *ratio*. This is the question of that which, as existence turned towards the consistent *which does not exist*, and which, as such, is always

already projected beyond mere subsistence, composes (with) the incalculable. (pp. 89–90)

Thus, the question of invention becomes a making as the active cultivation of "the difference between consistence and existence" (p. 92). It is a difference as singularity, and, therefore, "*incomparable*, and in this sense inexistent, reality (if by existing one understands calculable) of that difference, itself *improbable* (that is, which we do not know how to prove), between existence and subsistence" (p. 92).

The concern of Stiegler is to preserve the possibility of an existence with technology that has neither been reduced to that of adaptation and adjustment nor to the reassertion of a Sloterdijkian, archaic belonging. This is the preservation of a notion of spirit that is fundamentally distinct from the Schmittian critique of technology, as political theology. Spirit is not an ineffable and diffuse spiritualism—a return to an aspect of Schmitt's critique in *Political Romanticism*. Rather, it implies an inventiveness, enhancement, and intensification of knowledge, a theory of individuation that is also a relatedness to others—in other words, an associative coexistence, in contrast to the dissociation resulting from the exclusive connection of technology to a "knowledge economy," which is nothing more than an empty technological utopianism.

6

Political Theology and Democratic Constitutionalism

The establishment of the constitutional democracy of the German Federal Republic, after the collapse of National Socialism and the Nuremburg Tribunal, created the initial situation for the juridico-political reconsideration of Schmittian thought. The Federal Republic commenced by banning Schmitt from resuming an academic position within the German university system, which Schmitt, with the move to Plettenberg, symbolized as a more general "withdrawal" from participation in the institutions of the German Federal Republic. Schmittian thought becomes "extrinsic"—it remains outside the acceptable parameters of institutional, juridico-political reflection and Schmitt elaborates a position of critical intervention at variance with the German Federal Republic's philosophical, political, and juridical foundations and its insertion within the post–World War II international order. Thus, at the inception of the German Federal Republic there is no officially condoned attempt to engage with Schmittian thought.

The importance of the work of Ernst-Wolfgang Böckenförde (1930–2019) is due to his participation, from the late 1950s and the 1960s, in Schmitt's privately organized and funded seminars, and in the intellectual circle around Schmitt,[1] who sought to engage with Schmittian thought and to render it compatible, through a process of internal critique, with a framework of constitutional democracy. Böckenförde's critique represents a reconfiguration of the Schmittian conceptual framework that transforms the understanding and position of political theology in relation to constitutional social democracy. The transformation shifts political theology from the extrinsic Schmittian position to one *within* the framework of contemporary constitutional democracy. The internal critique, and the accompanying shift, are considered through Böckenförde's explicit juridical integration and regulation of the state of exception within a democratic constitution, the deflation of the Schmittian opposition between democracy and liberalism (*Rechtstaat*), and the reduction of the Schmittian opposition between discussion and decision as the counterpart of the deintensification of the friend/enemy distinction. The difficulties of the Böckenfördian theory of constitutional social democracy, flowing from the internal critique of Schmitt, will then be revealed through the presence of continuing tensions underlying an apparently coherent, unified theory.[2]

The Prolegomena: The Critique of the Relationship between Catholicism and National Socialism

The initial focus of Böckenförde's critical intervention is centered upon a fundamental critique of the relationship between both Catholicism and the Federal Republic and Catholicism and the conduct of Christians under National Socialism (Böckenförde, 2019a, 2019b, 2019c). It seeks, prior to its confirmation by the *De Libertate Religiosa* of the Second Vatican Council (1965), to reorient Catholic theology and Christian conduct, through the recognition of its essentially instrumental approach to the Weimar Republic and forms of accommodation with National Socialism, to relinquish any continued resort to instrumentalism within the German Federal Republic. The insistence upon the rejection of instrumentalism is accompanied by a critique of the theological "absolutism" from which it is held to be derived.

The theological "absolutism" arises from "a principled negation," the refusal to recognize the definitive effect of the French Revolution of 1789: "the 'organic' unity of the pre-Revolutionary orders had separated once and for all into 'society' and 'state'" (Böckenförde, 2019b, p. 102). The refusal furnishes the possibility for the misrecognition of National Socialism and its discourse as "a welcome ally in the struggle against the 'pernicious liberal spirit'" and for a Christian order that achieved the "full realization of natural law" (p. 102). In this misrecognition lies the origin of the subsequent acceptance of the National Socialist regime and its endorsement by the Catholic Church.

According to Böckenförde, the effect of, and responsibility for, this active support extends beyond the period of National Socialism. For while the institutions of the Catholic Church, and its *potestas indirecta*, retain their existence, the Catholic Church has exacerbated the "even more uncontested autocracy of liberal society they opposed" (p. 103). The inception of the Federal Republic confronts a conceptual horizon "so perverted and devalued" by the National Socialist regime that "all concepts of statehood, authority, and suprapersonal order" are confined to reestablishing a relationship between state and society predicated upon the state as "the servant of an unshackled economic and acquisitive society" (p. 103). The continued existence of the Catholic Church entails detachment—the "deep inner problem of the Church's *potestas indirecta*"—in which the Catholic Church "has never had any direct responsibility anywhere" (p. 104). The absence of direct responsibility enables the resumption of the refusal to attune itself to the reestablishment of the distinction and "structural co-existence" between society and state (p. 103).

In a footnote—itself a deliberate authorial gesture to distinguish Schmitt from the Catholic bishops and politicians dealt with in the main text (Gosewinkel, 2017, pp. 373–374), in "German Catholicism in 1933: A Critical Examination (1961)" (Böckenförde, 2019b)—Böckenförde indicates Schmitt's distinct position—"special path"—in German Catholicism:[3]

> Carl Schmitt followed a special path in affirming and supporting the Nazi state in 1933. He was neither a representative of Christian natural law nor did he stand on the ground of the organic state doctrine or Reich ideology. In 1931/2, in his capacity as constitutional law scholar, he legally defended the authoritarian government of the presidential cabinets for being—in his view—the last chance of the Weimar Constitution. Now, following the passage of the Enabling Act, he justified and defended the new order of the consolidating Nazi rule. In a sharp turn against the "democratic functionalism" of Weimar and the abstraction and substantive emptiness of the bourgeois *Rechtstaat*, he heightened the new trinity of "state, movement, *Volk*" as the characteristic political order of German people, in which substantive justice and a thinking in terms of "concrete orders" [*konkretes Ordunsdenken*] was once again becoming effective in opposition to the liberalistic dissolution. (Böckenförde, 2019b, p. 93, fn45)

This marks an interpretative distance that will inform the further engagement with, and internal critique of, Schmitt's work as an integral aspect of the subsequent development of Böckenförde's theoretical project.[4]

The Secular State and the Böckenförde-Diktum

Böckenförde's critique of the position of the Catholic Church in the early period of the Federal Republic is expanded into a reconsideration of the historical origin of the secular state as a process of secularization. The demonstration of the character and dynamics of this process is the historical foundation for the concluding formulation of the Böckenförde-Diktum: the structural dilemma that shapes the contemporary secular state.

In the presentation of the process of secularization that constitutes the secular state, the 1967 text (Böckenförde, 2019d) engages in a practice of citation that acknowledges the pertinent work of Schmitt and other members of the circle or other conservative thinkers while articulating an independent position. The independence is evident from Schmitt's subsequent reference to Böckenförde's text in *Political Theology II* (1970) (Schmitt, 2008c, p. 65), in the part devoted to the critique of Peterson's *Monotheism as a Political Problem: A Contribution to the History of Political Theology in the Roman Empire* (1935), in which a quotation is taken from the third, concluding section of the text: "Is it that the Christian belief, according to its inner structure, is a religion like any other religion and is therefore its valid manifestation like that of the public (polis) cult? Or does the Christian belief transcend all other religions known to date, and its effectiveness and relevance consist exactly in the fact that it leads rational people to their own freedom and the secular world by deconstructing mythical forms of religion and public belief in cults?" (p. 65; Böckenförde, 2019d, p. 165). Schmitt introduces the quotation to emphasize an absence in the conception of Christianity, in the preceding work of Peterson, by indicating the historically unique character of Christianity (Schmitt, 2008c). Böckenförde's question of Christianity's uniqueness, although "inevitable," is posed as "an implicit disjunctive alternative"—between ancient religions and Christianity—and is "too narrow" a definition of this uniqueness. For Schmitt, "The Church of Christ is not *of* this world and its history, but it is *in* this world. That means: it is localized and opens up a space; and space here means impermeability, visibility and the public sphere" (Schmitt, 2008c, p. 65). Thus, *Political Theology II* qualifies the pertinence of Böckenförde's question and, in this qualification, continues the elaboration of the critique of Peterson without proceeding to acknowledge the Böckenförde-Diktum of which the quotation is an essential preparatory aspect. In this manner, Schmitt implicitly avoids the necessity to confront the structural dilemma of the contemporary secular state with which the third section of Böckenförde's concludes.

The historical process and consequences of the emergence of the secular state, which Böckenförde traces, are elaborated independently of the Schmittian framework of political theology. The references to Schmitt relate entirely to citations of Schmitt's work that are held to confirm aspects of this distinct process of secularization that the text describes. The theoretical orientation is one that, commencing from the historically specific emergence of the state in Europe between the thirteenth and the late eighteenth or early nineteenth centuries, proceeds to a historical analysis centered upon the "detachment of the political order as such from its spiritual and religious origin and evolution" (Böckenförde, 2019d, pp. 152–153). The detachment, as a historical process, is the secularization of the state: the combination of the "separation of the political order from Christian religion"—the emergence of the state as an autonomous entity, conceptualized in secular terms, and separated "from any specific religion as its foundation" (pp. 152–153).

The historical reconstruction is predicated upon a neutral, descriptive presentation of the secularization of the state as the precondition for the understanding of "the fundamental problems of political order" encountered by the contemporary secular state (p. 153). The reconstruction presents secularization and the emergence of the secular state as a gradual process of the passage from the realm of the ideal to that of the real. The process is initiated by the Investiture Controversy (1057–1122) and proceeds to the "second stage," arising with the Reformation (1517/21–1648) and concluding with the French Revolution (1789–1799), which brings to completion the separate coexistence of religion and a secular state. The combined effect of the Declaration of the Rights of Man and the Citizen (1789) and the French Constitution of 1791 is to establish a state as "an organization of political power to protect the natural, prior rights of the individual" and the "free, self-determined individual person" as "a secular being emancipated from any necessarily religious destiny" (p. 163). Religion is preserved but detached from the state and relocated to the "sphere of society" in the form of the general individual freedoms of belief and worship. Thus, the state is "neutral with regard to religion, emancipating it from religion" and religion is "freed both from and by the state" (p. 163).

For Böckenförde the enduring importance of the French Revolution is that in each instance

> the state grants its citizens freedom of religion as a basic right—and doing so formed part of its "mandate" from the outset, even if it took some time for that freedom to materialize—these remarks apply. Freedom of religion as a right to liberty embraces not only the right to profess a religion privately and publicly, but also the right not to profess a religion without detriment to the citizen's legal position. It follows that the substance of the universality that the state is supposed to embody and protect can no longer be sought in religion or in a particular faith, but must be found independently of religion in secular goals and common interests. The extent to which freedom of religion is realized is thus a measure of the secularity of the state. (pp. 163–164)

It is this essential historical development that becomes the background against which further attempts to conceive and establish the relationship between religion and the state are determined.

The significance of the secularization process lies, according to Böckenförde, in the extent to which the separation of the state and religion marks a definitive privatization of religion—the freedom of religion—as the counterpart of a Christianity deprived of "its universal effectiveness and potential historical power" (p. 165). This transformation opens the question of the secular state's capacity, on a purely secular foundation, to guarantee and maintain "individual liberty, without a unifying bond antecedent to that liberty" (p. 166).[5]

The uncertain dynamics of the separation and co-existence of the state and religion revealed by the preceding historical development are then formulated as the enduring structural dilemma of the Böckenförde-Diktum: *"the liberal, secularized state is sustained by conditions it cannot itself guarantee"* (p. 167). The dilemma demonstrates the impossibility of either the secular state or religion asserting its absolute self-contained independence and the continued requirement for them to acknowledge their mutual interdependence.

The independence entails, on the part of the secular state, that the sphere of individual liberty is supplemented by "the moral substance of the individual and the homogeneity of society" (p. 167). The supplement originates and is sustained, beyond the secular state's limited and counterproductive "instruments of legal coercion and authoritative command," by "the inner impulses and binding forces that religious faith imparts to its citizens" (p. 167). This, in turn, requires that "Christians no longer see this state, in its secularity, as something alien, hostile to their faith, but as a chance for liberty, the preservation and realization of which is also their task" (p. 167).

The Böckenförde-Diktum establishes the necessity of the cooperative coexistence of the secular state and religion. The explicit intention is to present the Federal Republic, as an instance of the process of secularization, and, in this manner, to transform the detachment of the Catholic Church into genuine acceptance and participation. The implicit effect is to mark a distance from Schmittian political theology in both the conceptualization of the relationship between religion and the state and the institutional uniqueness of the Catholic Church.[6]

The Return to Schmitt I: Rethinking the State as an Ethical State

The Böckenförde-Diktum—the continuing dilemma posed by the separation of religion and the state—seeks the productive coexistence of religion and, in particular, the Catholic Church, with a secular, constitutional democracy. The integration of the Catholic Church[7] is the expression of a religious freedom that contributes to a positive coexistence of religion and the state as the counterpart of the Böckenfördian state as an ethical state (Böckenförde, 2017b).

The particularity of religious freedom becomes an aspect of, and a contribution to, the wider "sphere of the intellectual and ethical-moral freedom and self-realization of the individual" (Böckenförde, 2017b, p. 96). This sphere represents the conditions of the Böckenförde-Diktum, which the secular state can seek to protect and facilitate while being itself unable to create or guarantee these conditions. The protection and facilitation of these conditions, as the explicit purpose of the state, entails that the state is a "purpose-orientated institution" and "an ethical state" (p. 88). The determination of the ethical character of the state involves the explicit return to Schmitt and the designation, in a footnote, of *The Concept of the Political* as the fundamental conceptualization of the relationship between "the state as an entity of peace and the state as a political entity" (p. 88, fn7). For Böckenförde,

> the distinction that Carl Schmitt developed as the criterion of the political has been repeatedly misunderstood to this day

> as a normative theory of the political, as though his intent was to define the goal and content of politics as the so-called friend-enemy relationship. The text itself already refuses such an interpretation [Schmitt, 1996, pp. 33f.]. The friend-enemy theory is nothing more and nothing less than the phenomenological-empirical demonstration of a criterion of the political, namely that it is peculiar to political tensions and conflicts that they reach a level of intensity that includes the grouping of the people (groups of people) according to friend and enemy and thus the willingness to fight one another also with force of arms. Any look at the realities and events of the political world of earlier times and of today [1978] can only confirm this. It is the hallmark and tremendous achievement of the state as a political entity that it succeeds in keeping all internal disputes and conflicts between people and groups of people below the level of escalation into an extreme antagonism, that is, the friend-enemy relationship, and in so doing present itself as an entity of peace. (pp. 88–89, fn7)

The Schmittian position is, thus, incorporated into a theory of an ethical state, as the preliminary structural characteristic delineating an entity of peace, decision-making, and power (pp. 88–90). The incorporation is the reflection of a broader methodological purpose of the theory of an ethical state providing the complementary justification of the preliminary structural characteristic in the work of Hermann Heller (1891–1933).[8] In this manner, Böckenförde undertakes a methodological neutralization of the political and theoretical opposition between Schmitt and Heller, in the interwar period, in order to utilize their work as a common theoretical resource for the development of the theory of an ethical state.

The methodological neutralization enables the theory of an ethical state to be further delineated from a state as an "already existing and self-renewing entity of power" (p. 90) to a state as "an organization of authority" that is both "a postulate of security" and "a postulate of *freedom*" (p. 91). The delineation relies upon the preceding combination of Schmitt and Heller to legitimate the primacy and superiority of "the state's power of action and decision-making" (p. 90). This is the necessary corollary of the designation of a "counterforce" on the part of the citizens as illegitimate: "a theory of anarchy or self-empowerment of private or group force" (p. 91, fn10).[9]

The illegitimacy attributed to the emergence and existence of a "counterforce" to the state, as an entity of power, is accompanied by the circumscribed or qualified position attributed to democracy. Democracy—"the democratic organization of the state's decision-making power"—is the procedural combination of freedom and authority for the state's exercise of "authority toward individuals" (p. 91). The exercise of state authority—the entity of peace, decision-making, and power—toward individuals precedes, and is more fundamental than, its democratic organization.

The subordinate position accorded to democracy in the derivation of the elements of the Böckenfördian ethical state reflects the rejection of the democratic origin of the ethical state: the essential separability of the state from its democratic (self-)derivation. In this manner, the ethical state explicitly demarcates its derivation from Habermasian domination free discourse,[10] which is, in turn, designated as utopian (p. 91, fn13). The rejection is the counterpart of the integral connection, for Böckenförde, between the state as an entity of peace and as a decision-making entity. This essential interconnection reconfigures the Schmittian position of decision and sovereignty of *Political Theology* (1922) by resituating them *within* a theory of the state. The relationship between these elements of the ethical state is the guarantee of "the basic conditions of orderly human existence" (p. 91, fn9). The ethical state, as an entity of peace, requires the guarantee of conditions of peace through "valid norms and rules of behavior to determine how these disagreements are pursued" (p. 89). If the disagreement extends to these norms and rules themselves, then the decision-making aspect of the ethical state arises: the reestablishment of peace—the consensus upon norms and rules of behavior—through decision. The decision, as the implementation of the decision-making aspect of the ethical state, is the conventional, internal, and *institutional* "authority of having the 'last word' " (p. 89, fn9).[11]

The absence of any concordance with the Habermasian orientation, as the exemplification of the primacy of democracy,[12] is also the implicit adoption and reworking of the Schmittian distinction between liberalism and democracy (Schmitt, 1988). The ethical state, in the process of its derivation, recasts the Schmittian distinction by situating it within the Böckenförde-Diktum: the dilemma of the coexistence of the secular state and society. Thus, the Schmittian antagonistic relationship between liberalism and democracy is initially decentered and, thereby, deintensified by the primacy accorded to the derivation of the ethical state as an entity of peace, decision-making, and power. This, in turn, defines the position of democracy as a subordinate form of organization of the secular state and reconfigures liberalism as the sphere of freedom and self-realization of the individual within the domain of society.

The purpose of the determination and elaboration of these elements of the ethical state is to establish the preliminary condition of the ethical state as a "constraining and regulating authority ... for the realization of freedom" (Böckenförde, 2017b, p. 91). The capacity for the state, as an ethical state, to ensure the conditions for the realization of freedom entails the democratic, constitutional organization of the authority of the state. The juridification of the authority of the state, through a democratic constitution, transforms "the simple authority of power and decision-making ... into governance [*Herrschaft*]" (p. 92). This, in turn, modifies the form of authority exercised by the state toward individuals: "the link between governance and freedom is established" (p. 92).

The link expresses a relationship between the authority of the state and the individual as one in which state authority is oriented to "secure fundamental purposes of human life" as the corollary of the "freedom and self-realization of the individual" (p. 93). The orientation of state authority is differentiated by active intervention, at the level of "need and understanding" (p. 94), and a comparatively minimal protective approach, at the level of the freedom and self-determination of the individual.

The level of need and understanding designates the ethical state as a social welfare state. The ethical state as a social *Rechtstaat* is, for Böckenförde, the extension from the legally coordinated conciliation of the particular freedom of each individual (liberal *Rechtstaat*) to the "possibility of the realization of the legal freedom of the other" (p. 95, fn23). In this transition, the ethical state is oriented by the presupposition of the dependence of the full enjoyment and exercise of individual freedom and self-determination upon the existence of "specific social conditions among individuals themselves" (p. 95). The ethical state proceeds, beyond the parameters of the liberal *Rechtstaat*, to the acknowledgment that these specific social conditions, upon which individual freedom and self-determination are dependent, require active creation and maintenance. The acknowledgment is the counterpart of the recognition that the sphere of individual freedom and self-determination is unable to generate these conditions from within itself. The level of need and understanding encompasses the "common interests of all, which are prior to any particular interests," and entail the provision of "social security" and "intellectual education" (p. 95).[13]

The limits of the creation and maintenance of the common social conditions are apparent from the explicit qualification of state activity to some form of intervention in these areas of state provision. These limits are also prefiguratively concerned with the regulation and prevention of potentially "ungovernable" demands or expectations arising from existing forms of provision (p. 107, fn61). Thus, the Böckenfördian level of need and understanding, as the intersection of the political and ethical character of the state, is one determined by the state to ensure its compatibility with an industrial society. The focus is, therefore, upon the continuing viability of the ethical state, as a social *Rechtstaat* and industrial society, and the regulation of internal challenges.[14] The effect of industrial society upon nature—the dilemma of ecological coexistence—remains without a significant presence in the Böckenfördian conceptualization of the ethical state.[15] The absence indicates a continuity, in this aspect, with Schmittian thought, and effectively excludes the possibility that a challenge—"normative dissents within society" (Böckenförde, 2017e, p. 337)—to the ethical state would arise from the effect of industrial society upon nature.

An Excursus on Civil Religion

The Böckenfördian state, in order to remain an ethical state, is constrained, beyond intervention at the initial level of need and understanding, by a limit or "prohibition." The proscription applies to state intervention, to promote the freedom and self-realization of the individual, which seeks to generate "an unquestioned political faith as the foundation of the state" (Böckenförde, 2017b, p. 97).

The origin of this form of state intervention is attributed, by Böckenförde, to Rosseau's civil religion (*religion civile*) in book 4, chapter 8, of *The Social Contract* (p. 97, fn30).[16] The Rousseauian civil religion is the originary and exemplary false solution to the perceived effects of the separation of religion and the state: the "resolution" of the Böckenförde-Diktum through the forced coexistence of state and society.

For Böckenförde, civil religion forces the resolution of the dependence of the secular state, personified in the sovereign, upon the distinct sphere of society through the state's elaboration and promulgation of a set of dogmas—"sentiments of sociability"—that render possible the existence of the "good Citizen" or "loyal subject" (Rousseau, 1997, p. 150).[17] The dogmas of the civil religion, as a "purely civil profession of faith" (p. 150), replace religion, in particular Christianity, as that which enables the state to determine that individuals within society, in their adherence to these dogmas, relate to themselves and each other through moral duties. The strength and enduring character of this adherence is achieved through the combination of a form of individual identification—love of moral duties—and state (sovereign) sanction—banishment (for disbelief) or death (disavowal after public acknowledgment).

The Rousseauian "resolution" reveals an impasse that, for Böckenförde, is obscured by the force that underlies and maintains the civil religion: a love of moral duty that is enforced by the intolerance of sanction. The recourse to a civil religion is one in which "liberal appearance and totalitarian consequence already lie close together at the very origin" (p. 97, fn30). The intertwining of liberal appearance and totalitarian consequence arises from the return to antiquity—"a political faith modelled on the classic polis religion" (p. 97, fn10)—in order to ensure that the freedom and self-realization of the individual is determined by the dogmas of civil religion. The dilemma of the state's dependence upon the sphere of society and its distinct conditions of existence is "resolved" by a civil religion that "lays hold of the disposition of the individual" (p. 97).

Böckenförde presents all attempts to establish the coexistence of the state and society on the foundation of an unquestioned political faith—the state's determinate shaping of the freedom and self-realization of the individual—as positions that merely remain within and repeat the fundamental limitations of Rousseauian civil religion.[18] The rejection of recourse to civil religion is an aspect of the broader reinterpretation of Rousseau to conform with the parameters of the Böckenfördian ethical state. The Rousseauian notions of the general and particular will are retained and reconfigured (p. 93, fn18) to accord with the preservation of a sphere of freedom and self-realization of the individual beyond the purview of active state intervention.[19]

The Return to Schmitt II: Rethinking the State of Exception

The secular state, as an ethical state, depends upon coexistence with a sphere of freedom and self-realization of the individual, which the secular state can only delimit and regulate externally (Böckenförde, 2017b, p. 101). The ethical state, as the response to the coexistence of the secular state and society, preserves a sphere whose autonomy contains the possibility for the freedom and self-realization of the individual to assert itself in opposition to the state. The possibility, as a permanent condition of the coexistence of secular state and society, is one to which the ethical state responds by creating and maintaining consensual coexistence between state and society. Consensual coexistence is the reflection of the continued presence of the Böckenförde-Diktum within the ethical state. The underlying fragility of consensual coexistence is an integral aspect of the ethical state's relationship to society in which the Böckenförde-Diktum remains operative. The dilemma establishes a coexistence between the secular state and society in which the form of an ethical state cannot overcome the Böckenförde-Diktum without the collapse of coexistence.

The consensual coexistence rests upon the singular and combined effect of the democratic configuration of the ethical state (pp. 105–107) and the existence of state institutions that "endow the civic virtues with recognition and support" (p. 104). These elements are traversed by the inherent fragility of consensus—a contingent unity—dependent upon the interaction between state and society. The consensus of the democratic configuration of the ethical state, as a representative, party democracy, rests upon the "interplay" (p. 106), through elections, of the active citizenry and the legislature and executive: the "*two* representatives of the collective will and collective consciousness" (p. 106). It is the degree of openness of "the government, parliament and the political parties" that determines the capacity of the active citizenry to "articulat[e] itself and . . . to attain self-knowledge" (p. 106). The consensus, as the distinctive consensus of an ethical state, requires this particular relationship between the two representatives to endure.

The consensual recognition and support of civic virtues—"the public order of a polity" (p. 104)—between state and society requires that the sphere of individual freedom and self-realization extends beyond self-regarding individual interest" (p. 103) to encompass civic virtue. In this manner, the state "enables and helps to sustain subjectivity" (p. 105), in a broader ethical and moral sense, through "anchoring points" (p. 103) that facilitate their identification and adoption.[20] The durability of this consensus confronts the continued capacity for the sphere of individual freedom and self-realization to disengage from this broader ethical and moral sense: "individual interests are set free to unfold in a self-regarding way" (p. 103). The ethical state, through this form of consensual relationship with society, seeks to preserve the conception, as the counterpart of these "anchoring points," of the fundamental incompletion of the intellectual and moral formation of a self-regarding individual.

The ethical state remains a distinctive response to the coexistence of the secular state and society to the extent that these inherently fragile effects of consensual coexistence persist. The distinctiveness of the ethical state is the attempt to confront the Böckenförde-Diktum by preventing the state from becoming either the "mere executive organ of society" (p. 95) or "the regression to a primitive, nature-like state for the organization of political co-existence" (p. 105). Consensual coexistence is animated by an explicit acknowledgment that its fragile existence contains the continued potential for its collapse into either of these two forms of defective secular state.

The primacy of the interconnection between the ethical state and the Böckenförde-Diktum—the assumption and response to the dilemma of the coexistence of a secular state and society—displaces the centrality of the Schmittian correlation between sovereignty and exception. The sovereignty of the state, as the precondition for the further elaboration of the ethical state, is established without recourse to the notion of exception. The Schmittian insistence, in *Political Theology* (1922), upon the exception as both "a general concept in the theory of the state" (Schmitt, 2005, p. 5) and one that contains the "whole question of sovereignty" (p. 7), is absent from the Böckenfördian framework. The displacement of the Schmittian orientation arises from the substitution of the Schmittian "philosophico-historical or metaphysical" (p. 7) considerations of *Political Theology* (1922) by the Böckenfördian concentration upon the historical emergence and dynamics of the coexistence of a secular state and society.

In this displacement, the ethical state reconceives the relationship to the determination of an exception and the corresponding situation of exception or emergency.[21] The re-conception arises from a critical reflection upon the response, within the constitutional framework of the Federal Republic, to the extraparliamentary challenge from the activities of the Red Army Faction/Baader-Meinhof Group. The Böckenfördian approach is to selectively incorporate certain aspects of the Schmittian approach to the state of exception from within the constitutional framework of the Federal Republic.[22] The position of selective appropriation contributes to a broader process of situating the relationship between the norm and exception as a question of constitutional coordination. The question, oriented by the structure of the constitution of the Federal Republic, has ceased to center upon the juridical personification of a decision on the exception under Article 48 of the constitution of the Weimar Republic (Böckenförde, 2017c, 109). The Böckenfördian concern is to render the state of exception—the decision and the character and period of its duration—a coherent element of the ethical state (pp. 111–115).[23]

The coherence of the state of exception involves a comprehensive juridical determination that insists upon both a significant degree of juridical regulation and the retention of its exceptional character (p. 118). For Böckenförde, "the question we therefore confront concerns that of philosophy of law and the constitutional theory of the state of emergency" (p. 115). This philosophy of law considers the "interrelationship of the law and social reality as a *legal* problem" (p. 116) to be both the central determinant of law and the basis for its differentiation from ethics and morality (p. 116, fn30). The distinctive "normative ordering force" (p. 116, fn32) of legal norms is dependent upon the continued "correlational association" between the legal norm and the particular aspect of social reality to which it is directed (p. 117). The continued existence of this correlational association represents the orientation and regulation of social reality by legal norms. It is the interruption or collapse of this correlational association that deprives the legal norm of its "intended regulatory power" and, in turn, has the potential to become a political question as the correlational association is "the continuing existence of the state as an entity of peace, and thus the absence of political enmity within the state that is exercised in a dangerously aggressive way" (p. 117).

The state, as a constitutional state, acts, through its institutions, in conformity with "the rule of law and the separation of powers" (p. 117, fn35). The correlational association between legal norm and social reality is the counterpart of state activity that is itself legally defined and delimited (p. 118). Thus, the collapse of the correlational association confronts the constitutional state with a "*fundamental* discrepancy" in which the legal parameters and limits of its activity contend with a "serious threat that affects the state fundamentally as an entity of peace and the guarantor of the legal order" (p. 118). The fundamental discrepancy becomes the state of exception, which is, from the outset, posed *within* the framework of the legal order of the constitutional state. The development of the Böckenfördian approach consists of the further delineation of the "legal responses to the problem of the state of emergency" (p. 119).

The legal responses commence from a situation that, as an exception, cannot be "anticipated normatively" (p. 199) and, therefore, a comprehensive and definitive legal definition is unobtainable. The unforeseeable and unpredictable character of an exception is to be retained as an essential determinant of the legal response. The Böckenfördian approach is to insist that the exception, and the ensuing state of emergency, be conceived by according primacy to the legal situation of normality and peace. The decision, and consequent state of emergency, are understood as exceptional in relation to a constitutional and legal order that it is their sole purpose to restore.[24] This understanding is the corollary of the concern that the exceptional, in the process of restoration, leaves the normal untransformed: "safeguarding against a transformation of the law of normal state of affairs . . . into a new normal state characterized by the exception" (p. 121). The legal meaning attributed to the exception then orients the construction of the surrounding normative framework.

The construction of the framework is shaped by the three interrelated aspects: the preconditions, the decision, and the aims and constraints on the emergency powers (p. 119). The preconditions, as the juridical definition of a situation of emergency, are confined to "only the most extreme situation" whose "unforeseeability" is preserved by its expression in the form of a "relatively general clause" (p. 119). The decision, upon the basis of these preconditions, to declare a state of emergency is to be strictly separated from the substantive response to the state of emergency. The substantive emergency powers themselves are the aspect that retains a Schmittian influence, as Böckenförde utilizes the Schmittian distinction between law and measure to define the normative character of emergency powers as measures (p. 120). While measures are enforceable and authoritative, they are to remain, as a response to exception, "essentially and structurally different" (p. 120) from law that relates to the legal situation of normality and peace. The exceptionalism of measures prevents a juridification or "legal normalization" (p. 127) of the state of emergency. This exceptionalism is expressed in the specific normative form of measures that are to be formulated as temporary, specific, concrete responses to the particular situation of emergency as the legally regulated restoration of normality. Measures are immediately withdrawn or cease to be effective in conformity with the process of restoration. These three interrelated aspects are then overlain by the further concern that the fundamentally "unforeseeable" status of the exception, within the constitutional order of the ethical state, entails the "absence of precise substantive regulation of emergency powers" (p. 130). This enduring absence is then to receive a response in the form of "enhanced oversight" (p. 130), through procedural regulation, of these three interrelated aspects.

The Böckenfördian integration of the state of exception or emergency into the constitutional and legal order of the ethical state acknowledges that it "provides no absolute protection against the possible abuse of existing emergency powers" (p. 131). The limitation is itself the recognition that there are "no absolute protections against threats to legal and political freedom that arise from human co-existence" (p. 132). This position explicitly refers to the gloss in Hobbes's *De Cive*[25] (p. 132) and, in this reference, indicates the double displacement of other elements of Schmittian thought. In the recourse to this Hobbesian gloss on the term "absolute power," Böckenförde displaces the Schmittian appropriation of Kierkegaard—the "Protestant theologian"—in which the sense of the exception is the truth of the general (Schmitt, 2005, p. 15).[26] The displacement interrupts the preliminary indication of the continued pertinence of theological concepts for the conceptualization of sovereignty and the modern state: the initial Schmittian political theology. The Böckenfördian affirmation of the Hobbesian gloss displaces the emphasis of the Schmittian interpretation of Hobbes, in the later 1930s, upon the Hobbesian "mechanization of the state" (Schmitt, 2008c, 91). For Schmitt, from this Hobbesian transformation of the conception of the state arises the distinctive seventeenth-century state and the "essentially intellectual or sociological pre-condition for the technical-industrial age that was to come" (pp. 98–99). In place of this Schmittian prefigurative, historical position, the Böckenfördian emphasis is upon the enduring limits and fragility of the secular state confirmed by Hobbesian thought. The Böckenfördian position is the acceptance, in contrast to the Schmittian rejection, that "one day it may be shattered by civil war or rebellion" (p. 100). It is an acceptance, however, that furnishes the impetus to respond, rather than acquiesce, and, in this response, to situate Hobbes as the metonym for the Böckenfördian appropriation of Schmitt's *The Concept of the Political*.

Sin, Enmity, and the Böckenförde-Diktum

The ethical state, as the coordinated response to the dilemma of the coexistence of the secular state and society (the Böckenförde-Diktum), contains the continued possibility for challenges to, or failure of, this coordination. The possibility is located, by the remainder of the Hobbesian gloss, in the relationship between an "absolute power" and an imperfectible human nature whose dynamics underlie the relationship between individuals within society. The "absolute power" derives its specific characteristics from the incapacity of human nature to generate and guarantee the conditions of peace and normality from within itself. This incapacity is the corollary of an "absolute power" of sovereignty open to arbitrariness and abuse. The Böckenfördian inflection of this Hobbesian gloss—the dilemma of absolute power—interweaves it into the Schmittian conceptual framework of *The Concept of the Political*.

For Böckenförde, in this interweaving, an absolute sovereignty is retained, as the precondition for the ethical state, and it asserts itself, albeit temporarily, in the situation of exception and state of emergency: the survival of the state and restoration of the constitutional and legal order of the ethical state. The retention of a locus of absolute sovereignty is the retention of the Schmittian existential sense of the state that is revealed in the exception. This existential sense—the state's self-preservation—remains the correlate of a degree of enmity—the friend/enemy distinction—that exceeds the distinctive forms of pacific regulation and integration of the ethical state. The Böckenfördian regulation of the Schmittian position and, through this regulation, the differentiation and divergence of the Böckenfördian position, arises by designating the assertion of absolute sovereignty—the state of exception—as an even more exceptional situation: an unforeseeable event. For the emergence of the unrestrained enmity of the friend/enemy distinction—the necessary correlate of the state of exception—is itself rendered unforeseeable by the continued, enduring effect of the "theological points of orientation" (Böckenförde, 2019g, p. 271) of modern secular law in the normality of the ethical state (p. 267). An essential element of this orientation—"the damaged state of man from the power of sin" (p. 267)—is the implicit theological acknowledgment of the Hobbesian designation of a defective human nature. It is conceived as an internal division: "the human being is ambivalent in his habitus; he is not necessarily good and not necessarily evil, but instead carries both possibilities within himself" (p. 269).[27] Modern secular law, on the basis of an autonomous authority as law, assumes and responds to the damaged state of man through the provision of external normative orientation (p. 274). It is not simply an external order of constraint, but "the (external) system of preservation for human beings" in which "dignity and liberty" are guaranteed against a defective human nature (p. 277).

The guarantee of dignity and liberty, as the juridical protection of the sphere of individual freedom and self-development, encompassing the protection of freedom of belief, recognizes "divergent religious convictions . . . within the framework of the demands of fundamental social compatibility" (p. 273). The "legal space" created by this recognition assumes primacy over any invocation of "an objective order with a Christian imprint" (p. 273) or of a preexisting community. The relative homogeneity of the society that coexists with the ethical state arises from the primacy accorded to this legal space.

The concentration upon the question of "socio-cultural cohesion" (Polke, 2018, p. 123) is the transposition of the Schmittian relationship between order and crisis into the Böckenförde-Diktum. The dilemma of the coexistence of a secular state and society is superimposed upon the Schmittian conceptual framework and, in this superimposition, reconfigured to elaborate the possibility of coordinated coexistence in the form of an ethical state. The Böckenfördian orientation is the continual insistence upon both the possibility and contingency of this coordination: the essential fragility of the ethical state. It is this fragility, as the unsurpassable limit of a contemporary constitutional and legal order, that animates a constantly renewed reflection upon the conditions of its existence. Preservation of the ethical state is the Böckenfördian response that seeks to substitute coordination and fragility for order and crisis.

This substitution reflects the attempt to integrate Schmitt within a conventional juridico-political framework: to render Schmitt compatible with a theory of the contemporary constitutional state. It presents Schmitt as a background—a corpus of work for interpretation—that retains its pertinence only through this process of integration. It is an interpretative appropriation—a thinking with and beyond Schmitt—that enables the regulated transfer of Schmittian concepts and categories into a theory of an ethical state: the coordination of a constitutional order dependent upon the relationship between a secular state and a society into which religion has been transferred and transformed as freedom of belief and worship.

This interpretative position—the capacity to integrate Schmitt within a conventional juridico-political framework—rests upon the historical presentation of the separation of secular state and society and the ensuing limits imposed upon political and legal thought by the Böckenförde-Diktum. It is the degree of coherence and plausibility of both the historical presentation and the Böckenförde-Diktum that determine the capacity for the Böckenfördian position to establish itself *beyond* Schmitt. For it is through these central elements of the interpretative appropriation that Böckenförde seeks to achieve the integration of the Schmittian corpus within a constitutional theory. The integration explicitly acknowledges that it remains fragile and requires a constant effort and vigilance to ensure its preservation. This fragility, which is presented as a realism with regard to the expectations and limits of this integration, indicates the ease with which these Schmittian categories can reassert their primacy over the constitutional order with which they are sought to be regulated. It is these unresolved tensions of the Böckenfördian theory of constitutional democracy that indicate the more general challenges to contemporary democratic constitutionalism.

7

Political Theology and Contemporary Challenges to Democratic Constitutionalism

In this chapter, we propose to deepen our examination of some of the aporias and contradictions in democracy identified in the previous chapter. Our proposition is that the problems of coexistence between the secular state and what has for some time come to be known as post-secular society (see Habermas, 2008) can no longer be regulated, let alone resolved, through Böckenförde's notion of the "ethical state." These tensions are reflected in the way that today liberal democracies are challenged by political forces and antagonisms that emerge from inside and outside the political order and that they can no longer completely contain. Here we will focus on ethnonationalist populism, as well as extraparliamentary movements for social, racial, and environmental justice. Our claim will be that such forces and movements are not only symptomatic of the legitimation crisis of the secular constitutional order but also that they can be understood as contemporary modes of political theology. By this we do not mean that they are religiously inspired movements as such—although they often intersect with and draw upon religious beliefs, narratives, rituals, and symbols in various ways. Rather, they represent a kind of theologically inflected politics. They might be considered a secularized form of theology given political expression and performed in the public space. Contemporary movements that characterize the post-secular public space and that challenge the terms of the current economic, social, and political order express a desire for a sacred, transcendental meaning beyond the limits of this order. This might be the desire for a renewed and reinvigorated idea of national sovereignty and a purer and more unmediated articulation of the sacred "will of the people"; or it might be the demand for social justice and equality. It might be expressed in exclusionary or inclusionary terms, as a sanctification of the identity of majorities or the recognition of rights of minorities, or even of nonhuman communities. It might even be couched in quasi-theological terms: the Manichean opposition between the "pure" people and the corrupt "elites" characteristic of populism, or the messianic promise of justice and emancipation. However, these contemporary movements also represent two different and opposed orientations for political theology today: post-secular movements of the right, we argue, are essentially a repetition of the Schmittian model of political theology, based as it is on the desire for a strong authoritarian sovereign and a homogeneous political order; whereas post-secular movements of the left represent an alternative and more emancipatory direction for political theology, one inspired by the promise of justice. We intend to show that, contra Schmitt, political theology, while concerned with the question of political legitimacy, does not have to end up as an endorsement of an authoritarian sovereign state as an answer to this problem. Indeed, political theology might be engaged in a radical critique of state authority.

Political Theology and Post-industrial Society

Many of the political antagonisms emerging around us might be seen as symptomatic of deep-set structural weaknesses and long-term crises afflicting post-industrial societies: the withdrawal of the social democratic welfare state, which Böckenförde saw as a mechanism for mediating the tensions endemic to the liberal constitutional order; the financialization of the global economy and resulting economic precarity; as well as the looming environmental crisis. The prevalence of quasi-religious movements and narratives in secular societies, and the ideological antagonisms they reflect, all speak to a general sense of rancor and discontent, a general a loss of faith in the current political order. This has in many ways been accelerated by the pandemic, which has placed extreme pressures on political institutions and economic systems, exposing their inadequacies and weaknesses, and revealing deeper injustices and inequalities. The context of the pandemic has given rise to contagious, "viral" forms of political dissent, which spread rapidly across borders, as we saw in the spontaneous global protests in reaction to the police killing of George Floyd in the United States, or in the toppling of the statues of slave traders. We have also seen anti-lockdown and anti-vaccination protests in many parts of the world, where it is difficult to identify a clear or coherent ideology. However, such expressions of opposition reveal a much deeper legitimation crisis in the liberal political order, one that predates the pandemic, going back at least to the financial crisis of 2008 and the economic and political fallout from this. The inherent instability of global banking systems, and the decade or more of austerity that followed—a policy response that only exacerbated already entrenched wealth inequalities—showed the limitations of the neoliberal economic model and brought to a head the long-standing crisis of the welfare state.

Furthermore, as Bernard Stiegler has argued, the hyper-consumerist model of finance capitalism and the "creative destruction" wrought by neoliberal economic policy dominant since the 1980s—coupled with digitalization and our addiction to the internet (something that has also been exacerbated during the pandemic)—has produced a kind of general psychic regression: a condition of stupidity, irrationality, and unreason that he sees as characteristic of the post-industrial era (see Stiegler, 2015). Perhaps the most obvious sign of this today is the bewildering proliferation of conspiracy theories and movements, such as the anti-vaxxer and COVID conspiracies, or the bizarre and outlandish QAnon conspiracy, which can be perceived as a new form of religion. Understood in the broader context of "post-truth" condition, where there is a loss of faith in established sources of truth—the political class, the mainstream media, scientific authority—and a proliferation of alternative narratives and competing perspectives ("alternative facts"), conspiracy theories and political cults might be considered new modes of religious belief. In their deeply paranoid structure, there is the same desire to make sense of the world, to identify a deeper truth behind the veils of social reality, allowing believers to anchor themselves in a world that seems increasingly bereft of meaning and outside their control. We can apply Eric Voegelin's concept of "political religions" to an understanding of contemporary conspiracy movements and political cults.[1] While Voegelin developed this term in 1938 to characterize modern totalitarianism, especially National Socialism, he pointed to the way that modern secular societies had an underlying religious structure, and that political movements and ideologies bore a deep affinity with religious thinking. There is the same desire for inner-worldly community, transcendence and salvation, the same hope attached to the figure of the leader. As Voegelin said: "The language of politics is always interspersed with the ecstasies of religiosity and, thus, becomes a symbol in the concise sense by letting experiences concerned with the contents of the world be permeated with transcendental divine experiences" (2000, p. 70). Furthermore, according to Voegelin, followers of political cults continue to believe in the truth of their narrative, even if they are aware of the manipulations behind it: "As a consequence of the pragmatic elements of the inner-worldly faith, people following this type of religion will not allow their faith to be disrupted even though they know of the psychological techniques used for creating myths, the propaganda of myths, and the social dissemination" (p. 63). The followers of the Trump cult in the US—which shows no signs of abating despite his electoral defeat in 2020—may not literally believe his outlandish and prolific lies (perhaps even Trump does not believe them), and yet this does not dislodge their faith in him. The religious structure of faith that permeates political cults is not really concerned with literal truth but is, rather, about providing a point of identification and a guiding narrative that allows one to place oneself within a community of fellow believers. A different order of truth is at work here. The notion of revelation, which Voegelin identifies as part of the apocalyptic narrative of political religions, is also central to contemporary conspiracy movements. Adherents of conspiracy theories often talk about the "Great Awakening"—a theme they take from evangelical Christianity—to evoke the moment when the truth of the conspiracy will be revealed to the world.[2]

Populism and Political Theology

The contemporary right-wing populist insurgency[3]—which often has an intimate connection with conspiracy movements and theories—sits somewhere between, we would argue, political religion and political theology. While Voegelin had in mind the totalitarian movements of the 1930s and 1940s with his designation "political religions," and while today's populist movements are much more diffuse and lack a clear ideological orientation,[4] they nevertheless display certain aspects of a political religion. We can point to the political alliances formed between ethnonationalist populists and religious conservatives in many parts of the world—the US, Poland, Hungary, and Russia, for example. Populist discourse often mobilizes religious themes and images in its narrative, particularly the idea of defending a certain religious identity or heritage, associated with a homogeneous cultural, ethnic, national community, against the threat posed by immigration from alien cultures. The "Great Replacement" narrative, and the perceived need to defend European Christian identity against the influence of Islam, has loomed large in the discourse and imagination of national populists and the extreme right.[5] Whether this reflects a genuine religious affinity or a deliberate manipulation of religious themes by populists to galvanize political support, the point is that populism draws on religion and politicizes it (see also Arato & Cohen, 2017; Schmiedel & Ralston, 2021). Religious identity and tradition are often central to the idea of the national community that populists see as under threat.

Religious and theological themes and images are also present in other aspects of populist discourse. The idea, for instance, of the people as "sacred," as morally pure, is central to the narrative of populism. The people are seen as good, honest, hard-working, "salt of the earth" types with a strong affiliation and loyalty to their national community, in contrast to the elites, whether cultural, political, or economic, who are positioned as morally impure, corrupt, as representing liberal values—the "rootless cosmopolitans" who are loyal to nowhere and who have sacrificed national interests to the globalization and multicultural agenda. The "sacred" people are also pitted against minorities, whether immigrants or simply anyone who does not share the values of the majority, and who are seen to pose a threat to national cultural identity and to be enabled by elites. There is a Manichean imaginary at work here, in which good is pitted against evil. Furthermore, in populism there is a strong investment in the personality of the leader, who is seen as a sort of Messiah-like figure who promises salvation. In the politics of populism, the figure of the leader is absolutely central; the leader dominates over the party—indeed *is* the party[6]—and is seen to embody the "will of the people." The peculiar attraction of "strongman" leader types, characteristic of populism, might be interpreted in politico-theological terms as a desire for sovereignty, a desire for, as Schmitt would have it, a strong, decisive, unilateral will that can cut through the bureaucratic norms and procedures of the rule-bound state and "get things done." Indeed, populist leaders threaten to turn on the "administrative state" and the elites and civil servants who control it. Populism, as they say, is about offering simple solutions to complex problems. Hence the appeal of authoritarian figures like Trump, Bolsonaro, Duterte, Orbán, Putin, and many others. They convey, in their displays of strength, masculinity, and vitality, the fantasy image of sovereignty.[7] The populist leader—the one who is both of the people and yet transcends them—offers the promise of their salvation and redemption. He is the one who "knows how they feel," who shares their values, who expresses their true inclinations and defends their interests, who can deliver what they truly desire, and who is not afraid to transgress the established norms and practices of politics in doing so. As Margaret Canovan (1999) argued, populism represents, or seeks to represent, the redemptive, salvific face of democracy, in opposition to its more mundane, pragmatic, procedural face. It is symptomatic of the tension internal to democracy between this idealistic, passionate dimension—expressed in the romantic idea of popular sovereignty and the will of the people—and the more technocratic, institutional aspect that is concerned with real-world problem solving. The gap between democracy's message of salvation—the idea that the will of the people should prevail—and the actual realities of power, between promises made and promises broken, usually leads to disenchantment, a disenchantment that populists exploit. In promising to give the people "what they really want"—in contrast to the mainstream political establishment that, mired in technocratic and bureaucratic complexity, is unable or unwilling to carry out the wishes of the people—populism offers a "reenchantment" of democracy, claiming to restore its central message of redemption and hope. In this sense, populism might be understood as a kind of secularized messianism, even if its promise of salvation ultimately proves empty.

Populism might also be seen in terms of political theology in the more direct Schmittian sense (see also Arato, 2013). It reflects and, we would argue, *radicalizes* Schmitt's sovereign-centric, antipluralistic, and antiliberal model of politics. Populist politics represents a particular challenge to liberal constitutional democracy, in part because it emerges from within the democratic system, makes use of democratic mechanisms and institutions, and yet often represents a profoundly illiberal, at times authoritarian, agenda.[8] It accentuates the tensions that exist between liberalism, as a discourse of rights and institutional checks and balances on executive power, and democracy, as the idea of popular sovereignty and the unmediated will of the people. Hungary's Viktor Orbán likes to style himself as an "illiberal democrat" who defends socially conservative values and the Christian identity of the nation against the liberal agenda of individual rights, multiculturalism, pluralism, and open borders. In doing so, he has stripped out the constitutional framework of that country, undermining the independence of the judiciary, operating a state-run media, and, in

2020, in the context of the pandemic, giving himself unlimited emergency powers to bypass parliament and the constitution and to effectively rule by decree. Populism, particularly of the right-wing nationalist kind, fractures democracy from within, introducing a conflict over the very meaning and terms of democracy: is democracy about constitutional safeguards, the rule of law, and political pluralism; or is it only the expression of the "will of the people" that must always be obeyed? This was the internal tension within democracy that Schmitt himself explored and sought to accentuate.

Central to populism's imaginary is the idea of sovereignty. Sovereignty is a specter that reappears in our contemporary globalized, interconnected world more as a fantasy than a reality, but as an idea no less powerful and appealing for all that. In conditions of uncertainty and insecurity, there is a strong desire for sovereignty, as a protective force, an immunizing mechanism that will defend people against outside forces and restore national prestige and potency. Even in the context of the pandemic, when the incompetence of many populist governments in dealing with the public health crisis has been exposed, the populist message of securing national borders against immigrants, now seen as biohazards, has been a powerful and resonant one, and will continue to be so in the future. The image of sovereignty suffuses three key themes in populist discourse: the people as sovereign, the national community as sovereign, and the populist leader as sovereign. Populist discourse therefore bears a close proximity to Schmitt's sovereign-centric version of political theology. The populist leader is one in whom the fantasy of exceptional sovereignty is invested; the one in whom, as Schmitt put it, "the power of real life breaks through the crust of a mechanism that has become torpid by repetition" (2005, p. 15). Furthermore, the antagonistic logic central to populism—the way that the people are defined in opposition to elites (and minorities) and national identity is defined in opposition to outside interests—directly reflects Schmitt's friend/enemy distinction, where the political community becomes unified in opposition to a common foe. Indeed, populist politics—in both its parliamentary and extraparliamentary forms—seeks to intensify this friend/enemy opposition in a deliberate attempt to destabilize and internally fragment the political order.

Schmitt's constitutional theory is useful for thinking about the ambiguous relationship between populism and political order. In his *Crisis of Parliamentary Democracy* from 1923, Schmitt claimed that democracy is not essentially about parliamentary institutions or even about political parties, but, rather, about popular sovereignty and the will of the people, drawing attention once again to what he saw as the basic incompatibility between liberalism and democracy. Indeed, it was this tension that was the cause of the crisis of the constitutional order of the Weimar Republic, as we discussed in an earlier chapter.

According to Schmitt, parliament appeared increasingly as a great talking shop, a chamber of endless deliberation, and a means of satisfying special interests, which had nothing to do with democracy (1988, p. 8). If, by contrast, democracy is really about the expression of the "will of the people," how should this be understood? This is not an egalitarian idea, where there is the attempt to include and represent a plurality of interests and viewpoints but, on the contrary, an inegalitarian and exclusionary principle, or rather the idea that democratic equality is premised on *inequality*, on privileging one group over others. As Schmitt puts it: "Every actual democracy rests on the principle that not only are equals equal but unequals will not be treated equally. Democracy requires, therefore, first homogeneity and second—if the need arises—elimination or eradication of heterogeneity" (2000, p. 9). In other words, what is really central to democracy is *identity*—identity defined by the inclusion of one group and the exclusion of others. As in populist discourse, where the people do not include everyone and are defined through opposition to others (certain minorities—those who are not part of the people properly speaking)—the identity of the people can only ever be an exclusionary concept. For Schmitt, the democratic will of the people must be homogeneous.[9] This theme is also reflected in Schmitt's later work *Constitutional Theory* (*Verfassungslehre*) from 1928, where he argues that the legitimacy of the constitutional order derives entirely from the unmediated "will of the people" as a force external to the constitution and with the power to make and unmake it. Here the people are once again understood as a homogeneous unified identity that cannot be contained within the constitutional order and whose will cannot be adequately represented through the pluralistic mechanisms of political parties and parliaments (see 2008a).

Therefore, on Schmitt's account, the modern crisis of parliamentary democracy results from the failure to recognize the identitarian basis of democracy and constitution-making power:

> The crisis of the parliamentary system and of parliamentary institutions in fact springs from the circumstances of modern mass democracy. These lead first of all to a crisis of democracy itself, because the problem of a substantial equality and homo-

> geneity, which is necessary to democracy, cannot be resolved by the general equality of mankind. It leads further to a crisis of parliamentarism that must certainly be distinguished from the crisis of democracy. Both crises have appeared today at the same time and each one aggravates the other, but they are conceptually and in reality different. As democracy, modern mass democracy attempts to realize an identity of governed and governing, and thus it confronts parliament as an inconceivable and outmoded institution. If democratic identity is taken seriously, then in an emergency, no other constitutional institution can withstand the sole criterion of the people's will, however it is expressed. Against the will of the people especially an institution based on discussion by independent representatives has no autonomous justification for its existence, even less so because the belief in discussion is not democratic but originally liberal. (1988, p. 15)

In other words, there was, in Schmitt's view, no way that an institution like parliament, which seeks to represent a plurality of interests, can ever properly express the homogeneous will of the people. Schmitt's solution to this crisis of legitimacy was an authoritarian and, indeed, *populist* one. Because "the People" is a homogeneous identity, its will can only be conveyed through the singular person of the leader, with whom there is a direct and unmediated relationship. This was why Schmitt claimed that some form of dictatorship through plebiscite was compatible with democracy and, indeed, was a more meaningful and effective way of articulating the will of the people than parliamentary institutions and voting in elections (1988, pp. 16–17).

Populism proposes a close relationship of identification between the will of the people and the will of the leader, one that bypasses the mediating mechanism of political parties and institutions. This relationship is what Nadia Urbinati (2019) has paradoxically referred to as "direct representation." However, at the same time, this is a strictly hierarchical and transcendent relationship; populist leaders appear as sovereign over the people, who are expected only to support them at election time or to acclaim them at political rallies, rather than having any real say over the decisions they make. The last thing the populist leader wants is the direct participation of the people in democratic decision-making. If there is room for a form of democracy within Schmitt's sovereign-centric political theology, it is a highly singular, idiosyncratic, and reductionist one, in which there is little space for genuine democratic participation, let alone an accommodation of pluralism. Yet, it is this narrow conception of democracy that is increasingly reflected in the contemporary populist turn.

Post-secular Political Emancipation

Is there another way to think about democracy that avoids the problem of sovereign transcendence? And how can an alternative account of political theology allow us to formulate a nonpopulist understanding of democracy that, at the same time, has the power to transform the existing political order? There have been many experiments, particularly in recent times, in forms of direct democracy and consensus decision-making emerging from extraparliamentary protest movements, such as Occupy Wall Street, as well as the 15-M and Indignados movements in Spain, and elsewhere in the world, which emerged in the wake of the financial crisis of 2008. If such movements could be described as "populist" at all, they represented a very different kind of populism to the kind discussed earlier. Even the Occupy slogan of the "99% against the 1%," while seeming to resemble "the people" versus "the elites" narrative of populism, implied a much more inclusive conception of "the people" than the one proposed by national populists, and was based on the more heterogeneous figure of the precarious multitude rather than a homogeneous national community. More importantly, these movements were nonhierarchical and horizontally organized, without centralized leadership and even without a representative agenda, apart from a loose set of principles and decision-making procedures. As experiments in direct democracy, they implied an actively engaged form of public deliberation rather than political support or the acclamation of a leader. Even though, as in the case of the Spanish anti-austerity movements, political parties emerged from these protests, the movements themselves were fundamentally a rejection of conventional forms of political representation. Their orientation was to remain external to representative parliamentary democracy, to articulate a distinct political discourse, and to transform the parameters of conventional politics. They could be seen as a nonsovereign form of democracy that sought to open up alternative and autonomous political spaces outside state institutions.

These movements could not, properly speaking, be considered a form of constituent power insofar as they did not seek to create new state institutions or even to get rid of existing ones, but rather to suspend the political order, to delegitimize its authority. Revolutionary constituent power, while it emerges from outside the political order, thus having the authority to replace or change it, nevertheless ends up becoming part of a new political order. As we have seen with most revolutions, constituting power always ends up as *constituted* power, as political sovereignty. Instead, Agamben (2014) has proposed the notion of *destituent* or deinstituting power as an alternative concept that escapes this oscillation between the force that makes constitutions and the force that conserves and enforces them. In seeking to deinstitute or suspend the authority of the constitutional order, contemporary radical movements might be said to produce a "state of exception." However, unlike the Schmittian "state of exception," this is an anomic space without sovereignty. It is not created by a transcendent sovereign authority but rather comes from below. Nor does it seek to create a new form of sovereignty in place of the old.

If such movements and mobilizations could be considered a form of democracy without sovereignty, they were also a form of democracy without "the people." As we have suggested, "the people"—at least as it is deployed in populist conceptions of democracy—is an exclusionary category, based on a homogeneous (usually national and cultural) identity. Moreover, it is always attached to the figure of the leader who speaks for the people and who articulates their desires. "The people" is a monotheistic politico-theological category that is ultimately authoritarian and hostile to pluralism and difference. For democracy to be genuinely democratic it must, paradoxically, dispense with the figure of the people and organize itself around other symbols and principles. How can an alternative account of political theology allow us to reformulate a notion of democracy without a people? Indeed, is there a radical political theology that is compatible with a more radical and nonsovereign conception of democracy? As Jeffrey W. Robbins (2011, p. 6) puts it: "While radical democratic theory accomplishes the conceptual shift from the people as one to the multitude as many, a democratic political theology might serve as its critical and necessary supplement by drawing on alternative theological sources, specifically theologies of the weakness of God as opposed to those traditionally oriented around divine power. . . . A democratic political theology reveals democracy as the political instantiation of the death of God."

We will return to these alternative renderings of political theology. But in further exploring new forms of post-secular democratic politics, we need to consider some more recent political movements that we would also describe as "post-populist" (as well as post-secular)—which are no longer configured around the idea of "the people" but around other signifiers such as social and racial justice and emancipation, and the protection of the natural environment. Here we have in mind relatively recent movements like Black Lives Matter and Extinction Rebellion. Like the anti-austerity movements discussed earlier, BLM and XR are extraparliamentary movements of civil disobedience, which largely take the form of horizontal networks rather than organized political parties. They also appear in response to the current legitimation crisis of the liberal constitutional and economic order. BLM, which gained greater prominence with the global protests in reaction to the murder of George Floyd in 2020, is a civil rights movement that emerged in protest against lethal police violence targeted toward unarmed black men and women in the United States. It has drawn attention to the contradiction in a constitutional order that guarantees equal rights to all yet, in reality, fails to protect even the most basic rights of minorities. Its focus on racialized police violence, moreover, has also brought up broader issues about entrenched racial inequalities and the legacy of slavery. XR (along with its more recent off-shoot Insulate Britain) is a UK-based environmental activist movement that draws attention to the failure of the political order to respond adequately to the ecological crisis and the exigencies of the Anthropocene. Its key demand is that governments declare an environmental emergency and take appropriate action to radically reduce greenhouse gas emissions. Both movements, as different as they are, are motivated by a demand for justice, whether racial or environmental. Moreover, they have been given greater impetus in the context of the pandemic, which has brought up issues of social, economic, and racial inequality, as well as the environmental question.

What interests us primarily about these movements is their post-secular character. By this we are referring not only to the way that church groups and religious organizations often play an active role in both. We also mean that in their narrative structure, moral imagination, practices, and rituals, they exhibit a theological dimension that transcends secular political discourse—or, perhaps more accurately, blurs the line between the secular and the religious and embodies an alternative form of "spiritual activism." For instance, religious or quasi-religious rituals—such as prayers, public vigils, meditation, the pouring of libations—drawn from a variety of different traditions are often present in these protests (Skrimshire, 2019a; Vandenbloom, 2020). Furthermore, those who take part in such protests and gatherings regard it as a spiritual experience (see Kidwell, 2019). The convergence of bodies in public spaces—often in defiance of COVID restrictions on gatherings—suggests a desire for a communal, collective experience that goes beyond normal forms of political expression. The demand for justice—whether defined in terms of legal justice, rights recognition, freedom from violence and racial inequality, or the protection of the natural environment—expresses a kind of messianic promise of emancipation. Moreover, there is a strongly eschatological structure in the discourse of XR, which employs a deliberately millenarian "end of times" narrative in the motifs of extinction and the impending ecological apocalypse (see Skrimshire, 2019b; see also Rothe, 2020). As examples of post-secular politics, movements such as these display a desire for a sacred, transcendental experience through political activism. Like populism, they seek a reenchantment of the secular political space, albeit in a very different way and with very different aims. They might be considered, then, as examples of a more radical and emancipatory political theology.

A Political Theology of Emancipation

Thinking about contemporary social movements in this way suggests the need for a different, non-Schmittian rendering of political theology. Rather than being committed to the bolstering of sovereign authority in response to the crisis of the constitutional order, an alternative account of political theology would provide a theological justification for movements that challenge sovereign authority in the name of greater justice and emancipation. Can there be a political theology of resistance, rather than one that sacralizes political power?[10] In responding to this question we turn to a tradition of thought that emerged in Germany in the 1960s, associated with the "liberation theology" of figures like Johann Baptist Metz and Jürgen Moltmann.[11] Moltmann and Metz are significant figures in the debate about the relationship between theology and politics, and the broader public role of the church in secular societies. They also challenge, in different ways, the Schmittian model of political theology. Indeed, it is important to note here that both Schmitt and Böckenförde are critical, albeit for different reasons, of this new political theology. Böckenförde explicitly discounted the thought of Metz, Moltmann, and liberation theology as simply a form of Marxist-inspired social activist politics overlain with a superficial layer of theology: "It is not a theology of politics or political order, but provides a justification for and shape to the faith-motivated political-social activism of Christians; it is aimed directly at behavior and action" (Böckenförde, 2020, p. 254). Schmitt, for his part, in *Political Theology II*, takes this new political theology slightly more seriously; he agrees with Metz's critique of modern consumerist society with its commodification of values and its absolute faith in science and progress—a society Metz saw as "*hominising*" (see Schmitt, 2008c, p. 54). At the same time, according to Schmitt, in seeking to reconcile theology with a more progressive, pluralistic, and secular society, a society made up, as Schmitt puts it, of "a plurality of social groups in which everything becomes plurivalent," Metz simply affirms the nihilism of secular modernity, or at least is unable to transcend it: Metzian eschatology can therefore only be "imminent to the system and therefore progressive and plurivalent" (p. 54). In this way, from Schmitt's point of view, Metz's theology is a kind of eschatological utopianism, a "utopia on the principle of hope" (2008c, p. 54). Therefore, while Böckenförde believed that radical political theology was too political, Schmitt suspected that it was not political enough. Yet, as we shall see, it is precisely this principle of hope, which Schmitt derides in Metz, that contains genuine political potential.

Schmitt and Böckenförde represent, in their own ways, two largely conservative interpretations of political theology. For the former, political theology is a framework for legitimizing the authoritarian state encapsulated in the sovereign decision on the exception. For the latter, political theology becomes a way of coming to terms with the aforementioned "dilemma" posed by the liberal secular state and its inability to provide a unifying ethical principle—in the absence of a religious foundation—for its own existence. Thus, for both thinkers, political theology is a way of legitimizing the existing political order otherwise lacking a firm grounding in religion. By contrast, the political theology represented by figures like Moltmann and Metz is a much more radical response to the crisis of political legitimacy. It is not concerned with justifying the existing political order, less still with authorizing a strong sovereign state, but rather with challenging political authority and the structures of capitalist society. The thought of Metz and Moltmann emerged, like so much of postwar theology in Germany, as a response to the moral catastrophe of the Holocaust and to the silence of the Roman Catholic Church, and some Protestant churches, in the face of Nazi atrocities.[12] Both thinkers, moreover, aimed not only to redeem Christian theology "in the wake of Auschwitz" but also to make it more compatible with the demands of modern secular plural societies. Indeed, the processes of secularization and modernity were to some extent aligned with the liberating dynamics of Christian eschatology. At the same time, for Metz, influenced as he was by Frankfurt School Marxists like Adorno and Horkheimer, secular modernity and the Enlightenment were characterized by the dialectic between freedom and "instrumental rationality," which led to the objectification and domination of the subject. There was therefore an important role for theology and the church to play in providing a space for freedom and for the critique of political power (see Metz, 1969). Rather than the church being consigned to the private domain, Metz asserted its more active, politically engaged role in supporting struggles for social and economic justice, and against political oppression: here there was a central opposition between what he saw as "bourgeois religion"—characteristic of liberal capitalist societies—and the message of liberation and hope embodied in messianic Christianity (see Metz, 1981).

In a similar way, Moltmann also sought to come to terms with the tensions within liberal secular modernity, recognizing, on the one hand, its liberating potential while, on the other, remaining critical of its privatizing, individualizing, and relativizing tendencies. In developing a form of eschatological Christianity, he argued that theology must be public and political, and that the church should align itself with secular struggles for emancipation and social and ecological justice: "As the theology of God's kingdom, theology has to be public theology: public, critical and prophetic complaint to God—public, critical and prophetic hope in God. Its public character is constitutive for theology, for the kingdom of God's sake" (Moltmann, 1999, p. 5). Paradoxically Christianity asserts its political existence, as part of this new political theology, by maintaining a certain critical distance from both society and the state. It resists any kind of incorporation into, or alliance with, the state. Rather, its role here is to radically dissociate from the state, to condemn its abuses of power and thereby contribute toward a democratization of society. At the same time, Christianity should be something more than a privatized belief system that fits in with the existing social order without challenging it; the church should be something more than simply another private organization in society. The church retains a critical distance from both the state *and* society, from the institutions of political power and the market. This sort of autonomous space claimed by the church thus forms the basis of a new kind of political theology, radically different from Schmitt's. Indeed, in Moltmann's view, Schmitt's sovereign-centric political thinking is not really a political theology at all, in the sense that it has nothing to do with any genuine Christian theology. Rather, it is a *political religion*, or a religion of power, a way of justifying, using the language and metaphors of theology, an absolutist sovereign state. However, for Moltmann, in the wake of modern totalitarianism, this form of sovereign-centric political theology was no longer acceptable. Instead, he put forward a different conception of political theology where the aim was "to strip the magic from political and civil religion, and to subject to criticism the state ideologies which are supposed to create unity at the cost of liberty. In this way it places itself in the history of the impact of Christianity on politics, which means the desacralization of the state, the relativization of forms of political order, and the democratization of political decisions" (p. 44).

In Moltmann's hands, political theology is transformed into a critique of state power and domination, becoming the basis for secular social movements and struggles for social, economic, racial, and environmental justice. This alternative political theology is part of his broader commitment to human liberation and his defense of human rights. For Moltmann, human rights provide a language for human liberation, one that is international and cosmopolitan rather than confined to particular national communities or religious and cultural identities. Insofar as human rights invoke the idea of human dignity, they are genuinely universal. Moreover, human rights embody the fundamental principles of liberty and equality. According to Moltmann, these principles and values were already reflective of many religious traditions, particularly Christianity, Judaism, and Islam, which believe that all humans, both rulers and ruled, are created equally after God's image. And it was this idea of the equal recognition of human dignity that led to the humanization of politics and the emergence of constitutions designed to limit political authority and protect human dignity from violation: "The institutions of law, government and economy must respect this personal dignity, which is the endowment of all human beings, if they claim to be 'humane institutions'" (pp. 122–123). This theological idea of equal human dignity led to a democratization of European society and produced a new form of political legitimacy based on respect for the equality and liberty of all human beings: "Any exercise of rule must legitimate itself before other human beings" (p. 123). At the same time, Moltmann argues that liberalism, in its focus on individual rights, neglected questions of economic equality and the social dimension of freedom, which could only be realized collectively. Individual human rights and social rights must therefore be seen as inextricably linked, each deriving their meaning and significance from the other. Moltmann's political theology of human rights thus proposes a discursive and political interlinking of different struggles and political horizons—political, economic, ecological—that tends toward a genuine universality (p. 121). This schema of interlocking, or "intersectional," applications of human rights is aimed at human survival and the protection of human dignity. Human beings must be protected not only from political domination but also from nuclear annihilation and genetic manipulation. Their economic security must be guaranteed, which means that negative individual rights must go hand in hand with positive social and economic rights, such as the right to work and the right to an income. Furthermore, none of this is achievable without a recognition of the rights of the natural environment. We can see how this particular rendering of rights, central to Moltmann's political theology, supports the idea of a constitutional order that imposes legal limitations on political power, while at the same time transcending the liberal secular discourse in which it is generally framed. Here his conception of rights also goes beyond that of Böckenförde, who, while sharing Moltmann's concerns about the threat to human dignity and autonomy posed by bioengineering (see Böckenförde, 2020, pp. 339–353), believes that fundamental human rights are best preserved within the nation-state order. Moltmann has a more expansive and radical understanding of rights. Rights are not confined to national polities, where they are enjoyed by some and denied to others outside their borders, but should be genuinely universal, cosmopolitan, and enshrined in international legal structures. Moreover, social and environmental rights must accompany political rights and negative freedoms; rights are not only those of individuals but also of broader collective entities and, as such, are intended to protect common goods and resources.

These alternative renderings of political theology offered by Moltmann and Metz are still based on some idea of transcendence—but this is very different to the notion of sovereign transcendence central to Schmitt's model. The transcendence of God cannot be embodied in any particular political institution, as Schmitt would have it; indeed, this would be considered a form of idolatry from a Christian point of view.[13] Rather, it should be understood in an eschatological sense as embodied in the promise of justice and emancipation. Central to both thinkers, then, is an eschatology of hope that provides the ground for a universal ethical sensibility and for political action. One way to understand this is through Metz's idea of the historical memory of suffering, or the *memoria passionis*, which reminds us of Christ's suffering (see Metz, 1999).[14] This mutual acknowledgment of human suffering—something that we can all recognize regardless of religious or cultural differences—becomes the basis of a universal ethical standpoint that transcends plural positions and viewpoints without denying them in some totalizing or totalitarian fashion. Like Schmitt, Metz believes it is necessary to transcend the immanence of the world, with its economic, technological, and scientific processes and forces of rationalization that threaten to eclipse the subject. A universal ethics must be more than simply an "ethics of accommodation" that seeks to reconcile human action with the "practical circumstances" of the world, something that, according to Metz, would deprive us of any kind of ethical critique of biotechnology and its threat to human dignity and autonomy.[15] Transcending these forces and processes requires some form of authority, and even obedience, according to Metz, but this is an obedience to the authority *of those who suffer*, not to the authority of the sovereign state. Moreover, this recognition of human suffering also provides a universal point of resistance to injustice, oppression, racism, and violence. As Metz puts it: "Isn't it resistance to unjust suffering, largely inspired by respect for the authority of those who suffer, which brings humankind together from quite diverse religious and cultural worlds?" Here Metz calls for an ecumenism of religions around a praxis of resistance not only to racism, xenophobia, nationalism, and ethnoreligious fundamentalism but also to the global market in which the human being is drowned out by anonymous economic, technological, and communicative processes; a "global community in which world politics increasingly loses its primacy to a world economics whose laws of the market were long ago abstracted from 'human beings' themselves" (Metz, 1999, p. 233). Again, as with Schmitt, we find here a critique of the liberal capitalist global order. However, Metz does not propose, as a counterpoint to this, the idea of a national community defined by strong state sovereignty, but rather the universal moral authority of all human suffering. If this *is* a political theology of transcendence that Metz offers us, it is surely a strange one, in which the powerful submit to the powerless, in which authority comes not from above, not from on high, but from *below*, from those who suffer, those who are vulnerable, those who live in hope.[16]

At times it appears doubtful whether this acknowledgment of mutual suffering could act as an impetus for recognizing our global obligations. As the experience of populism has demonstrated, many people are only too willing to turn a blind eye to the suffering and precarity of others beyond their national borders, let alone to recognize that they might have ethical obligations toward them. The central message of populism is the privileging of the national community over everyone else, and the rejection of entanglements and responsibilities to the broader global community. It is essentially one of indifference to the outside world. This is a question we will pick up on again in the final chapter. Nevertheless, as we have seen with recent movements of emancipation, the acknowledgment of suffering—whether of minorities, the poor and excluded, and even of nonhuman species and natural ecosystems—has proved a powerful impetus for new forms of resistance.

Messianism and Radical Politics

However, the recognition of suffering is not on its own sufficient foundation for a politics and ethics of resistance. Any political theology oriented toward emancipation must also hold out some promise of hope and redemption. In their versions of eschatological Christianity, Moltmann and Metz offer a message of hope that human suffering will be redeemed, and that human and environmental liberation will be realized. Indeed, it is this idea of hope that really connects the Christian (and Judeo-Christian) messianic tradition with various forms of radical politics. Of course, the messianic promise of salvation and the coming kingdom of God can also operate as a principle of political quietism, even conservatism, where one "turns the other cheek" and meekly submits to the oppressions and injustices of this world as one waits calmly for the next. This was the gist of Marx's materialist critique of religion as the "opium of the people." On the other hand, as the history of Christian antinomian and millenarian heretical movements throughout the Middle Ages shows, the coming of the Messiah and the promise of the afterlife could at times be a powerful motivating narrative for rebellion against church and state authority. Indeed, for the Marxist Ernst Bloch, Christianity contained a utopian dimension of emancipation, an atheistic and rebellious potential that would continue to inspire revolutionary politics. While Karl Löwith (see 1949), and indeed many others, saw Marxism as a form of secularized Christianity, with its promise of salvation from the corruptions of the capitalist world in the apocalyptic revolt of the workers and the ushering in of communism,

Bloch saw Christianity as already embodying the hope of revolutionary emancipation. Moreover, it was this utopian potential within Christianity that could reconcile it with Marxism: "When Christians are really concerned with the emancipation of those who labor and are heavy-laden, and when Marxists retain the depths of the Kingdom of Freedom as the real content of revolutionary consciousness on the road to becoming true substance, the alliance between revolution and Christianity founded in the Peasant Wars may live again—this time with success" (Bloch, 2009, p. 256).

The promise of emancipation is also central to the Jewish messianic tradition, particularly in its more mystical strands. Angelus Novus, the famous figure that dominates Walter Benjamin's "On the Concept of History" (see 2003), is witness to the human suffering and catastrophe that history piles up before his feet; and yet "the angel of history" is blown off course from his desire to redeem mankind by the unstoppable storm of "progress." Here, in addition to the memory of human suffering, the *memoria passionis* invoked by Metz, we think also of the ecological catastrophe and the suffering of nonhuman species implicit within, and driven on by, the spirit of "progress." This was perhaps why Benjamin believed that the real revolutionary gesture was to call a halt to historical progress, to pull the "emergency brake" on the locomotive of history. In the context of the Anthropocene, we perhaps need to reevaluate the very idea of progress and reflect more seriously on the destructive forces it unleashes. Perhaps we also need to take account of the fact that, as Benjamin puts it, in an oblique reference to Schmitt, the "state of emergency in which we live is not the exception but the rule" (2003, p. 392). The climate emergency is a mundane feature of everyday life, as is lethal and arbitrary police violence, even in constitutional democracies.[17] The only way to end this everyday state of emergency, according to Benjamin, is to bring about a "real" of emergency—in other words a revolutionary rupture of the current order. We will elaborate further, in the following chapter, on what this revolutionary "state of emergency" might actually mean today in a time when the classical revolutionary model of politics seems to have irretrievably broken down. However, if a secular revolution can in any way be associated with the theological and messianic hope of redemption, then we need to understand how this moment features in Benjamin's peculiar version of messianism. In the Jewish messianic tradition, according to Benjamin, the moment of redemption does not come at the end of time, at some point in the future—as in Christian eschatology—but is, rather, something that can come at *any* time: "For every second was the small gateway in time through which the Messiah might enter" (Benjamin, 2003, p. 397). This suggests that the revolutionary moment of rupture, and the hope of emancipation and social justice invested within it, should not be seen as an event that comes at the end of history, as in the eschatological narrative of Marxism, but rather as a potentiality that exists in the spaces and movements of resistance that occur in the present moment.

This thought takes us away from the "political theology" of Marxism, as represented by Bloch, and closer, perhaps, to a "political theology" of *anarchism*. Anarchism has a particular, if paradoxical, significance for the investigation of political theology, in part because the very term "political theology" was coined not by Schmitt but by the nineteenth-century anarchist Mikhail Bakunin.[18] There is, furthermore, a complex and subterranean dialogue between Schmitt and anarchists like Bakunin and Proudhon, as we have already had the opportunity to remark upon. Indeed, it might be argued that Schmitt's politico-theological paradigm of the sovereign state of exception, in which power—detached from constitutional constraints—becomes in a sense "anarchic," is a weapon mobilized primarily against the threat of revolutionary anarchism, which, more so than liberalism, Schmitt considers his real ideological foe (see also Meier, 1998). As an anti-authoritarian, and generally atheistic, political tradition, in which the rejection of the sovereign state and religious authority is central, anarchism represents the extreme ethical and political counterpoint to Schmitt's political theology. However, there are clear anarchistic tendencies within Jewish, and even Christian (see Ellul, 1991), mystical traditions, which at the same time offer us an alternative theological understanding of revolutionary politics.

Here we could mention the thought of the German Jewish activist Gustav Landauer, a contemporary of Schmitt's, who combined an anarchist politics and ethics with strands of Christian and Jewish mystical philosophy. While Landauer had a clear affinity with anarchism, at the same time he abhorred the violent "propaganda by deed" it was at times associated with, including political assassination. Instead, Landauer invoked an inner mystical experience, where the goal was a sort of spiritual transformation of the self through which one achieved a form of autonomy or self-mastery (Landauer, 2010, p. 88). Taking the idea from the thirteenth- to fourteenth-century German theologian Eckhart von Hochheim (or Meister Eckhart), Landauer believed that this mystical experience involved a detachment from external social relations and even from oneself—a process that would lead not only to a redemption and renewal of the self but also to discovery of new forms of spiritual and political community:

> But we can only find the community that we need and long for if we—the new generation—separate ourselves from the old communities. If we make this separation a radical one and if we—as separated individuals—allow ourselves to sink to the depths of our being and to reach the inner core of our most hidden nature, then we will find the most ancient and complete community: a community encompassing not only all of humanity but the entire universe. Whoever discovers this community in himself will be eternally blessed and joyful, and a return to the common and arbitrary communities of today will be impossible. (p. 96)

This idea of a renewed spiritual community finds parallels with Martin Buber's Jewish messianic utopianism, in which there is also a desire for a mystical communion (see Buber, 1958). Yet, it is not an understanding of community that can take a distinct political form or identity—and, as such, is very different from the sovereign political community invoked by Schmitt. The mystical community, or "community of spirit" proposed by Landauer, is a kind of open, borderless community, defined by voluntary association or affinity rather than one determined by borders or national identity, or bound together through shared loyalty and obedience to the sovereign.

It seems to us that new forms of radical activism that we see emerging today in response to the crisis of legitimacy in the political and economic order embody a similar desire for an intense experience of community—one that is otherwise lacking in contemporary neoliberal societies characterized by atomized individualism. Yet, in contrast to the idea of national community asserted by the populists, the open communities that are evoked in social and environmental justice movements are defined by a different experience of solidarity and communion, where people converge around a shared recognition of suffering and injustice, as well as a sense of hope and a desire for emancipation.

Here, as we have argued, the messianic hope for future redemption is intrinsically bound up with the need to bring to a halt the violent and (self-)destructive drives of the current planetary order. The new forms of radical activism that we have discussed embody a fundamental distance from the constitutional, legal, and institutional framework of liberal democracy and its economic order. The distance is their experience of the crisis of this form of social order as one that is both national and global.

Political Theology and Contemporary Challenges | 159

The following, and final, chapter will explore the possibility of political redemption through a reconsideration of the notion of the *katechon*, the ambiguous figure in Pauline theology, as that which restrains the coming catastrophe.

8

Katechon and the Problem of Order

The previous chapter explored some contemporary challenges to the constitutional order in the form of populist politics and new movements for social and environmental justice. It was argued that these challenges were symptomatic of a crisis of legitimacy of liberal democracy and the (neo)liberal economic order with which it is associated. In the context of this crisis, and in thinking about how to respond to it, the chapter also explored a more radical articulation of political theology, one that sees the possibility of redemption in the promise of justice and emancipation rather than in the authority of a sovereign state.

Our investigation throughout this book has been centered around the themes of *crisis*, *order*, and *redemption*. As we have argued, the question of political theology emerges, in all its intensity, in response to a crisis of representation—in other words, when the current political order can no longer embody or contain the social antagonisms and forces that start to agitate it from within and spill over its edges. Here the political order is confronted with its lack of stable foundations, with its indeterminacy, contingency, and the specter of its own finality. Schmitt believed that in the modern era, defined by the lack of theological coordinates, adrift in the nihilistic seas of technology, capitalist economics, bourgeois individualism, and revolutionary politics, the state would not survive in its current constitutional form. His solution to this increasingly anarchic situation was for the state to in a sense *embody* this coming anarchy as a way of restraining it or warding it off. The state would have to free itself from constitutional constraints and legal limits—in other words, declare a state of emergency as a way of reimposing order and restoring its sovereign authority. In order to preempt the Apocalypse, the sovereign state must in a sense simulate and provoke it. It is no wonder that this particular way of reimposing order on society paved the way for the Nazi apocalypse and resulted in the total destruction of the German state. In an unstable world, Schmitt sought salvation and redemption in a theologically charged idea of sovereignty, seeing this as the only way of preventing disaster.

In our world today, no less unstable and crisis-ridden than in Schmitt's time, we are forced to return with renewed urgency to the question of redemption. But in what form? If the existing liberal constitutional order can no longer command the faith and loyalty of its citizens, if it can no longer protect them, or even protect itself, from the forces it has unleashed, should we seek to preserve it? And if so, how? How can an order that is in crisis preserve itself without at the same time hollowing itself out, that is, without violating the very principles and procedures upon which it is based? If, on the other hand, we seek salvation in a total transformation of our political and economic arrangements, what would this look like? What alternatives are on offer? In an age characterized by the collapse of the revolutionary metanarrative, where, given past experience, revolutionary eschatology is looked on with an understandable degree of suspicion, it is very unclear what this notion of total transformation would amount to and how it would be achieved. It seems evident, to us at least, that the solution to political and economic instability, not to mention ecological disaster, cannot be a new sovereign state of exception. If anything, the model of strong nation-state sovereignty that Schmitt was defending is not only unsustainable in the current globalized era, but is actually an *accelerator* of the coming crisis rather than a bulwark against it. On the other hand, while there is a real need for alternative political and legal structures, ones that transcend national borders, that rely on global cooperation and solidarity rather than geopolitical competition, there seems to be little impetus behind such measures, and the vision of a new planetary order remains just as hazy and obscure as ever.

In coming to terms with this dilemma, we will encounter two central theological figures that are opposed and yet inextricably bound together: the Apocalypse and the *katechon*. Our time, perhaps more so than any other, is haunted by the image of the Apocalypse, particularly in the era dominated by the Anthropocene and the looming threat of ecological disaster, not to mention the sense of uncertainty and finitude experienced in the COVID pandemic and other global events, such as the invasion of Ukraine and the prospect of nuclear armed conflict. The cumulative effect is to place political, social, and economic forms into fundamental question. Like those early Christian communities addressed by the Apostle Paul, whose forewarnings we will say more about, we are thrown into a state of agitation and uncertainty as we are faced with the end of the world. All political and legal authority, just like the Roman Empire in Paul's time, appears increasingly ephemeral, temporary, and finite as the end draws near. Of course, the difference in our experience today is that, unlike in Christian eschatology where the Apocalypse is the destructive event, or series of events, which at the same time precedes and *reveals* the Second Coming of Christ and thus the promise of salvation, for us there is no final horizon of redemption in ecological catastrophe. For us, living under the shadow of the Anthropocene, the end *really is* the end. But what does this mean for the messianic promise of redemption and the hope for future justice and emancipation?

The absolute finality of the end today places even more acute focus on the alternative idea of the *katechon*, the obscure and enigmatic figure from Pauline theology, as the power that delays the end of the world. However, in restraining the ascendancy of the Antichrist, the *katechon* also delays the coming of the Kingdom of Christ and the final victory over evil. The *katechon* therefore has an extremely complex and ambiguous place within Christian theology, and we will have more to say about this and about the political effects of this ambiguity later. However, it is important to note that the *katechon* is absolutely central to Schmitt's political theology, and indeed to any understanding of political theology. If we understand political theology broadly as the translation of theological concepts into political concepts, then without some idea of a force that delays the end of the world, there is no politics as such; there is only theology. In other words, the *katechon* creates an autonomous space for politics that escapes, even if momentarily, the eschatology that otherwise inexorably proceeds toward the end, rendering all politics pointless. The *katechon* interrupts this imminent, and immanent, logic, creating a space or gap in which political activity can take place. As that which holds off the coming of the end, the *katechon* is what gives meaning to human institutions and action. In other words, political activity ceases to have a purpose if the end of the word is inevitable. Such a realization would be entirely politically disabling and would lead only to apathy and indifference. The *katechon* as a gap, an interregnum, thus creates a space for politics. It is the force behind both the desire to preserve existing institutions, as well as the desire to transform them; it gives meaning to both conservative and revolutionary forms of politics, and even to a *revolutionary conservative* politics such as Schmitt's. Indeed, as we shall see, Schmitt, following a tradition of political theology that flowed from Tertullian to Hobbes, associates the *katechon* with political sovereignty, with, first, the Christian empire in the Middle Ages, and later with the modern state. This does not mean, however, that the *katechon* always translates into state sovereignty. There may be alternative, nonsovereign political arrangements that can play the role of the *katechon*—and, indeed, these alternatives will be explored in this chapter. At the same time, the *katechon* is a fundamentally ambiguous concept, any political consideration of which brings up a number of questions. What exactly is the *katechon*: is it a person, an institution, the law itself? Indeed, can it even take a distinct political form? And who or what is the Antichrist whose ascendency the *katechon* holds at bay; how should evil be understood in political terms today? Moreover, how exactly should we understand the relationship between the *katechon* and the Antichrist? While it might seem that these are distinct and opposed entities, as we shall see, they are intimately connected, one being immanent within the other. Finally, is the *katechon* itself on the side of good or evil? From the point of view of Paul's eschatology, this is fundamentally unclear. While, on the one hand, the *katechon* delays the reign of evil in the world, in so doing it also delays the final defeat of evil and the triumph of the good. Yet, it is this ambivalence that, we argue, makes the *katechon* a fundamental political, and politico-theological, category, one that allows for genuine political reflection and action.

The Coming Barbarism

These days it is hard not to think about the end of the world. The "end of times" dominates our imagination. We have the looming specter of ecological catastrophe. The environmental crisis is something that will make the planet unlivable, and indeed has already made it unlivable for people, not to mention for other nonhuman species, in many parts of the world. Rapid and uncontrolled climate change, with all its consequences, fundamentally reshapes our relation to the world and to ourselves, defining its absolute limit and haunting us with the prospect of civilizational collapse. The pandemic, which has served as the harbinger and symbol of this catastrophic horizon, has confronted us with our own mortality, with our frailty and finitude as human beings. More significant, perhaps, is the sense of social death—the feeling that life will never be the same again, that what were once normal social interactions and behaviors will never return; that our world, at least as we knew it, has already ended and we are living a strange, dimly lit afterlife bereft of hope, lacking the very qualities that make life worth living. We seem to be witnessing the disintegration of a once familiar social and political landscape as we enter onto an uncertain terrain without clear coordinates and ontological guarantees. No wonder that the prevailing experience today is one of overwhelming anxiety, coupled with a sense of powerlessness in the face of this existential threat.

Reading the book of Revelations, the divine mysteries revealed, as it is alleged, to John of Patmos, it is hard not to be struck by the contemporary resonance of his description of the Apocalypse.[1] There are scenes of devastation and destruction, with rivers and seas being poisoned, grasses and trees being burnt up, hunger, infestations of locusts, plagues of all kinds, earthquakes and hailstorms, people seeking refuge in caves. The final judgment that God visits upon the world cannot be dissociated from the idea of the natural world's final judgment over us. And yet, unlike in the biblical prophecy, there is, for us today, no possible redemption, no River of Life and Tree of Life that will heal us or miraculously repair the damage done to the planet.

The Apocalypse is a particularly powerful and resonant metaphor for some of the destructive forces and energies that—aside from climate change from which they cannot at the same time be disassociated—have been unleashed on our world. The coming barbarism[2] can be seen in many of the destructive trends immanent in the liberal capitalist global order, whose fragmentation we are currently witnessing with all the violence and instability this portends. The dynamics of neoliberal globalization have produced, on the one hand, the atomized individualism of the possessive and narcissistic consumer and, on the other, as part of the same dialectic, antagonistic and exclusionary forms of communitarianism. The telos of capitalist globalization seems to be playing itself out in the proliferation everywhere of barriers, borders, and other means of separation, from the crudest fences and walls to the most sophisticated surveillance and biometric technologies, which are designed to exclude certain people and restrict their movement. The demos is animated by the desire for division and separation into homogeneous communities. There is a renewed demand for sovereignty, or for the fantasy image of sovereignty, as a projection of enclosed, bordered communities and national identities. However, divisions and antagonisms over identity and culture return to the very heart of our societies, which at times seem to be verging on civil war. Contemporary societies appear increasingly fragmented and polarized, split along ideological and cultural lines. The global order is deteriorating into a sort of planetary civil war, with hatreds and antagonisms cropping up everywhere, within and between nation-states. The Russian invasion of Ukraine, fueled by messianic fantasies of restoring imperial sovereignty, highlights the extreme fragility of the international order.

Liberal democracies seem to be incapable of containing these tensions and antagonisms. Indeed, one of the main antagonisms emerging here is between liberal democracy and capitalism itself. While the idea of a capitalist economy and the liberal democratic constitutional order have historically gone together, it seems evident that they are now coming apart, and that capitalism is perfectly compatible with the most authoritarian and oppressive regimes, as the example of China demonstrates. Moreover, after decades of the neoliberal deracination of public institutions and the public space, upon which any coherent understanding of democracy rests (see Brown, 2015, 2019), Western democratic societies themselves are becoming increasingly illiberal, driven by authoritarian populist forces that want to restrict the rights of minorities and migrants, as well as by governments that are only too willing to impose draconian measures and limit civil liberties in response to emergencies, as we have seen all too clearly with the pandemic.

Capitalism, as an economic system, simply has no need for liberal democratic institutions and, indeed, would rather dispense with them altogether in order to allow the unfettered reign of the market and ever greater concentrations of wealth and power. Late modern capitalism is coming to resemble something more like feudalism, or techno-feudalism, in which the concentration of informational power in the hands of big tech coincides with an increasingly hierarchical and unequal social order. Our dependence on internet-based communication technologies and platforms, as an aspect of our technologically saturated and increasingly virtualized lives—particularly now as a result of the pandemic—gives an extraordinary degree of power to big tech companies. The way that computer algorithms and data analytics, particularly on social media, can be used to track movements; monitor interactions, interests, spending habits, internet search histories; predict behaviors; and shape preferences, even political preferences, points to a new age of authoritarian capitalism that is unhinged from any kind of democratic constraints or accountability.

The libertarian fantasies and messianic ruminations of tech entrepreneurs like Peter Thiel, founder of Palantir Technologies, whose data analytics software is used for surveillance purposes by military intelligence, national security agencies, police, hedge funds, banks, and even by public health authorities, are indicative of the general direction of late modern capitalism. Thiel believes that "creative monopolies" are good for society, and that democracy, with its quaint ideas of equality, only gets in the way of the market and technological innovation; in fact, he considers "capitalist democracy" to be an oxymoron (see Cohen, 2017). Like many other Silicon Valley messiahs, who are already "prepping" for the end of the world, building themselves state-of-the-art bunkers, Thiel speculates on the "end of times," invests money in cryogenic research as well as in projects to develop floating communities (known as "sea-steading")—independent city-states afloat on the waters of the world, like Noah's Ark after the Great Flood, outside the control of nation-states and not subject to the inconveniences of democracy.

These dystopian/utopian fantasies that our masters indulge in—including the colonization of other planets—reveal much, not only about the antidemocratic tendencies of late modern capitalism but also about the condition of nihilism characteristic of our time. The sense that the world is coming to an end is experienced in a general mood of pessimism, helplessness, and impotence. We feel unable to act when confronted with a world that appears to be spinning off its hinges and beyond any kind of human control. We witness a social order that is disintegrating before our very eyes, powerless spectators to the crises and catastrophes that seem to pile up day by day. This sense of impotence is channeled into different forms of psychic regression, from mental illness, depression, and anxiety—rates of which are increasing exponentially—to explosions of rage, hatred, and violence evident in mass shootings, terrorist outrages, racist attacks. We find it too in the sense of paranoia prevalent in conspiracy theories, particularly those that have emerged around COVID and vaccines. The general "post-truth" climate, where the symbolic order of truth, central to the liberal notion of public reason, collapses, and where reality is drowned out in a miasma of mis- and disinformation, competing perspectives, and "alternative facts," is an aspect of this nihilism. There is a widespread disdain for truth, a willingness to believe in whatever narrative best accords with one's prejudices or brings one the most satisfaction or enjoyment. Willful ignorance and stupidity[3] seem to reign everywhere. Nihilism also fuels a newfound religious intensity, seen in the return of religious fundamentalism or in new forms of religious belief and identification, akin to mass psychosis. Above all, the nihilism of our times is expressed in a callous indifference and the lack of care for the world, a lack of concern for the suffering of others within and beyond the borders of our communities or for the natural environment. Indeed, there is a desire among some to hasten the coming catastrophe, to intensify the destructive drives of capitalism, to extract and consume the very last drop of the earth's resources. Caught between paralyzing impotence and frenzied destruction, either believing in nothing or believing in everything, or, for the most part, simply absorbed in consumerist pleasures, we are like Nietzsche's last men of whom Zarathustra despaired.

We see signs of the Apocalypse all around us today: boatloads of refugees drowning in the Mediterranean or languishing in migrant camps; spiraling rates of contagion and death from COVID; geopolitical tensions, now over the supply of vaccines; populist demagogues stoking the fires of enmity and division; famines and humanitarian disasters; armed conflicts and civil unrest around the world; violent political repression; oceans littered with plastic and disposable masks; and the daily sounding of the death knell for the natural environment.

The Power That Restrains

It is in this context of the "end of times" that we encounter the figure of the *katechon*. The concept, which has a marginal and obscure place in Christian theology, first appears in Paul's address to the early Christian congregations in 2 Thessalonians:

> Now we beseech you, brethren, by the coming (*parousia*) of our Lord Jesus Christ, and *by* our gathering together unto him, that ye be not soon shaken in mind, or be troubled, neither by spirit, nor by word, nor by letter as from us, as that the day of Christ is at hand. Let no man deceive you by any means: for *that day shall not come*, except there come a falling away (*apostasia*) first, and that man of sin (*anomia*) be revealed, the son of perdition (*apoleia*); who opposeth and exalteth himself above all that is called God, or that is worshipped; so that he (*ho antikeimenos*) as God sitteth in the temple of God (*eis ton naon*), shewing himself that he is God. Remember ye not, that,

when I was yet with you, I told you these things? And now ye know what withholdeth (*to katechon*) that he might be revealed in his time. For the mystery of iniquity doth already work: only he who now letteth (*ho katechon*) *will let*, until he be taken out of the way (*ek mesou geneta*). And then shall that Wicked (*Anomos*) be revealed, whom the Lord shall consume with the spirit of his mouth, and shall destroy with the brightness of his coming (*parousia*): *even him* (*Anomos*), whose coming is after the working of Satan with all power and signs and lying wonders, and with all deceivableness of unrighteousness in them that perish; because they received not the love of the truth, that they might be saved. And for this cause God shall send them strong delusion, that they should believe a lie: that they all might be damned who believed not the truth, but had pleasure in unrighteousness (*adikia*). (Paul's Second Letter to the Thessalonians 2: 1–12, cited in Cacciari, 2018, pp. 119–120)

Paul is seeking to calm the religious enthusiasm of his fellow believers for the end of the world and the promised Second Coming of Christ. He says that the Day of the Lord would be preceded by the Antichrist, "the man of lawlessness," the "son of perdition" who will bring about a state of anomie. However, this in turn will be preceded by a mysterious power that withholds or delays the coming of the Antichrist until his proper moment is revealed. In other words, there is a divinely ordained sequence of events and things must be allowed to take their course. The *katechon*, as we have already remarked, has an enigmatic place in this eschatology. It is not clear what exactly the *katechon* is: is it an abstract force, "*that which* withholds" (τὸ κατέχον), or is it a person, "*the one who* withholds" (ὁ κατέχων)? Paul seems to invoke both meanings. Furthermore, who or what exactly is the Antichrist (*antikhristos*) that the *katechon* withholds? In the Christian theological tradition, the Antichrist is the "one who denies Christ" and is seen as a false prophet, or series of false prophets, who preach misleading doctrines, who seek to deceive the followers of Christ, and to set themselves up as the Messiah. In the history of the church, the Antichrist has been associated with various Roman emperors, heretics, and later on, after the Protestant Reformation, even with the pope himself. In contemporary evangelical Christian narratives, and in various conspiracy theories, the Antichrist is depicted as one who seeks to undermine Christian beliefs through the promotion of secular values and international institutions. The Antichrist is one who would establish a new order of unbelief (apostasy) and lawlessness (anomie), and would reign until such time as he would be revealed by Christ and removed by his breath, by the "Spirit of his mouth." The place of the *katechon* within this narrative is therefore highly ambiguous: on the one hand, its intervention arrests or delays the reign of evil and lawlessness; but on the other hand, it also delays the Coming of the Christ and the final victory of good over evil. Furthermore, Paul says that the "mystery of lawlessness is already operating." So how can it be that the *katechon* stops or delays what is already happening? Or is Paul here simply referring to the imminence of lawlessness, something that we see signs of but is not yet fully in effect? This would intimate a relationship of immanence—that the *katechon* and the Antichrist are opposed elements within the same phenomenon (see also Cacciari, 2018).

It is, however, the political, or politico-theological, implications of the *katechon* that we are concerned with here. There are two main interpretations to be considered. First, the *katechon* is crucial to Schmitt's understanding of political theology. Schmitt says in his writings from 1947, "I believe in the *katechon*: it is for me the only possibility as a Christian to understand history and find it meaningful. We have to be able to name the *katechon* for every epoch in the last 1948 years. The place has never been unoccupied, otherwise we would not be present anymore. . . . There are temporary, transient, splinter-like fragmentary bearers for this role" (cited in Szendy, 2016). Why was this obscure figure from Pauline theology so important for Schmitt? Following a line of thinking that extended from early theologians like Tertullian, who associated the *katechon* with the Roman Empire, to the theorist of the modern state, Hobbes, Schmitt identified the *katechon* with political sovereignty. The *katechon* is a placeholder that was occupied at various times by different political institutions, whether the Roman Empire, or the Christian empire of the Middle Ages, or the modern sovereign state. As a form of institutionalized authority, it not only delays the coming state of lawlessness and anarchy but actually gives meaning to history. Without the idea of something that defers the end of the world, history would simply have no meaning; we would live in empty time, waiting for the end, like those early Christians who are the subject of Paul's exhortation. The *katechon* interrupts this empty time, inserting within it a space for human activity, for politics. In *The Nomos of the Earth*, where the concept receives the most extensive treatment, Schmitt argues that the Christian empire of the Middle Ages played the historical role of the *katechon*. The Christian empire, even though it was not eternal and had an idea of its own end,[4] nevertheless fulfilled the role of historical placeholder, providing Europe with some form of identity and structure, bringing together, within the idea of a Christian republic, *imperium* (political authority) and *sacerdotium* (spiritual authority). Even though the Christian empire was not centralized—in fact, Schmitt describes its structure as "anarchic"—the *katechon* served as a unifying point of orientation and order for Europe, giving it meaning and substance. He says:

> The empire of the Christian Middle Ages lasted only as long as the idea of the katechon was alive. I do not believe that any historical concept other than katechon would have been possible for the original Christian faith. The belief that a restrainer holds back the end of the world provides the only bridge between the notion of an eschatological paralysis of all human events and a tremendous historical monolith like that of the Christian empire of the Germanic kings. (2006, pp. 59–60)

Here Schmitt once again reaffirms the significance of the *katechon* for his political theology: the intervention of the *katechon* interrupts the empty time of eschatology, in which all political life is otherwise paralyzed, and allows politics to take place. It thus provides a bridge between theology and politics, allowing theological concepts and ideas to take a political shape. This was, of course, something that Erik Peterson argued was impossible from the point of view of Christian doctrine. However, from Schmitt's perspective, political theology is made possible via this, albeit rather obscure, theological figure.

Thinking about the *katechon* in this way allows us to make better sense of the various figures of political order and legitimacy that Schmitt has deployed in his political theology, whether the aforementioned Christian empire, or the Roman Catholic Church itself, or the modern sovereign state defined through the state of exception. All these institutions had the function of uniting society around a representative image, providing it with a stabilizing, anchoring point, and preventing the coming nihilism and anomie, the reign of the Antichrist that Schmitt saw in the different guises of liberalism, technology, atheism, and revolutionary anarchism. The restraining of these forces was much more important, for Schmitt, than the fulfillment of Christian eschatology—a point made by Jacob Taubes: "[Schmitt] prays for the preservation of the state, since if, God forbid, it doesn't remain, chaos breaks loose, or even worse, the Kingdom of God!" (2003, pp. 69–70). In Schmitt's thinking, the *katechon* is always a form of sovereignty that conserves the political order.

Is there another way to interpret the *katechon*? In Agamben's alternative reading of Paul, he essentially downplays the significance and value of this concept: "Yet, the fact remains that despite its obscurity, this Pauline passage does not harbor any positive valuation of *katechōn*. To the contrary, it is what must be held back in order that the 'mystery of anomia' be revealed fully" (2005b, pp. 110). In other words, because the *katechon* is that which delays the revelation of the mystery of lawlessness, and thus ultimately delays the Parousia of Christ, it is precisely the *katechon* that must be held at bay. The *katechon* is not a positive force that wards off evil, but is part of the very structure of evil. As Paul says, the mystery of lawlessness is already at work in the world—so, logically speaking, the *katechon* must be part of this phenomenon. Or, on Agamben's account, it is the force behind which the principle of lawlessness or anomia hides. The *katechon* is therefore part of the same structure as the lawlessness it holds back:

> It is therefore possible to conceive of *katechon* and *anomos* not as two separate figures . . . but as one single power before and after the final unveiling. Profane power—albeit of the Roman Empire or any other power—is the semblance that covers up the substantial lawlessness [*anomia*] of messianic time. In solving the "mystery," semblance is cast out, and power assumes the figure of the *anomos*, of that which is the absolute outlaw. . . . This is how the messianic is fulfilled in the clash between the two *parousiai*: between that of the *anomos*, who is marked by the working of Satan in every power [*potenza*], and that of the Messiah, who will render energeia inoperative in it. (2005b, p. 111)

Messianic time, in Agamben's reading, is what renders all law inoperative. It produces a "state of exception," whose mystery must be revealed in order for the authority of the law to be brought to its end. The law is a machine that produces law and lawlessness as the two opposed sides of itself, and it is this machine whose workings are brought to a halt in this eschatology. Here there is an interpretation of the messianic fulfillment that closely parallels Walter Benjamin's notion of "divine violence"—the force that brings to an end to the continual oscillation between lawmaking and law-preserving violence, between constituting and constituted power, finally redeeming humanity, expiating guilt, and allowing us to live in the law's absence (see Benjamin, 1986).[5]

As with Benjamin's notion of divine violence, there is a clear anarchistic orientation in Agamben's reading of Paul's messianism, an orientation that we also find in Taubes's revolutionary interpretation of Paul (see 2003). For all these thinkers, the messianic moment coincides with the ending of legal sovereignty and the abolition of state power (Benjamin, 1986, p. 252). This is why, according to Agamben's reading, which is directly opposed to Schmitt's, the *katechon* is not a positive force but an institution of sovereignty that simply gets in the way of "the coming anarchy." Yet here, anarchy—or lawlessness—has two dimensions or sides, "bad" and "good": the *anarchy of power* and the *anarchy beyond power*.[6] There is a real ambiguity here. For Agamben, it is almost as if the secret of the anarchy of power—that is the way the structures of global economic and political power appear as increasingly directionless, unhinged, and chaotic, that the law is in effect but is "without significance" (see 1998)—must be revealed before another and more redemptive kind of anarchy can appear. However, this is little more than a vague allusion. Agamben never really expands on this more positive understanding of anarchy, and certainly there is little engagement in his writings with the anarchist political tradition or with anarchist proposals for a stateless society.

While we are sympathetic to Agamben's anarchistic, or anarcho-messianic, reading of Paul's eschatology, his interpretation of anarchy gives rise to a number of problems and ambiguities. As Massimo Cacciari argues, anarchy should not be conflated with anomie—that is, with the state of lawlessness mentioned by Paul. As Cacciari points out, the Antichrist is not an anarchist but an apostate, and his reign imposes a new kind of order, one in which lawlessness and instability coincide with a form of power, with a new nomos: "*Anomie* is a new order, a new *nomos*, that of the Antikeimenos. It is a 'society' founded upon his triumph, lasting throughout the end-time" (2018, p. 70). Moreover, under this reign, the last man, the "free" individual, in pursuing his sovereign self-interest, is at the same time caught

> solely in his own net, caught in the power of the Antikeimenos, incapable of lifting himself out of it. His epoch—which he claims will complete not only history but also the very species "man"—

> is that of the net in its precise metaphysical difference from the sign of the cross, in its radical "antichristicity." The former radiates out in a wholly horizontal manner and its "project" consists in annulling—in the *hic et nunc* of global space—the very meaning of eschatological-messianic time. . . . The last man has been "secured" in the net where every relation seems calculable and where what cannot be reduced to calculation is simply no-thing. (p. 73)

This seems to describe the condition of life under contemporary neoliberalism, where individual freedom is inscribed within a market rationality that governs life, that calculates and monitors behavior, the Foucauldian "conduct of conduct" (see 2008). The last man, under this condition, lives in a flattened-out space absent of meaning, concerned only with preserving his own security and consumer comforts. In other words, the reign of the Antichrist, which coincides with the neoliberal order, is also a condition of nihilism and the denial of eschatological-messianic time.

However, as we have argued, this smooth global space is today continually disrupted by new antagonisms that it has engendered but can no longer contain. According to Cacciari, all political orders, insofar as they have a catechontic function, are caught up in a tension between the need to stabilize themselves, to provide security, and to constantly transform themselves and expand beyond their own borders. The drive to stabilize and consolidate power unleashes forces of destabilization that eventually turn back on the political order itself and destroy it. Such has been the fate of every empire in history, and such is the fate, it would seem, of the current liberal "empire." As a form of legitimating authority, the liberal order seeks to "represent" the age, to contain and hold together the tensions that constantly threaten to disrupt it. However, it is becoming clear that this representative function is no longer effective, and that the liberal order is now subject to antagonisms that it can no longer manage. This is why, for Cacciari, the *katechon*, in its administrative-securitizing function, is not only impotent before the advancing anomie but in a sense is complicit with it. To defer the coming disorder, it has to embody it—as Schmitt made quite explicit in his notion of the state of exception, which he saw as the hidden truth of the constitutional order. Yet, in doing so, political orders end up destroying themselves in an autoimmune fashion. Therefore, "the katechon cannot fail to participate in the most intimate fashion with the principle it strives to withhold and delay, if not bring to a halt. It is impossible not to retain what you seek to contain. Every catechontic power must constitute itself within the dimension, even the cosmic dimension, of the principle of anomie that is destined to triumph" (Cacciari, 2018, p. 51). If it is the case, then, that the *katechon* is indeed complicit with the very forces of anomie, with the reign of lawlessness that it claims to hold at bay, then why invest any importance or value in it at all? Is Agamben right to think that the *katechon* should only be seen as something to be overcome rather than something to be preserved? Why not simply hasten the coming of the end, wherein also lies our redemption? The trouble with this messianic line of thinking where, in a sense, the worse it gets the better it gets, is that we cannot quite be sure of any promise of redemption. As we have suggested, the age of the Anthropocene places in doubt all messianic thinking. The end is simply unthinkable; it has an absolute finality, with little hope of redemption, with no promise of the Second Coming. In other words, in the age dominated by ecological crisis, where things can *always* get worse, we cannot afford to simply let events take their course, let alone to hasten the coming catastrophe in the hope of overcoming it according to some sort of vague promise of salvation. What this future salvation could mean in concrete political terms is very unclear, and, given the stakes involved, too risky to even contemplate. Rather, any possibility of salvation means acting *now*, in the present moment, and putting off, withholding, insofar as it is possible, the political and economic drives and forces that are otherwise impelling us toward destruction. The ability to act in the present moment, the capacity to experiment with new forms of politics, develop new conceptions of community, create a new kind of "order" means reinventing the *katechon*.

Care for the World

The *katechon*, we suggest, does not always have to be thought in the form of political sovereignty or according to the logic of the "lesser evil." There are alternatives to Schmitt's conservative interpretation of the *katechon*, as the antiutopian force that defends the political order and that is identified with the decision-making authority of the sovereign state (see Virno, 2008). Indeed, today, in the context of heightened geopolitical competition and tension between nation-states, driven by populist and authoritarian political forces, it would seem that sovereignty itself, rather than acting as a *katechon*, is more like an *accelerator* of the coming crisis. Contrary to Schmitt, state sovereignty appears more and more as a destabilizing force in our world today. This does not mean, on the other hand, that we are confined to the preservation of the current form of the liberal constitutional order. Rather, our aim should be to develop an alternative political project, or series of projects, oriented around an ethics of care and conservation—care for the world that exists and for those who live within it, and conservation of the natural environment threatened with serious depletion. In other words, the *katechon* today might be rethought as a politics of planetary care, which is also a recognition of our entanglement with the world and our broader ethical commitments and responsibilities toward others.

Elena Pulcini has argued for a new ethics of care and solidarity that extends beyond national borders. Capitalist globalization, she contends, because it means the loss of boundaries and markers of certainty and identity, gives rise to the conflicting tendencies of hyper-individualism and narcissistic consumerism, on the one hand, and closed and identitarian forms of communitarianism, on the other. The latter emerges as a regressive reaction to the former, but it also reflects a genuine need and desire for community in our atomized global world, as a form of protection from our exposure to uncertainty and insecurity. The predominant passion today is *fear*, fear of the outside world, a fear that often translates into hostility toward the other, the desire for closed, bordered nation-states, and the scapegoating of minorities and immigrants. The resurgence of national populism that we have explored in the previous chapter can be understood entirely from this perspective: the fear of a globalized and uncertain world is channeled into resentment toward minorities, who are seen to pose a risk to national identity, as well as into acting out an aggressive form of sovereignty. However, in Pulcini's psychological account of ethics, which draws on the thought of Günther Anders, fear can also be a productive emotion that can be transformed from fear *of* the world to fear *for* the world. Fear not only shakes us out of our individualistic consumerist slumber but can also remind us of our common vulnerability. Fear brings to the forefront the question of our own survival, forcing upon us moral and political tasks that we would otherwise rather ignore. In contrast to messianic eschatology, which is filled with hope and enthusiasm for future redemption and salvation, Pulcini sees fear as a more powerful motivator for human action (2013, p. 144). However, this sentiment of fear needs to be converted into a sense of ethical responsibility through the idea of contamination, or, as we would say, *entanglement*. Here the awareness of the extent to which we are proximate to others and to which our fate is inevitably bound up with others—an awareness that otherwise provokes fear and hostility—is transformed into a positive value, one that results in a greater recognition of, and hospitality toward, difference (p. 153). It is important to point out that this recognition of difference is not the same as "identity politics"—which is as much, if not more, a disposition of the political right as the left—but, on the contrary, something that troubles and disturbs the very boundaries of identity. As Pulcini says: "To recognize difference it is necessary first of all to put one's own identity at stake so as to avert all danger of absolutization" (p. 154).

The heightened awareness of our ecological entanglement, our dependence upon, and our vulnerability to, natural ecosystems, can act as an impulse for a greater sense of environmental responsibility. Indeed, as Hans Jonas argues, the future survivability of humanity is so obviously bound up with the future survivability of nature that self-interest alone imposes upon us a sense of responsibility toward the natural world:

> Care for the future of mankind is the overruling duty of collective human action in the age of a technical civilization that has become "almighty," if not in its productive then at least in its destructive potential. This care must obviously include care for the future of all nature on this planet as a necessary condition of man's own. . . . There is no need, however, to debate the relative claims of nature and man when it comes to the survival of either, for in this ultimate issue their causes converge from the human angle itself. Since, in fact, the two cannot be separated without making a caricature of the human likeness—since, rather, in the matter of preservation or destruction the interest of man coincides, beyond all material needs, with that of life as his worldly home in the most sublime sense of the word—we can subsume both duties as one under the heading "responsibility toward man" without falling into a narrow anthropocentric view. (1984, p. 136)

Fear, and even self-interest, can thus become the basis for care, and care can become the basis for a greater ethical responsibility toward the other and a new vision for global social justice. Pulcini considers the possible transformation of the egotistic individual, otherwise absorbed by consumerist pleasures and fearful of the other, to an individual "capable of taking care of the world since he is aware of the world's fragility and the nexus that today indissolubly links every single being to the destiny of humankind" (pp. 163-164). Part of the task of taking care of the world is being able to think the world in common, as a common ethical and political project, something that the dynamics of globalization have made possible; in other words, to imagine a new *world form* (see also Nancy, 2007). Caring for the world means preserving it against destructive forces that globalization has unleashed. As Pulcini says, "Care of the world therefore means, first of all, preservation of the world, protecting humankind against the specter of self-destruction and defending life" (p. 200). In other words, the politics and ethics of world care has, in our terms, a catechontic function—it preserves what is worthy of preservation, holding at bay the forces of nihilism and destruction. However, as Pulcini points out—and here we would agree—this is not a conservative political gesture but, rather, something emancipatory: "A far cry from having the static and anti-progressist sense of maintaining the status quo, here 'preservation' assumes the disruptive and emancipatory meaning of a preliminary moral task: to protect something that, in the absence of our attention and our care, we risk inevitably exposing to loss, orphaning us of the only dwelling place that we have been allowed to know thus far" (p. 200). Rather than simply maintaining the status quo, the politico-ethical—we could also say *politico-theological*—project invoked here is one of *conscious* and *active* care. It is not simply about preserving what currently exists, but creating a new world: "Entrusted to the individual creator of meaning, care of the world in itself sums up the moment of preservation and the moment of creation" (p. 207).

Pulcini's ethics of care of the world is defined not so much by abstract, rationalistic, and contractualist theories of justice and rights—those associated with Kant and Rawls for instance—but rather by an affective and emotional commitment to the well-being of others. Nor is it simply about sentiments like compassion and pity, which can be patronizing and disempowering to those who suffer, but, rather, an active and meticulous attention to the other. Care is associated with ideas of generosity, love, solidarity, through which the social bond is enhanced and intensified. As such, care goes beyond justice that, while important, tends to be confined to questions of the distribution of resources and the balancing of entitlements. While calculations of this sort are no doubt essential for addressing existing global inequalities, what separates justice from care, according to Pulcini, is that care also involves a commitment to the future—to future generations and to the future of the planet. Central to care, moreover, is a kind of excess or plenitude embodied in the idea of the gift and the gesture of giving, which transcends legalistic, egalitarian models of justice (p. 252).

There is certainly much of value in Pulcini's ethics of care. The awareness of our entanglement with the fate of others, and particularly with the natural environment, must surely supplement any vision of global social justice, as must the emotions of love, generosity, and solidarity that arise from this sense of common vulnerability. No doubt one of the limitations with liberal contractualist models of justice is their inability to adequately accommodate these affects. Indeed, these passions and affects are more easily and meaningfully expressed within the language of theology rather than within the liberal idea of public reason. As we saw from previous chapters, theological interpretations of justice have been based on the recognition of common suffering and vulnerability; for instance, Metz's notion of *memoria passionis*. Moreover, ecopolitical theological approaches such as Keller's and Moltmann's incorporate a notion of planetary and ecological entanglement into a deeper notion of social justice. Theology, to the extent that it is concerned with what exceeds secular political experience and discourse, can provide us with an alternative language in which to express the emotional commitments that Pulcini takes as central.

Cosmopolitical Theology

If the idea of planetary care is to become the ethical orientation for a new kind of politics—and indeed Pulcini insists on the public, that is to say, *political* dimension of care—we cannot imagine anything more different to Schmitt's sovereign-centric model. Sentiments such as care, love, solidarity are entirely alien not only to Schmitt's juridical way of thinking but also to his vision of the world of bordered national communities defined through relations of enmity, in which the only legitimate passion is obedience to the sovereign state. The idea of care and solidarity across borders, the recognition of shared responsibility for a world in common, is utterly inimical to Schmitt, who remained suspicious of even the thinnest notion of internationalism and global humanitarian ethics. Of course, his critique is pitched against the *liberal* international order, which, as we would agree, is a deeply flawed structure. However, as we have argued, the alternative cannot be to return to a geopolitical order defined by competing and antagonistic sovereign states. Rather, the crisis of representation experienced by the existing liberal order, which brings unparalleled dangers, also presents us with an opportunity to rethink globalization, to transform it in more positive ways through a reflection on our shared commitments to human and ecological survival. This would involve experimentation with new international and transnational legal institutions, new articulations of human and ecological rights, a just distribution of the world's resources, including medical resources, and so on. While such proposals and innovations seem detached and utopian now, they will become inevitable as the world contends with increasingly pressing global problems of climate change or, indeed, future pandemics.

The idea of caring for the world, for the welfare of others, for future generations, and for the natural environment beyond the borders of one's national community necessarily evokes a cosmopolitan ethical and political horizon. But of what kind? How should we think of cosmopolitanism today, in an era dominated by geopolitical competition and heightened antagonisms between communities, when the very notion of globalization has fallen into disrepute? How may we revisit the idea of cosmopolitanism—the vision of a global human community and global citizenship—without falling into the trap that Schmitt warned us about when he said, modifying the phrase of the anarchist Proudhon, "Whoever invokes humanity wants to cheat"? Schmitt's point was that not only was the idea of a liberal international order defined by universal humanitarian ethics untenable, but that it actually served as an ideological guise for the projection of particular geopolitical and strategic interests. In other words, global humanitarianism was often a cover for new forms of imperialism. Yet, what characterizes the current situation is the absence of any kind of imperial project or ambition, and perhaps this void in the global order of power also presents an opportunity for rethinking the cosmopolitan horizon and transforming it in a more radical and emancipatory direction.

Within the Christian tradition, as within other theological traditions, there is a cosmopolitan dimension. The possibility of salvation and redemption is, at least in theory, open to all, regardless of one's membership of a national community. The church is a universal community of believers, rather than one confined to a narrow ethnic or national identity. Indeed, Paul proposed a form of community of believers that was simply indifferent to identity altogether: "There is neither Jew nor Greek, slave nor free, male nor female, for you are all one in Jesus Christ."[7] In Augustine's two cities doctrine, which was influenced by the ancient Stoic tradition of cosmopolitanism, the City of God was separated from the worldly political affairs of the City of Men and reserved for sincere believers defined by their love of God rather than by membership or affiliation with any kind of particular political community.[8] This Stoic-Christian cosmopolitan horizon found its way into humanist and natural law traditions—in the case of Aquinas, Erasmus, and Grotius—and later into the Enlightenment Kantian vision of an international order of law and individual rights, as well as shaping modern conceptions of universal human rights (see Maritain, 1944).

Today, in an era defined by religious conflict, in which religious identification often maps onto a narrower ethnocultural communitarianism, the Stoic-Christian horizon of a universal community is irrecuperable. At the same time, this post-secular condition brings with it not only new divisions and antagonisms but also the possibility of new forms of identification and solidarity that transcend national borders. Étienne Balibar uses the term "cosmopolitics" to characterize a global terrain marked by competing cosmopolitanisms; even religious or theological conflict becomes *cosmopolitical* conflict insofar as it takes places on a universal, or potentially universal, horizon. Thus, for Balibar: "Contemporary cosmopolitics is a particularly ambiguous form of politics; it consists exclusively of conflicts between universalities without ready-made solutions. It does not prefigure the realization of a philosophical 'cosmopolitanism,' but neither does it purely and simply do away with the possibility of taking it as a point of reference. It would be more accurate to say that cosmopolitics clears the field for competition between alternative cosmopolitanisms" (2018, p. 48). If the global terrain is one on which all major conflicts over identity must be understood, then some sort of cosmopolitan dimension is inevitable. The cosmopolitical horizon, in this sense, is not only a condition of conflict but also the condition of its resolution; it is not merely the possibility of global antagonism but also the possibility of cross-border solidarity and cooperation. We take cosmopolitics to refer to the ambiguous political dimension of globalization itself, which gives rise not only to new divisions but also to new transnational and emancipatory political organizations and institutional innovations, as well as affiliations and alliances that transcend national borders (see also Ingram, 2013). The cosmopolitical horizon combines thought and action—the acknowledgment of responsibility as the counterpart of an ethical imperative.

The cosmopolitical combination of thought and action entails that the ethical imperative is neither pure duty nor a preconceived political project.

It is oriented by a number of propositions that express a provisional knowledge of transformation. *First*, it is not limited to constitutional design, or to the construction of new kinds of political and legal institutions. While these are essential, cosmopolitics also works on a more horizontal level of social movements that are transnational in character, and that attempt to build cross-border affinities and alliances as they contest different forms of inequality, violence, and domination. Over the decades we have seen many examples of these, from the anti-neoliberal alter-globalization movements of the 2000s and various global counter-summits such as Porto Alegre in Brazil to more recent movements for economic, environmental, and social justice. *Second*, cosmopolitics involves what Hauke Brunkhorst calls a globalization of democratic solidarity (see 2005). Highly pluralized, differentiated global societies have created the need for forms of solidarity no longer rooted in community identity but rather in democratic public legitimation, constitutionality, and human rights. In other words, what is required to deal with inclusion problems and inequalities generated by globalization—which are at the same time the source of its lack of legitimacy—is more than international law and legal institutions, but forms of egalitarian democratic solidarity that transcend national boundaries—a new kind of global civic republicanism (see also Bohman, 2001) and even what we might call "green republicanism" (see Fremaux, 2019). *Third*, cosmopolitics can be seen in struggles over human rights, and in attempts to expand the language and scope of human rights to include those hitherto excluded, even and especially those who, as Arendt put it with regard to stateless people, lack the right to have rights. Here we can also refer to the extension of rights to the natural environment and to nonhuman species. As we have argued, political, social, and economic rights are, in the Anthropocene era, meaningless without an accompanying conception of ecological rights. Cosmopolitics involves, therefore, not only the expansion of rights recognition across national boundaries but also the possible expansion of rights discourse beyond the conceptual boundaries of the human itself to other beings and life-forms who would also have to be recognized as members of the cosmopolis, given that our survival and well-being is intrinsically bound up with theirs.[9]

Conclusion

Indeed, cosmopolitics embodies an affective ethics and politics of *entanglement*. This is a key theme we have emphasized throughout the book. The idea that our interests are closely bound up with the interests of others, and that our survival depends on the fate of the natural ecosystems in which we are embedded, must be crucial to any cosmopolitan ethos that calls upon modes of identification beyond the atomized individual or a particular community. *Beyond* and *after* Schmitt's sovereign-centric political theology, defined by borders and boundaries, friends and enemies, cosmopolitical theology defines a different ethical, political, and, indeed, spiritual horizon of planetary entanglement.

The different horizon reconfigures the relationship between the theological and the political. It maintains the possibility of a conjunction beyond that determined by Schmittian parameters. In our alternative rendering of political theology, what is brought into connection here is not the church and the state, nor the theological origin of the conceptual categories of a theory of the state, nor the final "stasiology" of *Political Theology II*. Instead, we have sought an interpretation of the theological and its passage to the political, which has at the same time relinquished the Schmittian restoration of political authority. In other words, our investigation of the relationship between theological and political categories has identified a different understanding of the political, one based on the secular coexistence of justice and care.

Coda

This book was being concluded as one crisis—the COVID-19 pandemic—was ending and another beginning: the Russian invasion of Ukraine in February 2022. This has initiated the prospect, in the twenty-first century, of a protracted armed conflict in Europe, which only several months ago still seemed unthinkable. The effect of the conflict has extended beyond the infliction of death, injury, destruction, and the creation of refugees, to deepen the existing inequalities and insecurities of the geopolitical order and the global economy and to render them increasingly unstable.

These recent occurrences, when situated within the three-decade period inaugurated by the end of the Cold War, appear to indicate the demise of the last remnants of the particular combination of free trade, international law, and democracy that, under the term globalization, purportedly animated its progressive development. With their demise, these crises retrospectively reveal globalization as an attempt to project a philosophy of history—a world unity—upon developmental tendencies that it was incapable of fully comprehending.

The transformation of the geopolitical order and global economy is reflected in the most recent National Intelligence Council's *Global Trends* report (2021), which indicates the possible major challenges arising from potential developmental tendencies over the next two decades. Among these were: pandemics and other global public health crises, the impacts of climate change, disruptions to supply chains, food and resource scarcity, geopolitical competition, global migration, growing income inequality, mounting national debt, economic insecurity, unemployment resulting from the AI revolution, and the fragmentation and polarization of contemporary societies as a reaction to increased interconnectivity. Such threats would result in an unstable and contested world characterized by heightened geopolitical tensions. The report outlines a number of possible scenarios, but the general outlook is gloomy: an increasingly divided, directionless, and chaotic international order lacking the ability to manage its many and growing crises. Indeed, the incapacity of political institutions to respond adequately to these challenges, and the gap between the expectations of citizens and the actual capacity of states, would lead a crisis of legitimacy with growing disillusionment and distrust of governments, increased political volatility, ideological polarization and populism, and protest and civil unrest. This would be accompanied by a general decline in democratic governance, as liberal democracies would find themselves more vulnerable to instability and to competition from authoritarian regimes. As the report emphasizes: "Over the next two decades, the relationships between states and their societies in every region are likely to face persistent tensions because of a growing mismatch between what publics need or expect and what governments can or are willing to deliver" (2021, p. 80).

The report is explicitly presented as a source of orientation for a particular sovereign nation-state—each successive administration of the United States—and expresses the uncertain relationship between state sovereignty and the global order and global economy. The uncertainty of the relationship is reinforced from the perspective of the institutional architecture of international human rights law exemplified in the recent overview, by the UN High Commissioner for Human Rights, of the global human rights developments and the activities of the UN Human Rights Office.[1] The UN High Commissioner explicitly characterizes the present and immediate future as a globalization of division and increased polarization in which the common international, institutional architecture of international human rights law confronts the difficulty of ensuring its continued primacy in the determination of the relationship both between states and between states and the citizens and noncitizens within their territory. These difficulties relate to the guarantee of the effectiveness of the specific rights and freedoms contained in the UN Human Rights Conventions and to the maintenance of the broader normative frameworks represented by the 2030 Agenda for Sustainable Development Goals and Paris Climate Agreement.

The effect of this uncertainty, at the level of the subjects of international human rights law, is a "questioning not only [of] their own futures, but the future of their societies, and of our globe."[2] It is a placing into question not simply of their position as right-holders, their sense of themselves as legal subjects within a legal order, but of the sense of their wider existence within the global order. The depth and radicality of this questioning exceed the framework within which the UN High Commissioner seeks to respond to it. For it exceeds the capacity of the concept of globalization to circumscribe the boundaries within which this questioning is articulated and, through this circumscription, to designate the appropriate juridical and wider policy responses.

The depth and radicality of this questioning is more effectively comprehended as the corollary of the intensification of the tensions within the institutional configuration of the post–Cold War neoliberal global order. The emergence of this global order presented itself as a coherent and progressive intersection of free trade, international law, and democracy that would be reflected in a generalization of a particular form of democratic regime predicated upon the active reduction in the state's presence in the economy—the combination of privatization of state enterprises, the deregulation of the labor market, and the retraction or minimization of existing forms of social welfare provision. The tensions of this global order were initially represented by the continued existence of nondemocratic regimes and the increasing reversal of the phenomenon of democratization, the failure of the Doha round negotiations of the World Trade Organization to achieve a global framework for freer trade combined with the 2007–2008 global financial crisis, the persistence of armed conflict, and its exacerbation of nondemocratic regimes and the increasing reversal of the phenomenon of democratization. These tensions have resulted in a neoliberal global order that has increased rather than reduced inequality between and within states and can no longer justify itself on its own terms or satisfy the expectations and demands of its citizens.

Within the existing democracies of the neoliberal global order, these initial tensions have resulted in an increasing distance between a system of multiparty democracy and its governing institutions and the governed reflected in widespread voter apathy, alternative forms of political mobilization and expression, ideological polarization and "culture wars," the proliferation of conspiracy theories and dis- and misinformation, and the general breakdown of truth in public discourse. Perhaps the most significant element of this legitimation crisis is the detachment of neoliberalism from the liberal and democratic institutions from which it hitherto derived, even if only in a superficial and perfunctory sense, its political will formation. Neoliberalism appears to take on increasingly authoritarian forms today. From the violent and repressive policing of protests to the widespread use of state (and corporate) surveillance, and the increasing recourse to the adoption of emergency powers by the executive, the neoliberal state appears increasingly unhinged from democratic and constitutional constraints. Furthermore, the resurgence of right-wing national populist movements, in alliance with religious conservatives in many liberal democracies, represents a new kind of authoritarian neoliberal ideology, one that promotes a narrow conception of individual market freedom while supporting a socially conservative agenda with its particularly regressive effect upon the position of women and minorities. The policies of Trump, Bolsonaro, Modi, Orbán, and many other right-wing populist figures exemplify this type of agenda: introducing tax cuts for the wealthy and big corporations, eviscerating environmental regulations and consumer protections, removing the funding of public institutions and wider regulatory frameworks, while at the same time restricting the rights of minorities and empowering religious-conservative constituencies. Their disdain for democratic institutions, norms, and procedures suggests a form of reactionary neoliberal ideology that no longer seeks legitimation within the legally regulated public sphere of liberal democracies. This is accompanied by a weakening of institutional structures indicated by the lack of coherence and effectiveness in their public health response to the COVID-19 pandemic and to the wider response to environmental problems of the Anthropocene.

The situation is one in which the notion of sovereignty, both its absence and its reassertion, has reintroduced and reconfigured the dynamics of the neoliberal global order (Geva, 2021; Slobodian, 2021), which, in turn, reveal the underlying political dimension of neoliberalism (Biebricher, 2019). It is within this context that our study of Schmittian political theology has focused on this simultaneous absence and reassertion of sovereignty that Schmitt himself was acutely aware of in his time and sought to bolster and revivify sovereignty through the recourse to theology. The deployment of various politico-theological figures and tropes in Schmitt's thought—from the legal exception to the *complexio oppositorum* of the Roman Catholic Church, from the Christian empire to the modern nation-state, from the *katechon* to *stasis*—are all guided by the same imperative: to restore the principle of political order and authority and to prevent the coming anarchy. Yet, this project of reanimating sovereignty has been a failure. Conservative revolutions in both their Schmittian conception and their contemporary manifestation always undermine the political order that they seek to install by unleashing forces they cannot control. Indeed, it is the desire for strong sovereignty, fueled by both elite and populist passions and resentments, that is proving such a destabilizing force in politics today.

The loss of sovereignty has also been highlighted in a different sense. As we have shown, the sovereignty of the anthropocentric and theological figure of Man—the central subject of Schmitt's political theology—has been fundamentally displaced by the further transformation of technology on the one hand, and of nature on the other. Throughout the book we have pointed to the limits of the Schmittian conceptual framework and sought to proceed beyond them by indicating the various ways in which the conceptual boundaries of the subject are opened to new articulations of person and thing, man and animal, individual and community, and to ethical responsibilities toward human and nonhuman others. In tracing the limitations of Schmitt's sovereign-centric thinking, particularly in responding to contemporary conditions of the Anthropocene, we have also sought to reorient political theology around principles of social justice and emancipation, global solidarity, and planetary entanglement and care. We seek redemption not in some obscure messianic promise of a Last Judgment or Kingdom to come, but in new social movements and alliances that have arisen and that are currently transforming the political space. We believe that a global politics oriented by this ethos is the only adequate response to the current configuration of the neoliberal order.

However, our aim in this book has not been to develop a new systematic political theology or a new model for politics. We have sought neither to define a different role for religion, nor to outline an alternative program of political action. There is much more work to be done in thinking about how theology might transform, and in turn *be transformed by*, contemporary political practices in ways that are democratic and emancipatory. At a time when the forces of religious conservatism are on the ascendancy, and when the rights and freedoms of women and minorities are seriously threatened, even in liberal democracies, by powerful conservative constituencies,[3] the possibilities for a new post-secular form of radical politics seem unclear. Nor is the language of theology something that can be easily translated into the discourse of politics. This is the mistake that Schmitt made in his highly reductionist account of political theology. Rather, political theology should be thought of as an open space of inquiry into the meaning of politics and an ongoing ethical interrogation of its discursive limits. In highlighting the limitations of Schmitt's model—which continues to be dominant in political theology—and by showing how these limitations demand a rethinking, *with and beyond* Schmitt, of the terms of the debate, we have sought to contribute in a modest way to this field of inquiry.

Notes

Introduction

1. We cannot neglect the matter of Schmitt's anti-Semitism and its relevance to this question (see Gross, 2007).

2. We write this introduction amid the Russian invasion of Ukraine—an event that also poses an existential threat to the liberal world order as we have known it since the end of the Cold War. This existential threat can also be seen as an intimation of the revival of the Schmittian notions of the *pluriversum* and of the *Grossraum*.

3. Peterson (2011) argued that Schmitt's transcription of a triune God into the monotheistic figure of the political sovereign was incompatible with Christian doctrine and amounted to a form of paganism.

4. On the anarchistic tendencies of Jewish political theology, see also Loick, 2019; Rosenstock, 2010; Martel, 2012; Löwy, 2017.

Chapter 1. From States of Emergency to Forms of the Political

1. See also Derrida's idea of sovereign autoimmunity and its relationship with democracy (2005).

2. The Weimar political and constitutional context of these debates between Schmitt and Kelsen are covered by David Dyzenhaus (see 2000).

3. This is made clear in Schmitt's discussion of the political theology of Hobbes's Leviathan, in which it is argued that Hobbes gives us a decisionist theory of sovereignty (see Schmitt, 1996a).

4. This was the basis of Erik Peterson's (2011) critique of Schmitt, who queried the theological basis for Schmitt's monotheistic account of sovereignty, arguing that it was incompatible with the Christian Trinitarian doctrine, and accusing Schmitt of a kind of political heresy.

5. Juan Vargas (2021) has explored contemporary populism as a form of the politics of acclamation, or what Giorgio Agamben has called "glory"—a politics that bears little relationship to democracy and, indeed, is much closer to totalitarianism.

6. A similar point is made by Peter Uwe Hohendhal (see 2018).

7. See also Habermas's critique of Schmitt's idea of politics in "The Horrors of Autonomy" (1989).

8. A similar critique of Schmitt was made by Hans Blumenberg, who argued that the sovereign state of exception as an expression of the "primacy" of the political, was simply out of step with modernity: "When it is no longer possible to believe that the decision between good and evil is going to occur in history and is immediately impending, and that every political act participates in this crisis, the suggestiveness of the 'state of emergency' [*Ausnahmezustand*] as the normal political state disappears" (1985, pp. 91–92). Blumenberg also questioned Schmitt's use of the secularization thesis to justify the importation of theological categories into modern conceptions of politics. Rather, for Blumenberg, the legitimacy of the modern era stood on its own terms, and consisted in a radical innovation and self-assertion that displaced the old theological world.

Chapter 2. Who Is the Subject of Political Theology?

1. See Galli, 2012, originally published as the introduction to the Italian translation of Schmitt's *Hamlet or Hecuba: The Irruption of Time into the Play*.

2. The understanding of ethical responsibility and justice developed in this chapter furnishes the basis for the further reflection, in chapter 3, on fraternity by tracing its lineage from the notion of brotherhood in the Pauline Letter to Philemon. In tracing this lineage, it also interrupts the Schmittian appropriation of the Pauline notion of the *katechon* as the preparatory stage for the further reflection on the Schmittian notion of the *katechon* in chapter 8.

3. For the associated correspondence between Ball and Schmitt, see Wacker, 1996.

4. Both German versions are now contained in Ball's *Die Folgen der Reformation* (2005). It is the publication of this reworked version that Schmitt advises Ball not to publish and is the subject of a scathing review, by one of Schmitt's then graduate students, Waldemar Gurian (see Gurian, 1925). This leads to the termination of the relationship between Ball and Schmitt. For Gurian's later obituary for Ball, see Gurian, 1927. For Gurian's own break with and critique of Schmitt, see Gurian, 1934 (pseud. Müller).

5. The influence of Bakunin results from the unfinished work of Ball on Bakunin, undertaken in conjunction with his leading participation in Dada. See Ball, 2010. The brief mention of Bakunin in the extended review is entirely negative (Ball, 2013, pp. 68, 91).

6. For the discussion of this return to Catholicism from Bakunian anarchism, see Friedmann, 2019, and, more generally, Guerra, 2020.

7. See Galli, 2015, pp. 58–77, for a comprehensive analysis of the marginal position of Machiavelli in Schmitt, which attributes this position to an entirely different interpretative position from that of Ball.

8. For a sense of the degree of contraction involved in Ball's analysis of *Dictatorship*, see Kelly, 2016; and for an alternative origin of *Dictatorship* in Schmitt's experience during noncombat military service in World War I, see Rogers, 2016.

9. Ball (2013, p. 83) attributes this to the influence of Sorel.

10. On Ball's relationship to the Catholic Church, see Friedmann, 2020, and on the broader character of Ball's religious thinking, see Agazzi, 2009.

11. This is explicitly acknowledged by Schmitt himself in his correspondence with Carl Muth shortly after Ball's death in 1927. See Wacker, 1996, p. 239.

12. See Meier, 2006a, for the discussion of the "hidden" Schmittian response to Strauss's critique traced through the modifications of the original version of *The Concept of the Political* in its later editions.

13. It should be emphasized that polemic is the counterpart of a liberalism understood in its specifically Schmittian definition. See Galli, 2000.

14. For the wider discussion of the place of Hobbes in the Straussian trajectory, and the character of the Straussian interpretation of Hobbes, see Martinich, 2015; Meier, 2011. See also Paganini, 2015, for the discussion of the central importance of Hobbes's *De Motu, Loco et Tempore*, only discovered in 1973 (the year of Strauss's death), for both Hobbes's conceptualization of the relationship between philosophy and theology and Strauss's designation, in *Persecution and the Art of Writing* (1952), of the adoption, by early modern texts, of an oblique, "esoteric" mode of presentation.

15. See the 1962 preface to the English translation of Strauss's first work (1930), *Spinoza's Critique of Religion* (Strauss, 1997, pp. 1–31).

16. Here, the analysis leaves aside the more detailed examination of this development, and, within this, the work on Machiavelli, originally published in 1958 (Strauss, 1978). In particular whether the discussion of Machiavelli's approach to religion represents a further stage in this development, beyond Greek philosophy, or, whether it is to be understood as simply a reemphasis, in which the theological-political problem remains. See Meier, 2017, pp. 25–113.

17. For the character of this reflection, in the 1930s and 1940s, see Strauss, 2007a; Strauss, 2007b; Strauss, 2013a; Strauss, 2013b.

18. For the origins and early development of neoliberalism, see Biebricher, 2019; Dardot & Laval, 2014; De Carolis, 2016; Milanese, 2020; Milanese, 2020/21, pp. 47–68; Mirowski & Plehwe, 2009; Stiegler, 2019; Wiedemann, 2020/21, pp. 69–96.

19. It is Hayek's *The Road to Serfdom*, originally published in 1944, that involves the simultaneous acknowledgment and distance from Schmitt, and in Hayek's final work, *Law, Legislation and Liberty*, the development of Schmitt's legal thinking is held to reflect an inability to understand "the self-ordering forces of

society and the role of law in an ordering mechanism" (Hayek, 2019, p. 71). This provides the basis for the subsequent absence of sustained reference to Schmitt in the further development of neoliberalism.

20. Those regimes characterized by an explicit absence of response, whatever their associated characterization of the existence of COVID-19, represent the stronger adherence to the capacity of the neoliberal social order, without the assistance of the state, to endure.

21. This will be the subject of further extended analysis in chapter 4.

22. The political theology of fraternity is developed in chapter 3.

Chapter 3. Person, Identity, Transformation

1. For a comprehensive overview of the genesis and development of Maritain's philosophical approach, see Lorenzini, 2021.

2. Our critique of the Schmittian interpretation of the *katechon* is fully developed in chapter 8.

3. The analysis leaves aside the different approach of Vattimo, which is centered upon the notion of *kenosis* from Saint Paul's Letter to the Philippians 2: 5–11 and is, in fact the result of a further interpretative addition to Paul, taken from the Gospel of John, 15: 15 (see Vattimo, 1999, p. 26; 2002, 2007). The turn to *kenosis*, rather than *katechon*, is to present God's abasement in order to reorder the relationship to man as one of friendship, enabling, in turn, the introduction of the notion of *caritas*. The central purpose of this chapter is to utilize the Letter to Philemon in order to develop the notion of fraternity in contrast to that of friendship. This, in turn, is the preparatory step for the later reconsideration of the notion of *katechon*, in chapter 8, that detaches the *katechon* from its Schmittian attribution as a term of political sovereignty that functions as a "restrainer" within a wider logic of the "lesser evil."

4. Here, in contrast to Wolter, 2010, the analysis is, therefore, also less concerned with restoring this letter's central position by demonstrating its connection to the Pauline doctrine of justification.

5. It is exactly this transformative potential—the return of Onesimus to Philemon as a return to a relationship that is not (cannot be) the resumption of that between slave and master—that cannot be thought in an extensive history of Christian commentary on the Letter to Philemon, from Jerome to Luther, see Tolmie, 2017. For Agamben, this Christian commentary is a reflection of a more general elimination of "the messianic character of the Letters" that, in turn, is the neutralization of an aporia arising from "a messianic community that wants to present itself as an institution" (Agamben, 2005b, p. 1).

6. This is to be understood in the broad sense of the philosophical-theological framework of early modern philosophy as is evident from the fur-

ther discussion of the analogies and their historical development in chapter 3 of *Political Theology* (1922). In addition, early modern philosophy has rendered miracles a distinct philosophical-theological object of inquiry thereby detaching it from a necessary connection with the question of sainthood. The position of early modern philosophy is accompanied, during this period, by the Catholic Church's establishment, and increasing formalization of, the process of the investigation and determination of miracles as the essential precursor to the conferral of sainthood (Vidal, 2007).

    7. The analysis leaves aside here the question of the interpretative fidelity of Schmitt to the consideration of miracles in *Leviathan*. Compare, for example, Bertman, 2007; Curley, 1996; Pacci, 1988.

    8. Here, from the retrospective vantage point of the first five years of the National Socialist Regime, Schmitt's preceding presentation of the antagonistic relationship between liberalism and democracy, in *The Crisis of Parliamentary Democracy*, and the depoliticizing effect of liberalism's individualistic eschewal of state and politics, in *The Concept of the Political*, are now inserted within a broader historical trajectory that resists the characterization of the National Socialist Regime as the return of the Leviathan (Schmitt, 2008a, p. 71 and fn7, p. 76).

    9. The later Schmittian recourse to the Pauline notion of the *katechon* can be considered an attempt to identify this intertwining of Christianity and sovereignty in Pauline thought as an integral element of a broader Christian history.

    10. The character and conceptualization of this distinction is a central aspect of the divergent, contemporary interpretations of Badiou and Agamben. See, for example, Agamben, 2005b, pp. 52ff.

    11. This letter is, therefore, situated in an extrinsic position to the "hermeneutics of allegory" that Stanislas Breton considers underlying the mode of address of the Pauline letters (Breton, 2011, pp. 55–73). For while the Letter to Philemon has the purpose of an "education of religious consciousness" (p. 69), the mode of address is distinguished by its lack of allegory.

    12. This common brotherhood within the early Christian community, linked to Paul, remains traversed by the unequal vertical relationship with God: spiritual or divine authority. For Agamben, the sense in which Paul utilizes the term slave, in its formulation as "slave of the Messiah," which receives its exemplary formulation in 1 Corinthians 7: 20–23, "defines the new messianic condition for Paul, the principle of a particular transformation of all juridical conditions (which, for this reason, are not simply abolished)' (Agamben, 2005b, p. 13). This, in turn, for Agamben, is inextricably linked to Paul's own "messianic calling" (pp. 13–14).

    13. For the analysis of the Letter to Philemon within the wider context of ancient slavery, see Artz-Grabner, 2010; Barth & Blanke, 2020; Wessels, 2010.

    14. In addition, it would also be potentially possible to attribute this anti-Roman temper, in this critical reconstruction, to Paul's memory of both his

family's and his own situation and citizenship in Tarsus (Hengel, 2014, pp. 4–15), and a transformation in his understanding of it once he becomes a Christian.

15. Verse 23 of the Letter to Philemon, in which Paul indicates a proposed, future visit to Philemon and the community in Colossae, beyond its hopeful reassurance that Paul will eventually be freed from prison, could also express Paul's own acknowledgment that the entreaty will require to be accompanied by a future visit in order to establish conformity between the Pauline understanding and Onesimus's treatment by Philemon and the community.

16. This juridico-political abolition is symbolic because it exists in parallel with a history of its highly qualified application from the period immediately after abolition, reconstruction (Foner, 2012; Vorenberg, 2004), and extends to contemporary situations of modern slavery (Azmy, 2002).

17. See Williams, 2012a, for an analysis of the history of interpretation of the Letter to Philemon and Williams, 2012b, for a broader discussion of this interpretative sensibility in relation to the Pauline letters.

18. The analysis leaves aside Derrida's critical engagement with this Schmittian extract from *Ex Captivitate Salus* in *The Politics of Friendship* (1997), as the analysis is concerned with the Pauline concept of brotherhood that Schmitt is unable to recognize in the Pauline letters. This is evident from Taubes's account of his encounter and discussion with Schmitt concerning the first Pauline Epistle to the Romans, in which Schmitt deems 11: 28 to indicate an exclusive relationship of enmity between the gospel and the Jews (Taubes, 2003, p. 51). This for Taubes indicates Schmitt's adoption of "the folk traditions of antisemitism" (p. 51) and, as that the discussion is held when Schmitt is in his late eighties, its continued persistence. See also, for other approaches Monod, 2012; Ojakangas, 2003. A further element that is absent from both *Ex Captivitate Salus* and the Schmittian texts on Hobbes (Schmitt, 2008a) is Hobbes's discussion of Cain and Abel in the Latin version of *Leviathan*. See Thornton, 2002.

19. Esposito traces a path through Freud's thought in which the essay *A Phylogenetic Fantasy: Overview of Transference Neuroses* intimates the path from *Totem and Taboo* to the final work of *Moses and Monotheism*.

20. Derrida's extended reflection upon friendship, and, in particular the reticence with regard to fraternity (Derrida, 1997, pp. 227–270), is left aside as Nancy's reconsideration of fraternity is a reconsideration of this reticence.

21. The reserve reflects the enduring suspicion of fraternity that extends, beyond enmity, to include its Christian, sentimental, and utopian aspects (Nancy, 2013, p. 119).

22. Here, a further difference arises between Nancy and Esposito with regard to the conceptualization of birth. For Esposito, in *Bíos*, birth, through a combination of reference to Arendt and Simondon, is situated beyond an essential reference to the family. See Esposito, 2008, pp. 177–182.

23. For Nancy, it is marriage that is the "veritable site and stamp of the birth of the law" (2013, p. 122).

24. Here, Nancy's analysis refers to the earlier work, conducted together with Lacoue-Labarthe, originally published in two edited volumes in the 1980s, *Rejouer le politique* and *Le Retrait du politique*, that received a later, partial, English translation (Lacoue-Labarthe & Nancy, 1997).

25. See also the preceding and subsequent considerations on democracy in Nancy, 2010, and Bouthors & Nancy, 2019.

26. For Nancy, it represents a "signal: it is pointing out that the social, juridical and political order cannot take the register of sense upon itself. It can only open up points of approach or access. But it is essential for it to do that much, and for it to do that much, it must know itself well enough to indicate that beyond the law, sense springs forth" (Nancy, 2013, p. 122).

27. The recent emergence of the social movements associated with Black Lives Matter and Extinction Rebellion exemplify, in their distinctiveness, instances of this universalism. A further, extended reflection upon them both is provided in chapter 7.

28. Further iterations of this suspicion underlie the later, post–World War II work *The Nomos of the Earth* (Schmitt, 2006) and *Political Theology II* (Schmitt, 2010b), which, in addition, reaffirms ineradicable antagonism (pp. 122ff.).

29. See Galli, 2000, for the discussion of Schmitt's distinctive understanding and critique of liberalism.

30. For Balibar, the coexistence of these notions, as the "proposition of equaliberty" (Balibar, 2011, p. 12), is a dynamic and unconditioned proposition that "refers to *de jure* universality" (p. 11). See also Balibar, 1994; Balibar, 2014.

Chapter 4. Political Theology and the Anthropocene

1. A point that was brought home in the compromises on decarbonization commitments that marked the ignominious conclusion to the COP climate change summit of 2021.

2. The Anthropocene is also the *Capitalocene* (see Moore, 2016), and, while the ecological damage wrought by human activity cannot be reduced to capitalism, it cannot be entirely separated from it either. The coordination of all economic activity according to the profit motive has led to the treatment of the natural environment and global commons as an externality that can be commercially exploited without limit or accountability. Moreover, the implications of rapid decarbonization, and the transition from fossil-fuel-based industries to those based on renewable energy sources, not to mention dramatic limits to human consumption and production, may already signal a shift into a postcapitalist economy.

3. Here our interpretation of Schmitt differs from Michael Northcott's, who suggests that it is this telluric dimension of Schmitt's thought—in other words, the idea that concepts of law and justice are rooted in the earth and biblically sanctioned—that makes his political theology instructive for understanding the politics of climate emergency (see Northcott, 2013).

4. As an alternative to Schmitt's anthropocentric geopolitical and telluric worldview, Donna J. Haraway proposes an earth-centric vision of the planet, which she calls Terrapolis, and which she describes as "open, worldly, indeterminate, and polytemporal," and a place that "makes space for unexpected companions." Unlike Schmitt's vision of politics centered around sovereign autonomy, "Terrapolis is the sf [science fiction] game of response-ability" (2016, p. 11). This would imply not only an ethical responsibility to the planet we inhabit but also a deeper sense of co-belonging and mutual interaction with the ecosystems we are intrinsically part of. This sense of co-belonging is based on Haraway's alternative ontology of what she calls the Chthulucene, which evokes a different relationship to the soil—not one of appropriation and extraction, but rather one of *entanglement*. This is what she refers to as "making kin" with nonhuman entities, animals, plant life, and biological organisms of all kinds, a different kind of rootedness in the soil and the earth in which we are *part of* terra, not transcendent over it.

5. The current debate about the global distribution of vaccines is exemplary of this: as we all know, vaccination programs only work if they are coordinated globally and if vaccines are made available to all, that, as the saying goes, no one is protected until everyone is protected. Aside from its injustice, there is simply no point in wealthy countries hoarding vaccines and privileging their own citizens over populations in poorer parts of the world.

6. Jacques Derrida, for instance, points to the way that our concepts of sovereignty are premised on an undecidability between the human sovereign and the animal in the history of Western political philosophy. We think, for instance, of Leviathan the great sea serpent, which Hobbes turned into the visual metaphor for the modern state, and whose politico-theological significance Schmitt himself devoted extensive study to (see 1996a); or of Machiavelli's figures of the fox and the lion, or the strange composite figure of the Centaur, half-man half-animal, as an embodiment of the qualities and characteristics the prince must possess in order to rule. Derrida himself points to the parallel between the beast and the sovereign, particularly in their exceptional relationship to the law—the sovereign being above the law, the animal beneath it. With reference to Schmitt's theory of the sovereign exception, Derrida says that the right to place oneself outside the law "runs the risk of carrying the human sovereign above the law, towards divine omnipotence (which will moreover most often have grounded the principle of sovereignty in its sacred and theological origin) and, because of this arbitrary suspension or rupture of right, runs the risk of making the sovereign look like the most brutal beast who respects nothing, scorns the law, immediately situates

himself above the law, at a distance from the law" (2009, pp. 16–17). The state of exception, which Schmitt identifies at the heart of sovereignty, brings the human sovereign closer to God, and yet also, and no doubt contrary to Schmitt's intentions, closer to the animal. This strange proximity between God, man, and animal points toward a different kind of political theology—a zoo-political theology, in which the figure of the animal, as a supplement to the anthropocentric concept of sovereignty (that is both human and divine) at the same time deconstructs it and pulls it down into the mire of nature, the world beyond law and human institutions. This troubling relationship between the beast and the sovereign is, for Derrida, "like a coupling, an ontological, onto-zoo-anthropo-theologico-political copulation: the beast becomes the sovereign who becomes the beast" (2009, p. 18).

7. See also Cimatti on the Anthropocene, in which he argues that a virus's domination of man—rather than man's domination of nature—in the era of COVID-19 indicates that the age of the Anthropocene has already been surpassed (2020c).

8. Another way of approaching this question would be to place humans and animals on the same continuum, considering the ways that humans "become animal" and animals "become human" through various forms of play, for instance. This is precisely what Brian Massumi does. His aim is to break down the anthropomorphic divide by identifying the "animal" dimension in the human and the "human" dimension in the animal—something that can produce new forms of politics: "Expressing the singular belonging of the human to the animal continuum has political implications, as do all questions of belonging" (see Massumi, 2014, p. 3).

9. Laura Bazzicalupo (see in Cimatti, 2020b, pp. 263–280), for instance, talks about the possibility of a new kind of "intersectionality" of struggles—based on an immanent pluralist ontology—around the environment, involving different classes, genders, excluded minorities, along with nonhuman species.

10. See for instance the recent interventions from Andreas Fischer-Lescano (2020), Malte-Christian Gruber (2020), and Christoph Menke (2020) over the question of the recognition of nature as a legal person and the extension of legal rights to nonhuman species.

11. We might think of the example of St. Francis of Assisi preaching a sermon to the birds, where we find a veneration and respect for all living things as creatures of God. Cimatti refers to Francis's "mystical animalism" in which nonhuman beings are regarded as spiritual brothers, rendered in the fact that he speaks to them, thus recognizing them as equals. Furthermore, as Cimatti (2020b, p. 25) argues, this spiritual communion sought with nonhuman beings celebrates life in its immanence rather than transcendence: "In general, for Francis animal life is a life of complete holiness in the sense of a completely immanent life. A life in immanence, or better yet a life of immanence, is a life beyond, a life without, time—precisely, a life of immanence is a life without transcendence (a holy life has no need of God, because it already coincides with God)." In this

nontranscendent, nonanthropomorphic conception of life, God does not stand outside and above creation but is, rather, immanent within it.

12. This peculiar attitude was nicely satirized in the recent movie *Don't Look Up*, in which the imminent collision of a comet with the earth is largely met with a shrug of the shoulders.

Chapter 5. Technology as Political Theology

1. The influence of Däubler (1876–1934) is gradually displaced, during the 1920s, by the growing affinity with the poetry of Konrad Weiß (1880–1940) and the retrospective transformation in the understanding of Däubler's symbol of the Northern Lights in the poem "Der Nordlicht" by the later encounter with an essay, in 1938, by Proudhon (Schmitt, 2017b, pp. 39–45).

2. The period 1917–1920 represents the final years of Weber's life and, in this period, Weber's Munich lectures (public and university) are "Science as a Vocation," "Politics as a Vocation," "Economy and Society (Positive Critique of the Materialist Conception of History)," "The Most Universal Categories of the Science of Society," "Universal Social and Economic History," "General Theory of the State and Politics (Sociology of the State)," and "Socialism." For this period of Weber's academic work and wider intellectual engagement, see Hübinger, 2009.

3. While the analysis will leave the question of the limits of the Schmittian interpretation of Weber aside, it would require a return to examine the Weberian references in the early works of Schmitt (Vinx & Zeitlin, 2021) and to compare them with the work of Ghosh, 2008, 2014, 2016, 2019; Trieber, 2020.

4. Although Schmitt was unaware of Weber's 1910 outline for a sociological survey of the press, it is evident that it indicates a far more complex position than that ascribed by Schmitt to the press. See Weber, 1998; Hennis, 1998.

5. There is an ambivalence with regard to degree and character of this state control, which is held to pertain to the state's "courage" rather than juridical considerations of the limitation upon basic rights (Schmitt, 2008, p. 207) under the Weimar Constitution.

6. Here, the overtly anti-Semitic conference, The Jews in German Jurisprudence (*Das Judentum in der deutschen Rechtswissenschaft*), in 1936, marks its final expression.

7. In both texts, it is the essays of after 1936 to 1940/1 that are relevant here.

8. This Schmittian appropriation of the Pauline notion of the *katechon* will be the subject of extended reflection in the final chapter.

9. It is also indicative that the epigraph for the section on Weimar is a quotation from Ernst Jünger's *Das Abenteuerliche Herz: Figuren und Capriccios* (Sloterdijk, 1988, p. 384).

10. The English translation has replaced the reference, in the German title, to Taoism, with "Infinite Mobilization" (Sloterdijk, 2020a).

11. Sloterdijk returns to consider the notion of religion in *Gottes Eifer: Von Kampf der drei Monotheismen* (2007; English translation: *God's Zeal: The Battle of the Three Monotheisms* [2009b]); *Schatten des Sinai; Fußnote über Ursprünge und Wandlungen* (English translation: *In The Shadow of Mount Sinai* [2015]); *Nach Gott: Glauben und Unglaubensversuche* (2017; English translation: *After God* [2020b]), and *Den Himmel zum Sprechen bringen: über Theopoesie* (2020). The earlier text on Nietzsche, *Über die Verbesserung der guten Nachricht: Nietzsches fünftes Evangelium. Rede zum 100. Todestag von Friedrich Nietzsche* (2000; English translation: *Nietzsche Apostle* [2013a]) should also be considered to belong to this consideration.

12. For Sloterdijk, "the position of philosophical anthropology that humans are "here" loses its validity—we may no longer carelessly assume that "existence" and "being-in-the-world" can be attributed to humans. The presumption that "human beings" are already "in the world" and "exist" becomes corrected by a Socratic maieutic method that deals with arriving on earth and generating worlds, as well as the risk of failure associated with both efforts (2020a, p. x).

13. As Sloterdijk emphasizes, "The question of humanism is more than the bucolic assumption that reading improves us. It is, rather, no less than an issue of anthropodicy: that is, a characterization of man with respect to his biological indeterminacy and his moral ambivalence. Above all, however, from now on the question of how a person can become a true or real human being becomes unavoidably a media question, if we understand by media the means of communion and communication by which human beings attain to that which they can and will become" (2016a, p. 16).

14. For Sloterdijk, these are the chirotope, the phonotope (or logotope), the uterotope, the thermotope, the erototope, the ergotope (or phallotope), the alethotope (or mnemotope), the thanatotope or theotope, and the nomotope (2016c, pp. 339–340).

15. This reworking, originally published in German in 2001, is contained in Sloterdijk's *Not Saved: Essays After Heidegger* (2016b).

16. Religion is the subject of the later eighth dimension—the thanatotope/theotope (Sloterdijk, 2016c, pp. 411–436). In relation to the dimension of the erotope, the examination of the Sloterdijkian interpretative appropriation of Mühlmann's work and the further question of the coherence of this appropriation in relation to Sloterdijk's reliance upon the earlier German tradition of philosophical anthropology (Max Scheler, Helmut Plessner, Arnold Gehlen) is left aside.

17. For Sloterdijk, these attributes are "neglectful of immunity, preferential towards the foreign, inclusive, unselective, symmetrical, duty-free, as well as compressible and reversible at will" (2013b, p. 263).

18. Sloterdijk only indicates in *You Must Change Your Life* that, rather than being the original expression of Schmitt, it is a Schmittian emendation of an original quotation from Proudhon in which Schmitt substitutes "humanity" for "God" (Sloterdijk, 2013c, p. 449).

19. Both of the Sloterdijk translated texts utilize the word "deceive" in place of "cheat."

20. See also Sutherland, 2019. It is also instructive, despite the explicit endnote references to Roberto Esposito's *Communitas* and *Immunitas*, in *Foams* (Sloterdijk, 2016c, p. 25, fn14; p. 183, fn99; p. 502, fn31), that Esposito's critique, in *Immunitas*, of the German tradition of philosophical anthropology is unacknowledged. This lack of acknowledgment is accompanied by the absence of Esposito's explication of the negative logic of the appropriation of an immunological approach predicated upon inclusion by exclusion. For Esposito, the logic of exclusionary inclusion is one that, beyond the question of the institution of a process of inclusion by exclusion, is one of increasingly destructive extension and intensity. "The more life is hounded by a danger that circulates without distinction throughout all its practices, the more its response is concentrated into the mechanisms of a single device: as risk of the common becomes increasingly extensive, the response of the immune defense becomes increasingly intensive" (Esposito, 2011, p. 5).

21. Stiegler with the notion of grammatization explicitly introduces a degree of critical distance between his work and that of Derrida (see Stiegler, 2000). It is from this distance that the notion of grammatization is introduced through reference to the work of Sylvain Auroux. Critical distance should be understood here, in the words of Stiegler, as complexification of the initial Derridean approach (in Derrida's *De la grammatologie*), as is evident from Stiegler, 2014, p. 108, fn25).

22. The process is derived from Stiegler's critical appropriation of Gilbert Simondon whose analyses are accorded a central position throughout Stiegler's work.

23. While the period in which *Constitutional Theory* is written is that of the final years of silent cinema, it is the Schmittian opposition between a non-technological speech and thought, combined with the mediation of writing and printing, and cinema, that is the focus here. In addition, by the time of the essays of the early 1930s, although this is not explicitly stated, Schmitt's acceptance of the state's adoption of film technology relates to films that have become both image and sound: the "talkies."

24. The concept of hyper-industrialization is explicitly formulated in opposition to the notions of an "affluent society," a "leisure society," or a "post-industrial society" (Stiegler, 2011b, pp. 103ff.).

25. The Stieglerian position in *Technics and Time III* is the further development and generalization of the reflection upon the transformation of the relationship between science and technology in the biological sciences undertaken in *Technics and Time II* (Stiegler, 2009).

26. This identification of the presence of the negative is itself set within a broader consideration, by Stiegler, of the transition from a disciplinary society (Foucault) to a control society (Deleuze) that is left aside here (Stiegler, 2011b, 2013).

Chapter 6. Political Theology and Democratic Constitutionalism

1. Böckenförde's personal contact with Schmitt began in 1953, prompted by the reading of Schmitt's *Constitutional Theory* (*Verfassungslehre*) and continuing from this point onward. It is also the basis for the subsequent invitation to participate in the events of the wider intellectual circle constituted by the Ebrach seminars (1957–1968) organized by Ernst Forsthoff (1902–1974). See Gosewinkel, 2017.

2. The indication of these unresolved tensions then forms the basis for the transition to the discussion in chapter 7 of political theology and the challenges to contemporary democratic constitutionalism.

3. For the particular Catholic circle—the Siedlinghauser Circle—in which Schmitt participated in the 1930s and 1940s and the dynamics of its relationship with National Socialism, see Dietka, 2020.

4. The further consolidation of the National Socialist regime represented by the Nuremburg laws (1935), and their explicit Schmittian justification (see Zarka, 2005), is the subject of Böckenförde's much later text (2017d). The Böckenfördian approach is without direct reference to, or citation of, Schmitt, but the critical presentation, as one of civic betrayal, has the explicit intention of emphasizing the rejection of the anti-Semitic elements of Schmittian thought (Gosewinkel, 2017, pp. 371–372).

5. These questions will be posed again, without knowledge of Böckenförde's work or Schmittian political theology, but provided with a different response, in the work of Marcel Gauchet (1985).

6. The implicit distance is also evident in the manner of reference to and citation of Schmitt's work. This is exemplified in the final reference to Schmitt's *Tyranny of Values* (*Die Tyrannei der Werte*) (1967) (Schmitt, 2018c), which suggests that it centers upon a critique of all attempts, within a secular state, to establish the essentially supplementary conditions of homogeneity through recourse to values (Böckenförde, 2019d, p. 167, fn48). The narrowness of this interpretation is revealed through comparison with the understanding of Schmitt's text as a far more fundamental critique of the Federal Republic and reaffirmation of Schmitt's extrinsic position; see Zeitlin, 2020.

7. For Agamben, the Böckenfördian position would be a reaffirmation of the loss of the "messianic experience of time" originating in the "reorientation to stabilize the institutional and juridical organization of the early Church" in response to the "inexplicable delay" of the "imminent arrival of the messiah" (Agamben, 2018, p. 4).

8. Böckenförde refers to Heller's final, unfinished, and posthumously published *Staatslehre* (1933). The importance of Heller for Böckenförde is emphasized by Jouanjan (2018, 2019). For the contextual understanding of Heller's left-wing position in interwar Germany, see Llanque, 2019. In addition, see Gosewinkel, 2017, p. 387.

9. This is itself a particular conceptualization of anarchy and anarchism that, in the German tradition of the social sciences (*Geistwissenschaften*), originates with Stammler's *Die Theorie des Anarchismus* (1894). For an alternative conception, see the critical remarks on Stammler contained in Gustav Landauer's "Anarchismus in Deutschland" (1895) (Landauer, 1976).

10. The exclusion is predicated upon the assumption that the Habermasian approach remains unaltered from the period of Habermas's work of the 1970s and would require an extensive reconsideration, in particular, on the basis of Habermas's *Between Facts and Norms: Contributions to a Discourse Theory of Law and Democracy* (1996).

11. For Böckenförde, this institutional, higher authority, depending upon the structure of the constitution, will be passed to a court, if "it envisages a constitutional court with the authority to decide the constitutionality and thus the validity of laws and constitutional changes" (Böckenförde, 2017b, p. 89, fn9).

12. In this Böckenfördian rejection is also contained, from the Derridean thematics of democracy, the whole difficulty posed by the question: "Can one/must one speak democratically of democracy?" (Derrida, 2005, p. 71).

13. Böckenförde draws upon the conception of the social *Rechtstaat* in the work of Lorenz von Stein (1815–1890), and his interpretation of Stein and the further characterization of the social *Rechtstaat* are developed in Böckenförde, 1991a and 1991b. The further contrast with Schmitt arises from the comparison with Schmitt, 1995.

14. In the later work of the 1990s (Böckenförde, 2017e), the fundamental external challenges of globalization and Europeanization together with an accelerated individualization are considered to confront the preceding conception of the ethical state. The purview of the response expands, reaffirming the pertinence of statehood and democracy, while acknowledging the heightened difficulty of preserving the configuration of the ethical state (pp. 336ff.).

15. The attempt to acknowledge and respond to the ramifications of the ecological question is present in the work of Tine Stein, one of the editors of the *Selected Writings* of Böckenförde; see, for example, Stein, 2011 and 1998. However, it is evident that these positions represent a significant divergence from the Böckenfördian position.

16. Böckenförde maintains and reiterates the same position, twenty-nine years later, in Böckenförde 2019e, pp. 229–230. For alternative approaches that provide a more complex presentation of the Rousseauian *religion civile*, see Ber-

nardi, 2009, and Bachofen, 2011; and in regard to the equally complex relationship of Rousseau to the Bible and Christianity, see Di Rosa, 2016.

17. Rousseau considers that "the dogmas of the civil Religion ought to be simple, few in number, stated with precision, without explanations or commentary. The existence of the powerful, intelligent, beneficent, prescient, and provident Deity, the life to, the happiness of the just, the punishment of the wicked, the sanctity of the social Contract and the Laws; these are the positive dogmas. As for the negative dogmas, I restrict them to a single one; namely, intolerance: it is a feature of the cult we have rejected" (Rousseau, 1997, pp. 150–151).

18. The notion of an American civil religion, introduced and developed in the work of Robert Bellah, remains unacknowledged by, and beyond the purview of, the Böckenfördian critique as it is elaborated, in contrast to the Rousseauian notion, within a detached, sociological reflection upon the character and difficulties of this civil religion within a complex, modern society (see, for example, Bellah et al., 2007). The more fundamental divergence in approach and scope between Böckenförde and Bellah becomes evident from Bellah's final work (2011).

19. The approach to Rousseau marks a further reinterpretation of Schmitt that effectively considers only the approach to Rousseau in Schmitt's *Verfassungslehre* (Schmitt, 2008b) and excludes the other aspects of the Schmittian characterization of Rousseau as a distinctive and constitutively antidemocratic figure. See Schmitt, 2013, pp. 96–111, and Schmitt, 2018d.

20. Böckenförde considers that these "anchoring points" involve a wide spectrum of provision by the state: "the way in which laws about fundamental life orders and life relationships, such as marriage, family, and work, but also tenant law and land law, are shaped; the way in which planning and formative activity of the administration is carried out, for example in the area of old-age provision, family-suitable housing, and the care of guest workers; how state support is directed and how the public sector—according to its justifying idea, the institution in which people make the care for the concerns of the community in general their personal commitment—is organized and represents itself" (2017b, p. 104).

21. From a historical perspective, the Schmittian position arises within the context of the creation of the Weimar Republic and the suppression of the Berlin and Munich soviets (Schmitt, 2013, 2005), and then concerns the juridical definition and delineation of a state of exception or emergency, under Article 48 of the Weimar Constitution (Schmitt, 2013, pp. 180–226; 2008a). In contrast, the Böckenfördian position develops within the context of a significant separation between the creation of the constitution of the Federal Republic and the subsequent emergence of extraparliamentary challenge.

22. The further development of this conceptualization of the state of exception and its application to the constitution of the Federal Republic is undertaken in Böckenförde, 1981a, 1981b.

23. This Böckenfördian "integration" of the state of emergency into the constitutional and legal order of the ethical state is in contrast to the approach of Agamben (1998, 2005a) for whom the Böckenfördian "integration" would remain a deficient response.

24. Thus, the Böckenfördian position is the rejection of both the Schmittian attribution of the exception as sovereignty—the pathos and personification of decision—and the juridical unintelligibility of the state of exception within a conventional constitutional order. In this double rejection, the state of exception is to be juridically defined, it exists *within* the conventional constitutional order, and, in this, it asserts the juridical primacy of the conventional constitutional order over the state of exception.

25. "For he that hath strength enough to protect all, wants not sufficiency to oppress all."

26. The work to which Schmitt refers is Kierkegaard's *Repetition* (1843). On Schmitt's relationship to Kierkegaard, see Conrad, 2009, and Löschenkohl, 2019.

27. Within the theological framework, Böckenförde insists upon the coexistence of this fundamental deficiency with "God's obliging and justifying grace" (Böckenförde, 2019g, p. 269).

Chapter 7. Political Theology and Contemporary Challenges to Democratic Constitutionalism

1. We are not, however, equating this with political theology; while there are certain parallels, there are also important conceptual differences. See Gontier, 2013.

2. QAnon followers believed that Joe Biden's inauguration would be the occasion when the ringleaders of the Democrat-led pedophile network would be arrested, and Trump would be sworn in as their true president.

3. Our focus here is on right-wing nationalist populism as opposed to left populism. While left and right populism share a common narrative—"the people" versus "the elites"—they are in other respects very different. Where both forms of populism are critical of economic globalization and assert national interests against those of liberal global elites, left-wing populism does so in the name of a redistributionist economic agenda, whereas right-wing populism does so in the name of an exclusionary and homogeneous national community, narrowly defined in cultural and ethnic terms. The figure of the people, common to both forms of populism, can take on different meanings and can be constructed in different ways, in terms that are more or less inclusive, more or less hospitable to pluralism.

4. Populism, if indeed it has any ideology to speak of, may be described as a "thin-centered" ideology based around the narrative of "the people" versus "the elites" (see Mudde & Kaltwasser, 2017), or as Jan-Werner Müller (2016) describes it, a "moralistic imagination of politics," one that pits the "morally pure," homo-

geneous people against the "morally corrupt" and decadent elites and minorities, who have betrayed national interests to the globalist and multicultural agenda.

5. See for instance the Identitarian movement, a European-wide far-right network that sees itself as defending European civilization against Islam and immigration Muslim countries. Furthermore, the Norwegian right-wing terrorist and mass killer Anders Behring-Breivik was influenced by the "Eurabia" conspiracy theory that talked about the Islamic takeover of Europe.

6. As Donald Trump Jr. said about his father at a political rally, "This is not the Republican Party, this is Donald Trump's Republican Party."

7. This could be seen particularly in their expressions of indifference to the virus, deliberately downplaying its dangers: Bolsonaro compared it to a "little flu" from which he would be protected by his natural athletic constitution; Trump said when he contracted the virus that it was a blessing from God, a way of testing his strength and fortitude.

8. This is similar to what Derrida would refer to as the "autoimmune" impulse of democracy, whereby democratic regimes, in their openness, give rise to antidemocratic and authoritarian political forces and movements who use democratic mechanisms—elections, free press, and so forth—to gain influence, thereby destroying democracy from within (see Derrida, 2005).

9. Here he invokes Rousseau's concept of the general will (*volonté générale*). But there is a clear conceptual confusion here. While Rousseau believed that his democracy best functioned in homogeneous societies, at the same time the general will presupposes difference and individuality. People have different interests and perspectives, but, for Rousseau, these differences ideally cancel one another out as one thinks about the common interest when making political decisions. It is also the case that in Rousseau's republic, laws are made to apply equally to everyone and must not discriminate against some to the advantage of others. Furthermore, the civil religion that Rousseau proposes as part of his political theology forbids intolerance. The Rousseauian principle of democratic equality has little in common with the narrow, exclusionary, populist model proposed by Schmitt.

10. Jordan E. Miller (2019, p. 13) argues that theology *is* resistance: "After the transitional phase of modernity, in our time, resistance is the theological enacted politically. It is the expression of the theological—of desire for an alternate, less disappointing world—within the political sphere. Theology is the impulse toward resistance brought into the political ordering of life. Resistance takes up the meaning-making function of religion within the sphere of the political. Resistance is the political act through which the desire for a world that does not disappoint becomes expressed. Resistance is the activity through which theology animates the political. Theology itself is thus insurrectionary."

11. Liberation theology refers to a broader tradition of theology, associated also with figures like Dorothee Sölle, as well as the Marxist-inspired theology of Gustavo Gutiérrez and Leonardo Boff that emerged in the Latin American context.

12. There were of course some notable exceptions, most famously the Protestant theologian Dietrich Bonhoeffer who was involved in anti-Nazi resistance and who was executed in a concentration camp.

13. Precisely the same objection was raised by Erik Peterson in his famous critique of Schmitt (see 2011).

14. See also Metz's notion of "anamnestic reason," which seeks to keep alive the remembrance of past suffering and opposes the idea that what is past is past and therefore no longer represents an ethical challenge to the present (see 1992).

15. A similar point about the threat of biotechnology and genetic manipulation is made by Moltmann (see 1999, p. 100).

16. Judith Butler has proposed a similar notion of human suffering and vulnerability as the basis for a new ethics of solidarity and resistance to violence: "When the world fails us, when we ourselves become worldless in the social sense, the body suffers and shows its precarity; that mode of demonstrating precarity is itself, or carries with it, a political demand and even an expression of outrage. To be a body differentially exposed to harm or to death is precisely to exhibit a form of precarity, but also to suffer a form of inequality that is unjust. So, the situation of many populations who are increasingly subject to unlivable precarity raises for us the question of global obligations. If we ask why any of us should care about those who suffer at a distance from us, the answer is not to be found in paternalistic justifications, but in the fact that we inhabit the world together in relations of interdependency. Our fates are, as it were, given over to one another" (2020, p. 42).

17. In his "Critique of Violence" Benjamin talks about the way that the "law-preserving" (and "lawmaking") violence of the police is not exceptional at all but utterly normal and mundane. It is an "all-pervasive, ghostly presence in the life of civilized states" (1986, p. 287).

18. In his polemics against the Italian statesman Giuseppe Mazzini, Bakunin accuses him essentially of being a "political theologian" in illegitimately mixing together Christianity and politics (see Bakunin, 1871).

Chapter 8. *Katechon* and the Problem of Order

1. Catherine Keller has recently drawn on the contemporary parallels between the book of Revelations and the contemporary climate Apocalypse (see 2021).

2. A reference to the title of Isabelle Stengers's book *In Catastrophic Times: Resisting the Coming Barbarism* (see 2015).

3. Bernard Stiegler associates the contemporary condition of stupidity with the stupefying effects of digital technologies on the individual, leading a reduction of the human condition: "And such torpor becomes, in our time, a

stupor—and our stupefaction in the face of the state of shock provoked by digital technology leads not only to functional stupidity, but to a catastrophic and disastrous . . . destruction of noesis itself by automatic proletarianization" (2020, p. 58).

4. Julia Hell (2009) argues that the *katechon* in Schmitt functions as a way of thinking about the duration of empires, their rise and fall, whether the Roman Empire, the German Christian empire, and even the Third Reich, thus forming part of the European imperial imaginary.

5. Or rather, as James Martel argues, it leads to a nonfetishistic, "anarchist" approach to law (see 2014).

6. Agamben says (2019, pp. 66–67): "Against the anarchy of power, I do not intend to invoke a return to a solid foundation in being: even if we ever possessed such a foundation, we have certainly lost it or have forgotten how to access it. I believe, however, that a clear comprehension of the profound anarchy of the societies in which we live is the only correct way to pose the problem of power and, at the same time, that of true anarchy. Anarchy is what becomes possible only when we grasp the anarchy of power. Construction and destruction here coincide without remainder."

7. Paul's radical universalism is also commented on by Alain Badiou, who interprets it as a transversal of differences and particularisms, through the experience of love and truth, into a new kind of spiritual communion (see 2003).

8. It is telling that Schmitt criticizes Erik Peterson's use of Augustine's two cities doctrine to reject the idea of political theology (see Schmitt, 2008b).

9. Martha Nussbaum has argued for the inclusion of nonhuman animals within a cosmopolitan ethics and politics: "Typically the [cosmopolitan] tradition grounds our duties in the worth and dignity of moral/rational agency. This is not even a very good approach for the human kind, since it excludes humans with severe cognitive disabilities, who are certainly our fellow citizens and ought to be viewed as equal in worth. And it certainly excludes non-human animals. . . . We need an international politics that is truly cosmopolitan, and such a politics, I argue, must be grounded in the worth and dignity of sentient bodies, not that of reason alone" (2019, pp. 16–17).

Coda

1. "Oral Update on Global Human Developments and the Activities of the UN Human Rights Office," June 13, 2022, https://www.ohchr.org/en/statements/2022/06/oral-update-global-human-rights-developments-and-activities-un-human-rights.

2. "Oral Update on Global Human Developments."

3. As exemplified by the increasingly restrictive approach to women's reproductive rights in the recent decision of the conservative-dominated US Supreme Court in *Dobbs v. Jackson Women's Health Organization* to overturn

the Supreme Court's decision in *Roe v. Wade* that upheld the constitutional right to abortion. There is also the further suggestion, in the concurring opinion of Justice Clarence Thomas, that the Supreme Court should eventually proceed to reconsider its previous decisions upholding the further constitutional rights to contraception access, same-sex relationships, and same-sex marriage, https://www.supremecourt.gov/opinions/21pdf/19-1392_6j37.pdf.

References

Agamben, G. (1998). *Homo sacer: Sovereign power and bare life* (D. Heller-Roazen, trans.). Stanford University Press.
Agamben, G. (2004). *The open: Man and animal* (K. Attell, trans.). Stanford University Press.
Agamben, G. (2018). *The church and the kingdom*. Seagull Books.
Agamben, G. (2005a). *State of exception*. (K. Attell, trans.). University of Chicago Press.
Agamben, G. (2005b). *The time that remains: A commentary on the Letter to the Romans*. Stanford University Press.
Agamben, G. (2014). "What is a destituent power (or potentiality)?" (S. Wakefield, trans.). *Environment and Planning D: Society and Space 32*, 65–74.
Agamben, G. (2019). *Creation and anarchy: The work of art and the religion of capitalism* (A. Kotsko, trans.). Stanford University Press.
Agamben, G. (2020a, March 17). Clarifications. *Coronavirus and philosophers*. Special Issue of *European Journal of Psychoanalysis*. Accessed April 12, 2021, from https://www.journal-psychoanalysis.eu/coronavirus-and-philosophers/.
Agamben, G. (2020b). *The kingdom and the garden* (A. Kotsko, trans.). Seagull Books.
Agamben, G. (2021). *Where are we now? The epidemic as politics*. Eris.
Agazzi, E. (2009). Religion und Geistlichkeit im Werk von Hugo Ball. In Porombka, S., & Vietta, S. (Eds.), *Ästhetik, Religion, Säkularisierung II: Die Klassische Moderne* (pp. 125–138). Wilhelm Fink.
Altman, W. H. F. (2007). Leo Strauss on "German nihilism": Learning the art of writing. *Journal of the History of Ideas, 68*(4), 587–612.
Aquinas, St. T. (2018). *Commentary on the letters of Saint Paul to the Philippians, Colossians, Thessalonians, Timothy, Titus, and Philemon*. Emmaus Academic.
Arato, A. (2013, Spring). Political theology and populism. *Social Research, 80*(1), 143–172.
Arato, A., & Cohen, J. L. (2017). "Civil society, populism and religion. *Constellations 24*, 283–295.

Artz-Grabner, P. (2010). How to deal with Onesimus? Paul's solution within the frame of ancient legal and documentary sources. In Tolmie, D. F. (Ed.), *Philemon in Perspective: Interpreting a Pauline letter* (pp. 113–142). De Gruyter.

Auroux, S. (1995). *La révolution technologique de la grammatisation*. Mardaga.

Azmy, B. (2002). Unshackling the Thirteenth Amendment: Modern slavery and a reconstructed civil rights agenda. *Fordham Law Review, 71*(3), 981–1061.

Bachofen, B. (2011). La religion civile selon Rousseau: une théologie politique négative. In Waterlot, G. (Ed.), *La théologie politique de Rousseau* (pp. 37–62). Presses Universitaires de Rennes.

Badiou, A. (2003). *Saint Paul: The foundation of universalism* (R. Brassier, trans.). Stanford University Press.

Bakunin, M. (1871). *The political theology of Mazzini and the international* (S. E. Holmes, trans.). Accessed March 13, 2021, from http://wiki.libertarianlabyrinth.org/index.php?title=The_Political_Theology_of_Mazzini_and_the_International.

Balakrishnan, G. (2000). *The enemy: An intellectual portrait of Carl Schmitt*. Verso.

Balibar, É. (1994). *Masses, classes, ideas: Studies on politics and philosophy after Marx*. Routledge.

Balibar, É. (2011). *Politics and the other scene*. Verso.

Balibar, É. (2014). *Equaliberty: Political essays*. Duke University Press.

Balibar, É. (2018). *Secularism and cosmopolitanism: Critical hypotheses on religion and politics*. Columbia University Press.

Balibar, É. (2020a). *On universals constructing and deconstructing community*. Fordham University Press.

Balibar, É. (2020b). *Secularism and cosmopolitanism: Critical hypotheses on religion and politics*. Columbia University Press.

Ball, H. (1984). Der Künstler Und Die Zeitkrankheit. In *Der Künstler und die Zeitkrankheit: ausgewählte Schriften* (pp. 102–149). Suhrkamp.

Ball, H. (2005). *Die Folgen der Reformation: Zur Kritik der deutschen Intelligenz*. Wallstein.

Ball, H. (2010). *Michael Bakunin: Ein Brevier*. Wallstein.

Ball, H. (2013). Carl Schmitt's political theology. *October, 146*(3), 66–92.

Barth, M., & Blanke, H. (2020). *The Letter to Philemon*. Wm. B. Eerdmans Publishing Company.

Basu, A. (2020). *Hindutva as political monotheism*. Duke University Press.

Bazzicalupo, L. (2016). Economy as logic of government. *Paragraph, 39*(1), 36–48.

Bazzicalupo, L. (2018). Ambiguity of the neoliberal government, including selective inclusion and re-territorialization. *Soft Power Journal/Revista euro-americana de teoria e historia de la politica y del derecho, 6*(1), 39–50.

Bazzicalupo, L. (2020). From Renaissance ferinity to the biopolitics of the animal-man: Animality as political battlefield in the Anthropocene. In Cimattti, F., & Salzani, C. (Eds.), *Animality in contemporary Italian philosophy* (pp. 263–280). Palgrave Macmillan.

Beavis, M. A. (2021). *The first Christian slave: Onesimus in context*. Cascade Books.
Biebricher, T. (2019). *The political theory of neoliberalism*. Stanford University Press.
Bellah, R. (2011). *Religion in human evolution: From the Paleolithic to the Axial Age*. Harvard University Press.
Bellah, R., Madsen, R., Sullivan, W. M., Swidler, A., & Tipton, S. M. (2007). *Habits of the heart: Individualism and commitment in American life, with a new preface* (3rd edition). University of California Press.
Benjamin, W. (1986). Critique of Violence. In Demetz, P. (Ed.), *Reflections: Essays, aphorisms, autobiographical writings* (E. Jephcott, trans.; pp. 277–300). Schocken Books.
Benjamin, W. (1998). *The origin of German tragic drama* (J. Osborne, trans.). Verso.
Benjamin, W. (2003). On the concept of history. In Eiland, H., & Jennings, M. W. (Eds.), *Selected writings* (vol. 4: 1938–1940; E. Jephcott, trans.; pp. 389–400). Harvard University Press.
Benvenuto, S. (2020, March 20). Forget about Agamben. *European Journal of Psychoanalysis*. https://www.journal-psychoanalysis.eu/coronavirus-and-philosophers/.
Berg, Anastasia. (2020, March 23). Agamben's coronavirus cluelessness. *Chronicle of Higher Education*. https://www.chronicle.com/article/giorgio-agambens-coronavirus-cluelessness/.
Bernadi, B. (2009). La religion civile, institution de tolérance? In Mostefai, O. (Ed.), *Rousseau and l'Infâme: Religion, toleration, and fanaticism in the Age of Enlightenment* (pp. 153–172). Brill.
Bertman, M. (2007). Hobbes on miracles (and God). *Hobbes Studies, 20*(1), 40–62.
Biebricher, T. (2019). *The political theory of neoliberalism*. Stanford University Press.
Bloch, E. (2009). *Atheism in Christianity: The religion of the exodus and the kingdom* (J. T. Swann, trans). Verso.
Blumenberg, H. (1985). *The legitimacy of the modern age* (R. M. Wallace, trans.). MIT Press.
Böckenförde, E.-W. (1981a). Ausnahmerecht und demokratischer Rechtstaat. In Hans-Jochen Vogel, H.-J., et al. (Eds.), *Die Freiheit des Anderen: Festschrift für Martin Hirsch* (pp. 259–272). Nomos.
Böckenförde, E.-W. (1981b). Rechtstaatliche politische Selbstverteidigung als Probleme. In Böckenförde, E.-W., et al. (Eds.), *Extremisten und öffentlicher Dienst: Rechtslage und Praxis des Zugangs zum und der Entlassung aus dem öffentlichen Dienst in Westeuropa, USA, Jugoslawien und der EG Studie der Friedrich-Erbert-Stiftung* (pp. 9–33). Nomos.
Böckenförde, E.-W. (1991a). In *State, society, liberty* (pp. 47–71). Berg Publishers.
Böckenförde, E.-W. (1991b). Lorenz von Stein as theorist of the movement of state and society towards the welfare state. In *State, society, liberty* (pp. 115–145). Berg Publishers.

Böckenförde, E.-W. (2017a). The concept of the political: A key to understanding Carl Schmitt's constitutional theory (1988). In *Constitutional and political theory: Selected writings* (pp. 69–85). Oxford University Press.

Böckenförde, E.-W. (2017b). The state as an ethical state (1978). In *Constitutional and political theory: Selected writings* (pp. 86–107). Oxford University Press.

Böckenförde, E.-W. (2017c). The repressed state of emergency: The exercise of state authority in extraordinary circumstances (1978). In *Constitutional and political theory: Selected writings* (pp. 108–132). Oxford University Press.

Böckenförde, E.-W. (2017d). The persecution of the German Jews as a civic betrayal (1997). In *Constitutional and political theory: Selected writing* (pp. 309–317). Oxford University Press.

Böckenförde, E.-W. (2017e). The future of political autonomy: Democracy and statehood in a time of globalization, Europeanization, and individualization (1998). In *Constitutional and political theory: Selected writings* (pp. 325–342). Oxford University Press.

Böckenförde, E.-W. (2019a). The ethos of modern democracy and the church (1957). In *Religion, law, and democracy: Selected writings* (pp. 61–76). Oxford University Press.

Böckenförde, E.-W. (2019b). German Catholicism in 1933: A critical examination (1961). In *Religion, law, and democracy: Selected writings* (pp. 77–104). Oxford University Press.

Böckenförde, E.-W. (2019c). Types of Christian conduct in the world during the Nazi regime (1965/2004). In *Religion, law, and democracy: Selected writings* (pp. 105–114). Oxford University Press.

Böckenförde, E.-W. (2019d). The rise of the state as a process of secularization (1967). In *Religion, law, and democracy: Selected writings* (pp. 152–167). Oxford University Press.

Böckenförde, E.-W. (2019e). The secularized state: Its character, justification, and problems in the twenty-first century (2007). In *Religion, law, and democracy: Selected writings* (pp/ 220–236). Oxford University Press.

Böckenförde, E.-W. (2019f). Political theory and political theology: Comments on their reciprocal relationship (1981). In *Religion, law, and democracy: Selected writings* (pp. 248–258). Oxford University Press.

Böckenförde, E.-W. (2019g). Reflections on a theology of modern secular law (1999). In *Religion, law, and democracy: Selected writings* (pp. 259–279). Oxford University Press.

Böckenförde, E.-W. (2020). Political theory and political theology: Comments on their reciprocal relationship. In *Religion, law, and democracy: Selected writings* (pp. 248–258). Oxford University Press.

Böckenförde, E.-W. (2020). *Religion, law, and democracy: Selected writings* (M. Kunckler & T. Stein, eds.). Oxford University Press.

Bohman, J. (2001). Cosmopolitan republicanism: Citizenship, freedom and global political authority. *The Monist, 84*(1), 3–21.
Bornkamm, G. (1990). *Paul.* Hodder and Stoughton.
Bouthors, J.-F., & Nancy, J.-L. (2019). *Démocratie! Hic et nunc.* Bourrin.
Breton, S. (2011). *A radical philosophy of Saint Paul.* Columbia University Press.
Brody, S. H. (2018). *Martin Buber's theopolitics.* Indiana University Press.
Brown, W. (2015). *Undoing the demos: Neoliberalism's stealth revolution.* Zone Books.
Brown, W. (2019). *In the ruins of neoliberalism: The rise of antidemocratic politics in the West.* Columbia University Press.
Brunkhorst, H. (2005). *Solidarity: From civic friendship to a global legal community* (J. Flynn, trans.). MIT Press.
Buber, M. (1958). *Paths in Utopia* (R. F. C. Hull, trans.). Beacon Press.
Burns, T. (2011). Leo Strauss and the origins of Hobbes's natural science. *The Review of Metaphysics, 64*(4), 823–855.
Butler, J. (2020). *The force of non-violence: An ethico-political bind.* Verso.
Cacciari, M. (2018). *The withholding power: An essay on political theology* (E. Pucci, trans.). Bloomsbury Academic.
Calarco, M. (2008). *Zoographies: The question of the animal from Heidegger to Derrida.* Columbia University Press.
Caldwell, P. (1994). National Socialism and constitutional law: Carl Schmitt, Otto Koellreutter, and the debate over the nature of the Nazi state, 1993–1937. *Cardozo Law Review, 16,* 339–427.
Callahan, A. D. (2007). The Letter to Philemon. In Segovia, F. F., & Sugirtharajah, R. S. (Eds.), *A postcolonial commentary on the NT writings* (pp. 329–337). T & T Clark.
Campanini, M., & Di Donato, M. (Eds.). (2021). *Islamic political theology.* Lexington Books.
Canovan, M. (1999). Trust the people! Populism and the two faces of democracy. *Political Studies, 47*(1), 2–16.
Carrino, A. (1999). Carl Schmitt and European juridical science. In Mouffe, C. (Ed.), *The challenge of Carl Schmitt* (pp. 180–194). Verso.
Cassidy, R. J. (2001). *Paul in chains: Roman imprisonment and the letters of St. Paul.* Crossroad.
Cimatti, F. (2017). Biopolitics or biolinguistics? On language and human nature (with some glosses on Agamben and the "sovereign power"). *Italian Journal of Philosophy of Language (RIFL), 11*(1), 168–182.
Cimatti, F. (2020a). *Unbecoming human: Philosophy of animality after Deleuze* (F. Gironi, trans.). Edinburgh University Press.
Cimatti, F. (2020b). Animality and immanence in Italian thought. In Cimatti, F., & Salzani, C. (Eds.), *Animality in contemporary Italian philosophy* (pp. 21–50). Palgrave Macmillan.

Cimatti, F. (2020c). Beyond the Anthropocene: Emergence, migrations, and perspectivism. In Achella, S., & Palatinus, D. L. (Eds.), *Perspectives in the Anthropocene: Beyond nature and culture?*(pp. 47–65). Itinerari.

Cimatti, F. (2021). *Il postanimale: La natura dopo l'Antropocene*. DeriveApprodi.

Cobb, J. B. (1975). *Christ in a pluralistic age*. Westminster Press.

Cobb, J. B., & Griffin, D. R. (1979). *Process theology: An introductory exposition*. Westminster Press.

Cohen, N. (2017, December 27). The libertarian logic of Peter Thiel. *Wired Magazine*. Accessed March 25, 2021, from https://www.wired.com/story/the-libertarian-logic-of-peter-thiel/.

Colliot-Thélène, C. (1999). Carl Schmitt versus Max Weber: Juridical rationality and economic rationality. In Mouffe, C. (Ed.), *The challenge of Carl Schmitt* (pp. 138–153). Verso.

Cone, J. (2019). *Black theology and Black power*. Orbis Books.

Conrad, B. (2009). Kierkegaard's moment: Carl Schmitt and his rhetorical concept of decision. In Palonen, K. (Ed.), *Redescriptions: Yearbook of political thought, conceptual history and feminism* (pp. 145–171).

Cristi, R. (1998). *Carl Schmitt and authoritarian liberalism: Strong state, free economy*. University of Wales Press.

Crutzen, P. J., & Stoemer, E. F. (2000). The Anthropocene. *Global Change Newsletter, 41*(May), 17–18. http://www.igbp.net/download/18.316f1832132347017758000 1401/1376383088452/NL41.pdf.

Cudworth, E., & Hobden, S. (2018). *The emancipatory project of posthumanism*. Routledge.

Cullinan, C. (2010). The legal case for the universal declaration of Mother Earth. Accessed February 25, 2021, from https://therightsofnature.org/wp-content/uploads/pdfs/Legal-Case-for-Universal-Declaration-Cormac-Cullinan.pdf.

Curley, E. H. (1996). Calvin and Hobbes, or, Hobbes as an Orthodox Christian. *Journal of the History of Philosophy, 34*(2), 257–271.

Dardot, P., & Laval, C. (2014). *The new way of the world: On neoliberal society*. Verso.

De Carolis, M. (2016). Il neoliberalismo, la crisi e la rifeudalizzone della società. *Politica & Società, 1*, 73–90.

De Carolis, M. (2017). The neoliberal (counter) revolution: Its parabola and decline. *Phainomena, 26*(102–103), 141–152.

Deleuze, G., & Guattari, F. (1987). *A thousand plateaus: Capitalism and schizophrenia* (B. Massumi, trans.). University of Minnesota Press.

Derrida, J. (1997). *The politics of friendship* (G. Collins, trans.). Verso.

Derrida, J. (2005). *Rogues: Two essays on reason* (P.-A. Brault & M. Naas, trans.). Stanford University Press.

Derrida, J. (2008). *The animal that therefore I am* (M.-L. Mallet, ed.). Fordham University Press.

Derrida, J. (2009). *The beast and the sovereign, volume one* (M. Lisse, M.-L. Mallet, & G. Michaud, eds.; G. Bennington, trans.). University of Chicago Press.

Diehl, J. (2012). Empire and epistles: Anti-Roman rhetoric in the New Testament epistles. *Currents in Biblical Research, 10*(2), 217–263.

Dietka, N. (2020). *Der Siedlinghauser Kreis: Carl Schmitt, Konrad Weiß, Josef Pieper und Friedrich Georg Jünger treffen auf Gleichgesinnte.* Duncker & Humblot.

Di Rosa, G. (2016). *Rousseau et la Bible: Pensée du religieux d'un Philosophe des Lumières.* Brill.

Doremus, A. (2004). La théologie politique de Carl Schmitt vue par Hugo Ball en 1924. *Les Études philosophiques, 68*(1), 57–63.

Dyzenhaus, D. (2000). *Legality and legitimacy: Carl Schmitt, Hans Kelsen and Herman Heller in Weimar.* Oxford University Press.

Ellul, J. (1991). *Anarchy and Christianity.* Wm. B. Eerdmans Publishing.

Esposito, R. (2008). *Bíos: Biopolitics and philosophy.* University of Minnesota Press.

Esposito, R. (2010). *Communitas: The Origin and Destiny of Community* (T. Campbell trans). Stanford University Press.

Esposito, R. (2011). *Immunitas.* Polity.

Esposito, R. (2015). *Persons and things: From the body's point of view.* Polity Press.

Esposito, R. (2021). *Instituting thought: Three paradigms of political ontology.* Polity Press.

Fischer-Lescano, A. (2020). Nature as a legal person: Proxy constellations in law. *Law and Literature, 32*(2), 237–262.

Foner, E. (2012). The Supreme Court and the history of reconstruction—and vice-versa. *Columbia Law Review, 112*(7), 1585–1606.

Foucault, M. (2008). *The birth of biopolitics: Lectures at the Collège de France 1978–1979* (M. Senellart, ed., G. Burchell, trans.). Palgrave Macmillan.

Fremaux, A. (2019). *After the Anthropocene: Green republicanism in a post-capitalist world.* Palgrave Macmillan.

Friedmann, R. (2019). Paradoxe Freiheit: Zum Verhältnis von Anarchismus und Katholizismus bei Hugo Ball. *Hugo-Ball-Almanach, 10*, 39–74.

Friedmann, R. (2020). Wider den irdischen Wirrwar und Plunder: Hugo Ball und die Katholische Kirche. *Hugo-Ball-Almanach, 11*, 82–106.

Galli, C. (2012). Hamlet: Representation and the concrete. In Hammill, G., & Lupton, J. R. (Eds.), *Political theology and early modernity* (pp. 60–83). Chicago University Press.

Galli, C. (2015). *Janus's gaze: Essays on Carl Schmitt* (A. Minervini, trans.). Duke University Press.

Galli, C. (2000). Carl Schmitt's anti-liberalism: Its theoretical and historical sources, and its philosophical and political meaning. *Cardozo Law Review,* 5–6, 1597–1617.

Gauchet, M. (1985). *Le Désenchantement du monde: Une histoire politique de la religion.* Gallimard.

Geva, D. (2021). Orbán's ordonationalism as post-neoliberal hegemony. *Theory, Culture and Society, 38*(6), 71–93.

Gosewinkel, D. (2017). Biographical interview with Ernst-Wolfgang Böckenförde (2011). In Böckenförde, E.-W., *Constitutional and political theory: Selected writings* (pp. 371–406). Oxford University Press.

Ghosh, P. (2008). *A historian reads Max Weber: Essays on the Protestant ethic.* Harrassowitz.

Ghosh, P. (2014). *Max Weber and "The Protestant Ethic": Twin histories.* Oxford University Press.

Ghosh, P. (2016). From the "spirit of capital" to the "spirit" of capitalism: German social and economic thought between Lujo Brentano, Karl Marx and Max Weber. In *Max Weber in context: Essays in the history of German ideas c. 1870–1930.* Harrassowitz, 17–82.

Ghosh, P. (2019). History and theory in Max Weber's "Protestant Ethic." *Global Intellectual History, 4*(2), 121–155.

Gontier, T. (2013). From "political theology" to "political religion": Eric Voegelin and Carl Schmitt. *Review of Politics, 75*(1), 25–43.

Graham, E. (2013). *Between a rock and a hard place: Public theology in a postsecular age.* SCM Press.

Gross, R. (2007). *Carl Schmitt and the Jews: The "Jewish question," the Holocaust, and German legal theory.* University of Wisconsin Press.

Gruber, M.-C. (2020). Why non-human rights. *Law and Literature, 32*(2), 263–270.

Guerra, G. (2020). *L'acrobata d'avanguardia: Hugo Ball tra dada e mistica.* Quodlibet.

Guilhot, N. (2020). Automatic Leviathan: Cybernetics and politics in Carl Schmitt's postwar writings. *History of the Human Sciences, 33*(1), 128–146.

Gurian, W. (under pseudonym P. Müller). (1934). Entscheidung und Ordnung zu den Schriften von Carl Schmitt. *Schweizerische Rundschau, 34*(71), 566–576.

Gurian, W. (1925, January 30). Die Folgen der Reformation. *Augsberger Postzeitung*, Sontags-Deilage Nr. 5.

Gurian, W. (1927, September 25). Hugo Ball. *Kölnische Volkszeitung* Nr. 705.

Gutiérrez, G. (1998). *A theology of liberation.* Orbis Books.

Habermas, J. (1989). The horrors of autonomy: Carl Schmitt in English. In Nicolsen, S. W. (Ed.), *The new conservatism: Cultural criticism and the historians' debate* (pp. 128–139). MIT Press.

Habermas, J. (1996). *Between facts and norms: Contributions to a discourse theory of law and democracy.* MIT Press.

Habermas, J. (2008). Notes on post-secular society. *New Perspectives Quarterly, 25*(4), 17–29.

Habermas, J. (2011). "The political": The rational meaning of a questionable inheritance of political theology. In Butler, J., Habermas, J., Taylor, C., & West, C., *The power of religion in the public sphere* (E. Mendieta & J. Van Antwerpen, eds.; pp. 15–33). Columbia University Press.

Habermas, J., & Ratzinger, J. (2006). *The dialectics of secularization: On reason and religion* (B. McNeil, C.R.V., F. Schuller, ed.). Ignatius Press.

Haraway, D. J. (2016). *Staying with the trouble: Making kin in the Chthulucene*. Duke University Press.

Hayek, F. A. (2019). *Law, legislation and liberty: A new statement of the liberal principles of justice and political economy*. Routledge.

Head, M. (2016). *Emergency powers in theory and practice: The long shadow of Carl Schmitt*. Ashgate.

Heinrichs, S. (Ed.) (2019). *Unsettling the world: Biblical experiments in decolonization*. Orbis Books.

Hell, J. (2009). Katechon: Carl Schmitt's imperial theology and the ruins of the future. *Germanic Review: Literature, Culture, Theory, 84*(4), 283–326.

Heller, H. (2015, May). Authoritarian liberalism? (1933). *European Law Journal, 21*(3), 295–301.

Hengel, M. (1997). *Paul between Damascus and Antioch: The unknown years*. SCM Press.

Hengel, M. (2014). *The pre-Christian Paul*. SCM Press.

Hennis, W. (1998). The media as a cultural problem: Max Weber's sociology of the press. *History of the Human Sciences, 11*(2), 107–110.

Hesse, M. (2016, May 31). Peter Sloterdijk: Der Philosoph spricht über sozial demokratie und migration. *Berliner Zeitung*. https://www.berliner-zeitung.de/kultur/peter-sloterdijk-der-philosoph-spricht-ueber-sozialdemokratie-und-migration.24148132.

Hohendahl, P. U. (2018). *Perilous futures: On Carl Schmitt's late political writings*. Cornell University Press.

Honneth, A. (2009, September 24). Fataler Tiefsinn aus Karlsruhe: Zum neuesten Schrifttum des Peter Sloterdijk. *Die Zeit*. https://www.zeit.de/2009/40/Sloterdijk-Blasen.

Hooker, W. (2009). *Carl Schmitt's international thought: Order and orientation*. Cambridge University Press. http://www.consecutio.org/wp-content/uploads/2021/11/CR9.

Hübinger, G. (2009). Einleitung. In Weber, M., *Allgemeine Staatslehre und Politik (Staatssoziologie)* (pp. 1–39). J. C. B. Mohr.

Ingram, J. D. (2013). *Radical cosmopolitics: The ethics and politics of democratic universalism*. Columbia University Press.

IPCC. (2021). Sixth assessment report. Accessed August 23, 2021, from https://www.ipcc.ch/report/ar6/wg1/.

Jacobson, E. (2003). *Metaphysics of the profane: The political theology of Walter Benjamin and Gershom Scholem*. Columbia University Press.

Johnson, M. V. (2012). Onesimus speaks: Diagnosing the Hys/Terror of the Text. In Johnson, M. V., Noel, J. A., & Williams, D. K. (Eds.), *Onesimus our brother: Reading religion, race and culture in Philemon* (pp. 91–100). Fortress Press.

Johnson, M. V., Noel, J. A., & Williams, D. K. (Eds.). (2012). *Onesimus our brother: Reading religion, race and culture in Philemon*. Fortress Press.

Jonas, H. (1984). *The imperative of responsibility: In search of an ethics for the technological age*. University of Chicago Press.

Jouanjan, O. (2018). Between Carl Schmitt, the Catholic Church, and Hermann Heller: On the foundations of democratic theory in the work of Ernst-Wolfgang Böckenförde. *Constellations, 25*(2), 184–195.

Jouanjan, O. (2019). Enjeux de la théorie hellérienne de l'État. *Jus Politicum, 23*. http://juspoliticum.com/article/Enjeux-de-la-theorie-hellerienne-de-l-Etat-1295.html.

Kalyvas, A. (2008). *Democracy and the politics of the extraordinary: Max Weber, Carl Schmitt and Hannah Arendt*. Cambridge University Press.

Kahn, P. W. (2011). *Political theology: Four new chapters on the concept of sovereignty*. Columbia University Press.

Keller, C. (2015). *Cloud of the impossible: Negative theology and planetary entanglement*. Columbia University Press.

Keller, C. (2018a). Lines in the innumerable: Enmity, exceptionalism and entanglement. *Literature and Theology, 32*(2), 131–141.

Keller, C. (2018b). *Political theology of the earth: Our planetary emergency and the struggle for a new public*. Columbia University Press.

Keller, C. (2021). *Facing Apocalypse: Climate, democracy and other last chances*. Orbis Books.

Kelly, D. (2016). Carl Schmitt's political theory of dictatorship. In Meierhenrich, J., & Simons, O. (Eds.), *The Oxford Handbook of Carl Schmitt* (pp. 217–244). Oxford University Press.

Kidwell, J. H. (2019). Re-enchanting Political Theology. *Religions, 10*(550), 1–14.

Künkler, M., & Tine, S. (2018). Carl Schmitt in Ernst-Wolfgang Böckenförde's work: Carrying Weimar constitutional theory into the Bonn Republic. *Constellations, 25*(2), 225–241.

Lacoue-Labarthe, P., & Nancy, J.-L. (1997). *Retreating the political*. Routledge.

Landauer, G. (1976). Anarchismus in Deutschland. In Link-Salinger, R. (Ed.), *Gustav Landauer: Erkenntnis und Befrieung: Ausgewälte Reden und Aufsätze* (pp. 7–17). Suhrkamp.

Landauer, G. (2010). *Revolution and other writings: A political reader* (G. Kuhn, ed. & trans.). PM Press.

Landauer, G. (2011). Anarchy in Germany. Accessed on February 9, 2011, from libcom. org, https://theanarchistlibrary.org/library/gustav-landauer-anarchism-in-germany.

Latour, B. (2017). *Facing Gaia: Eight lectures on the new climatic regime* (C. Porter, trans.). Polity Press.

Latour, B. (2021). How to remain human in the wrong space? A comment on a dialogue by Carl Schmitt. *Critical Inquiry 47*, 699–718.

Latour, B., & Lenton, T. M. (2019). Extending the domain of freedom, or why Gaia is so hard to understand. *Critical Inquiry 45*, 659–680.

Llanque, M. (2019). Hermann Heller and the republicanism of the left in the Weimar Republic. *Jus Politicum, 23*. http://juspoliticum.com/article/Hermann-Heller-and-the-Republicanism-of-the-Left-in-the-Weimar-Republic-1317.html.

Loick, D. (2019). *A critique of sovereignty* (A. DeMarco, trans.). Rowman & Littlefield International.

Lorenzini, D. (2021). *Jacques Maritain and human rights: Totalitarianism, anti-Semitism and democracy (1936–1951)*. Saint Augustine's Press.

Löschenkohl, B. (2019). Occasional decisiveness: Exception, decision and resistance in Kierkegaard and Schmitt. *European Journal of Political Theory, 18*(1), 89–107.

Lovelock, J. (2000). *Gaia: A new look at life on earth*. Oxford University Press.

Lovelock, J. (2009). *The vanishing face of Gaia: A final warning*. Basic Books.

Löwith, K. (1949). *Meaning in history*. University of Chicago Press.

Löwy, M. (2017). *Redemption and utopia in Jewish libertarian thought in Central Europe: A study in elective affinity*. Verso.

Marder, M. (2010). *Groundless existence: The political ontology of Carl Schmitt*. Continuum.

Maritain, J. (1944). *The rights of man and natural law*. The Centenary Press.

Martel, J. R. (2012). *Divine violence: Walter Benjamin and the eschatology of sovereignty*. Routledge.

Martel, J. R. (2014). *The one and only law: Walter Benjamin and the Second Commandment*. University of Michigan Press.

Martinich, A. P. (2015). Leo Strauss's Olympian interpretation: Right, self-preservation, and law in the political philosophy of Hobbes. In Schröder, W. (Ed.), *Reading between the lines: Leo Strauss and the history of early modern philosophy* (pp. 77–97). Walter de Gruyter.

Massumi, B. (2014). *What animals teach us about politics*. Duke University Press.

McCormick, J. P. (1999). *Carl Schmitt's critique of liberalism: Against politics as technology*. Cambridge University Press.

McCormick, J. P. (2011). Post-Enlightenment sources of political authority: Biblical atheism, political theology and the Schmitt–Strauss exchange. *History of European Ideas, 37*(2), 175–180.

Mehring, R. (2014). *Carl Schmitt: A Biography*. Polity Press.

Meier, H. (1998). *The lesson of Carl Schmitt: Four chapters on the distinction between political theology and political philosophy* (M. Brainard, trans.). University of Chicago Press.

Meier, H. (2006a). *Carl Schmitt and Leo Strauss: The hidden dialogue*. Chicago University Press.

Meier, H. (2006b). *Leo Strauss and the theologico-political problem* (M. Brainard, trans.). Cambridge University Press.

Meier, H. (2011). Introduction: The history of Strauss's Hobbes studies in the 1930s. In Strauss, L., *Hobbes's critique of religion and related writings* (pp. 1–20). University of Chicago Press.

Meier, H. (2017). *Political philosophy and the challenge of revealed religion*. University of Chicago Press.

Meierhenrich, J., & Simons, O. (Eds.). (2017). *The Oxford handbook of Carl Schmitt*. Oxford University Press.

Menke, C. (2020). Why rights? A commentary on Malte-Christian Gruber. *Law and Literature, 32*(2), 271–276.

Metz, J. B. (1969). *Theology of the world* (W. Glen-Doepel, trans.). Herder & Herder.

Metz, J. B. (1981). *The emergent church: The future of Christianity in a post-bourgeois world* (P. Mann, trans.). Crossroads Publishing Company.

Metz, J. B. (1992). Anamnestic reason: A theologian's remarks on the crisis in the *Geisteswissenschaften*. In Honneth, A., McCarthy, T., Offe, C., & Wellmer, A. (Eds.), *Cultural-political interventions in the unfinished project of enlightenment* (pp. 189–194). MIT Press.

Metz, J. B. (1999). In the pluralism of religious and cultural worlds: Notes toward a theological and political paradigm (J. Downey & H. Wiggers, trans.). *Crosscurrents 49*(2), 227–236.

Milanese, A. (2020). *Walter Lippmann, d'un néolibéralisme à l'autre: Changement social et leadership libéral*. Classiques Garnier.

Milanese, A. (2020/21). Les sources lippmanniennes du problème néolibéral de la démocratie: la démocratie "reconstruite" de 34. *Consecutio Rerum, 9*(1), 47–68.

Miller, J. E. (2019). *Resisting hope: Secular political theology and social movements*. Palgrave Macmillan.

Mirowski, P., and Plehwe, D. (Eds.). (2009). *The road from Mont Pèlerin: The making of the neoliberal thought collective*. Harvard University Press.

Moltmann, J. (1971). Political theology. *Theology Today, 28*(1), 6–23.

Moltmann, J. (1985). *God in creation: An ecological doctrine of creation: The Gifford lectures, 1984–1985*. SCM Press.

Moltmann, J. (1999). *God for a secular society: The public relevance of theology* (M. Kohl, trans.). SCM Press.

Monod, J.-C. (2012). Hostility, politics, brotherhood: Abel and Cain as seen by Carl Schmitt and Jacques Derrida. In Radunović, D., & Bahun, S. (Eds.), *Language, ideology, and the human: New interventions* (pp. 95–112). Routledge.

Moore, Jason, W. (Ed.). (2016). *Anthropocene or capitalocene? Nature, history and the crisis of capitalism*. PM Press.

Mouffe, C. (1999). Deliberative democracy or agonistic pluralism? *Social Research, 66*(3), 745–758.

Mouffe, C. (2000). *The democratic paradox*. Verso.

Mouffe, C. (2013). *Agonistics: Thinking the world politically*. Verso.

Mouffe, C. (2018). *For a left populism*. Verso.
Mudde, C., & Kaltwasser, C. R. (2017). *Populism: A very short introduction*. Oxford University Press.
Mühlmann, H. (2003). *The nature of cultures: A blueprint for a theory of culture genetics*. Springer.
Mühlmann, H. (2005). *MSC maximal stress cooperation: The driving force of cultures*. Springer.
Müller, J.-W. (2016). *What Is Populism?* University of Pennsylvania Press.
Münkler, H. (2016, February 11). Wie ahnungslos kluge Leute doch sein können. *Die Zeit*.
Nancy, J.-L. (2007). *The creation of the world or globalization* (F. Raffoul & D. Pettigrew, trans.). State University of New York Press.
Nancy, J.-L. (2010). *The truth of democracy*. Fordham University Press.
Nancy, J.-L. (2013). Fraternity. *Angelaki, 18*(3), 119–123.
Nancy, J.-L. (2020, February 27). The viral exception. *On Pandemics*: Special Issue of *European Journal of Psychoanalysis*. Accessed on April 12, 2021, from https://www.journal-psychoanalysis.eu/on-pandemics-nancy-esposito-nancy/.
National Intelligence Council. (2021, March). *Global trends: A more contested world*.
Northcott, Michael S. (2013). *A political theology of climate change*. William B. Eerdmans Publishing Company.
Nussbaum, M. C. (2019). *The cosmopolitan tradition: A noble but flawed idea*. The Belknap Press of Harvard University Press.
Odysseos, L., and Petito, F. (Eds.) (2007). *The international political thought of Carl Schmitt: Terror, liberal war and the crisis of the global order*. Routledge.
Ojakangas, M. (2003). Carl Schmitt's real enemy: The citizen of the nonexclusive democratic community? *European Legacy, 8*(4), 411–424.
Pacci, A. (1988). Hobbes and biblical philology in the service of the state. *Topoi, 7*(3), 231–239.
Paganini, G. (2015). Art of writing or art of rewriting? Reading Hobbes's *De motu* against the background of Strauss' interpretation. In Schröder, W. (Ed.), *Reading between the lines: Leo Strauss and the history of early modern philosophy* (pp. 99–128). Walter de Gruyter.
Pasquino, P. (2016). Remarks on Rousseau's dictatorship: Between Machiavelli and Carl Schmitt. In Deneys-Tunney, A., & Zarka, E. C. (Eds.), *Rousseau between nature and culture: Philosophy, literature, and politics* (pp. 101–110) *Storia del pensiero politico* (2013), no. 1, 145–154.
Peterson, E. (2011). *Theological tractates* (M. J. Hollerich, ed. & trans.). Stanford University Press.
Piketty, T. (2014). *Capital in the twenty-first century* (A. Goldhammer, trans.). Harvard University Press.
Plehwe, D., Slobodian, Q., and Mirowski, P. (Eds.). (2020). *Nine lives of neoliberalism*. Verso.

Polke, C. (2018). Böckenförde's Dictum and the problem of "value fundamentalism." *Oxford Journal of Law and Religion, 7*(1), 109–123.

Pulcini, E. (2013). *Care of the world: Fear, responsibility and justice in the global age*. Springer.

Punt, J. (2012). Postcolonial approaches: Negotiating empires, then and now. In Marchal, J. A. (Ed.), *Studying Paul's letters: Contemporary perspectives and methods* (pp. 191–208). Minneapolis: Fortress Press.

Quélennec, B. 2018. *Retour dans la caverne: philosophie, politique et religion chez le jeune Leo Strauss*. Hermann.

Rasch, W. (2019). *Carl Schmitt: State and society*. Rowman & Littlefield International.

Rashkover, R., & Kavka, M. (2013). *Judaism, liberalism and political theology*. Indiana University Press.

Reinecke, V., & Uhlaner, J. (1993). The problem of Leo Strauss: Religion, philosophy and politics. *Graduate Faculty Philosophy Journal, 16*(1), 189–208.

Robbins, J. W. (2011). *Radical democracy and political theology*. Columbia University Press.

Rogers, M. (2016). The development of Carl Schmitt's political thought during the First World War. *Modern Intellectual History, 13*(1), 123–149.

Rosenstock, B. (2010). *Philosophy and the Jewish question: Mendelssohn, Rosenzweig and beyond*. Fordham University Press.

Roth, U. (2014). Paul, Philemon, and Onesimus: A Christian design for mastery. *Zeitschrift für die Neutestamentliche Wissenschaft, 105*(1), 102–130.

Rothe, D. (2020). Governing the end times? Planet politics and the secular eschatology of the Anthropocene. *Millennium: Journal of International Studies, 48*(2), 143–164.

Rousseau, J.-J. (1997). *The social contract and other later political writings*. Cambridge University Press.

Runciman, D. (2020, March 27). Coronavirus has not suspended politics—it has revealed the nature of power. *The Guardian*. Accessed February 20, 2022, from https://www.theguardian.com/commentisfree/2020/mar/27/coronavirus-politics-lockdown-hobbes.

Runciman, D. (2021). *Confronting Leviathan: A history of ideas*. Profile Books.

Scheuerman, W. E. (1996). Legal indeterminacy and the origins of Nazi legal thought: The case of Carl Schmitt. *History of Political Thought, 17*(4), 571–590.

Scheuerman, W. E. (2020). *The end of law: Carl Schmitt in the twenty-first century* (2nd edition). Rowman & Littlefield International.

Schmiedel, U., & Ralston, J. (Eds.) (2021). *The spirit of populism: Political theologies in polarized times*. Brill Academic.

Schmitt, C. (1986). *Political romanticism* (G. Oakes, trans.). MIT Press.

Schmitt, C. (1990). The plight of European jurisprudence. *Telos, 195*, 35–70.

Schmitt, C. (1995). Die Stellung Lorenz von Steins in der Geschichte des 19. Jahrhunderts (1940). In *Staat, Großraum, Nomos: Arbeiten aus den Jahren 1916–1969* (pp. 156–165). Duncker & Humblot.
Schmitt, C. (1996a). *The Leviathan in the state theory of Thomas Hobbes: The meaning and failure of a political symbol* (G. Schwab & E. Hilfstein, trans.). Greenwood Press.
Schmitt, C. (1996b). *The concept of the political*. University of Chicago Press.
Schmitt, C. (1996c). The visibility of the church: A scholastic consideration. In *Roman Catholicism and political form* (pp. 45–60). Greenwood Press.
Schmitt, C. (1996d). *Roman Catholicism and political form* (G. L. Ulmen, trans.). Greenwood Press.
Schmitt, C. (1988). *The crisis of parliamentary democracy* (E. Kennedy, trans.). MIT Press.
Schmitt, C. (2001). The Way to the Total State. In *Four Articles 1931–1938*. Plutarch Press.
Schmitt, C. (2003). Machtpositionen des modernen Staates. In *Verfassungsrechtliche Aufsätze aus den Jahren 1924–1954: Materialien zu einer Verfassungslehre* (pp. 367–374). Duncker & Humblot.
Schmitt, C. (2005). *Political theology: Four chapters on the concept of sovereignty* (G. Schwab, trans.). University of Chicago Press.
Schmitt, C. (2006). *The nomos of the earth in the international law of the jus publicum Europaeum* (G. L. Ulmen, trans). Telos Press.
Schmitt, C. (2007a). The age of neutralizations and depoliticizations (M. Konzen & J. P. McCormick, trans.). In *The concept of the political* (G. Schwab, trans.; pp. 80–96). University of Chicago Press.
Schmitt, C. (2007b). *The concept of the political* (G. Schwab, trans.). University of Chicago Press.
Schmitt, C. (2008a). *The Leviathan in the state theory of Thomas Hobbes: Meaning and failure of a political symbol*. University of Chicago Press.
Schmitt, C. (2008b). *Constitutional theory* (J. Seitzer, trans.). Duke University Press.
Schmitt, C. (2008c). *Political theology II: The myth of the closure of any political theology* (M. Hoelzl & G. Ward, trans.). Polity.
Schmitt, C. (2009). *Theodor Däublers "Nordlicht" Drei Studien über die Elemente, den Geist und die Aktualität des Werkes* (3rd edition). Duncker & Humblot.
Schmitt, C. (2010a). *Political romanticism*. Transaction Publishers.
Schmitt, C. (2010b). *Political theology II: The myth of the closure of any political theology*. Polity Press.
Schmitt, C. (2013). *Dictatorship: From the origin of the modern concept of sovereignty to proletarian class struggle* (1921). Polity Press.
Schmitt, C. (2014). *Positionen und Begriffe, im Kampf mit Weimar—Genf—Versailles 1923–1939*. Dunkler & Humblot.

Schmitt, C. (2015). *Land and sea: A world-historical meditation*. Telos Press.
Schmitt, C. (2017a). *Ex captivitate salus: Experiences, 1945–47* (A. Kalyvas & F. Finchelstein, eds., M. Hannah, trans.). Polity Press.
Schmitt, C. (2017b). *Über Schuld und Schuldarten: Eine terminologische Untersuchung: Mit einem Anhang weiterer strafrechtlicher und früher rechtsphilosophischer Beiträge* (2nd edition). Duncker & Humblot.
Schmitt, C. (2018a). On the TV democracy: The aggressiveness of progress. In *The tyranny of values and other texts* (pp. 200–205). Telos Press.
Schmitt, C. (2018b). The historical structure of the contemporary world opposition: Notes on Ernst Jünger's text: The Gordian Knot. In *The tyranny of values and other texts* (pp. 100–135). Telos Press.
Schmitt, C. (2018c). The tyranny of values: Reflections of a jurist on value philosophy. In *The tyranny of values and other texts* (pp. 26–41). Telos Press.
Schmitt, C. (2018d). To the true Johann Jakob Rousseau. In *The tyranny of values and other texts* (pp. 167–174). Telos Press.
Schmitt, C. (2021a). *Gesammelte Schriften 1933–1936: Mit ergänzenden Beiträgen aus der Zeit des Zweiten Weltkriegs*. Duncker & Humblot.
Schmitt, C. (2021b). *Staat, Großraum, Nomos: Arbeiten aus den Jahren 1916–1969*. Duncker & Humblot.
Schröder, W. (Ed.). (2015). *Reading between the lines: Leo Strauss and the history of early modern philosophy*. Walter de Gruyter.
Singh, A. (2012). The political theology of Navayana Buddhism. In Losonczi, P., Luoma-Aho, M., & Singh, A. (Eds.), *The future of political theology: Religious and theological perspectives* (pp. 159–172). Routledge.
Skrimshire, S. D. (2019a). Extinction rebellion and the new visibility of religious protest. Open Democracy. https://www.opendemocracy.net/en/transformation/extinction-rebellion-and-new-visibility-religious-protest/.
Skrimshire, S. D. (2019b). Activism for end times: Millenarian belief in an age of climate emergency. *Political Theology, 20*(6), 518–536.
Slobodian, Q. (2021). The backlash against neoliberal globalization from above: Elite origins of the crisis of the new constitutionalism. *Theory, Culture and Society, 38*(6), 51–69.
Sloterdijk, P. (1988). *Critique of cynical reason*. Verso.
Sloterdijk, P. (2009a). Rules for the human zoo: A response to the letter on humanism. *Environment and Planning D: Society and Space, 27*(1), 12–28.
Sloterdijk, P. (2009b). *God's zeal: The battle of the three monotheisms*. Polity.
Sloterdijk, P. (2009c, June 13). Die Revolution der gebenden Hand. *Frankfurter Allgemeine Zeitung*. https://www.faz.net/suche/?query=Die+Revolution+der+gebenden+Hand [https://petersloterdijk.net/2009/06/die-revolution-der-gebenden-hand/].
Sloterdijk, P. (2010, December 2). Warum ich doch recht habe. *Die Zeit*. https://www.zeit.de/2010/49/Sloterdijk-Reichensteuer.

Sloterdijk, P. (2011). *Bubbles, spheres volume I: Microspherology*. Semiotex(e).
Sloterdijk, P. (2013a). *Nietzsche apostle*. Semiotex(e).
Sloterdijk, P. (2013b). *In the world interior of capital: For a philosophical theory of globalization*. Polity.
Sloterdijk, P. (2013c). *You must change your life*. Polity Press.
Sloterdijk, P. (2014). *Globes, spheres volume II: Macrospherology*. Semiotex(e).
Sloterdijk, P. (2015). *In the shadow of Mount Sinai*. Polity.
Sloterdijk, P. (2016a). Rules for the human park: A response to the letter on humanism. In *Not saved: Essays after Heidegger* (pp. 193–216). Polity.
Sloterdijk, P. (2016b). *Not saved: Essays after Heidegger*. Polity.
Sloterdijk, P. (2016c). *Foams, spheres volume III: Plural spherology*. Semiotext(e).
Sloterdijk, P. (2016d, January 28). Es gibt keine moralische Pflicht zur Selbstzerstörung. *Cicero*. https:/ https://www.cicero.de/innenpolitik/peter-sloterdijk-ueber-merkel-und-die-fluechtlingskrise-es-gibt-keine-moralische.
Sloterdijk, P. (2016e, March 3). Primitive reflexe. *Die Zeit*. https://www.zeit.de/2016/11/fluechtlingsdebatte-willkommenskultur-peter-slotedijk/seite-3.
Sloterdijk, P. (2017, January 13). Der weite Weg zur Weltgesellschaft. *Handelsblatt Hamburg*. http://www.handelsblatt.com/my/politik/international/essay-von-peter-sloterdijk-der-weite-weg-zur-weltgesellschaft/19245112.html.
Sloterdijk, P. (2020a). *Infinite mobilization: Towards a critique of political kinetics*. Polity.
Sloterdijk, P. (2020b). *After God*. Polity.
Smith, M. J. (2012). Utility, fraternity, and reconciliation: Ancient slavery as a context for the return of Onesimus. In Johnson, M. V., Noel, J. A., & Williams, D. K. (Eds.), *Onesimus our brother: Reading religion, race and culture in Philemon* (pp. 47–58). Fortress Press.
Spector, C. (2016). *Éloges de l'Injustice: La philosophie face à la déraison*. Seuil.
Stein, T. (1998). Does the constitutional and democratic system work? The ecological crisis as a challenge to the political order of constitutional democracy. *Constellations, 4*(3), 420–449.
Stein, T. (2011). Sustainability of democracy: A consideration on the basis of its leading differences. In Raube, K., & Sattler, A. (Eds.), *Difference and democracy: Exploring potentials in Europe and beyond* (pp. 83–89). Campus.
Stengers, I. (2010). Including nonhumans in political theory: Opening Pandora's box? In Braun, B., & Whatmore, S. J. (Eds.), *Political matter: Technoscience, democracy, and public life* (pp. 3–34). University of Minnesota Press.
Stengers, I. (2015). *In catastrophic times: Resisting the coming barbarism* (A. Goffey, trans.). Open Humanities Press/Meson Press.
Stiegler, B. (1998). *Technics and time 1: The fault of Epimetheus*. Stanford University Press.
Stiegler, B. (2000). La fidélité aux limites de la déconstruction et les prothèses de la foi. *Alter: Revue de Phénoménologie, 8*, 237–263.

Stiegler, B. (2008). *Économie de l'hypermatériel et psychopouvoir*. Fayard.
Stiegler, B. (2009). *Technics and time 2: Disorientation*. Stanford University Press.
Stiegler, B. (2011a). *Technics and time 3: Cinematic time and the question of malaise*. Stanford University Press.
Stiegler, B. (2011b). *The decadence of industrial democracies: Disbelief and discredit, volume I*. Polity Press.
Stiegler, B. (2013). *Uncontrollable societies of disaffected individuals: Disbelief and discredit, volume II*. Polity Press.
Stiegler, B. (2014). *Symbolic misery, volume 1: The hyperindustrial epoch*. Polity Press.
Stiegler, B. (2015). *States of shock: Stupidity and knowledge in the 21st century*. Polity.
Stiegler, B. (2019). *"Il faut s'adapter," sur un nouvel impératif politique*. Gallimard.
Stiegler, B. (2019a). *The age of disruption: Technology and madness in computational capitalism*. Polity Press.
Stiegler, B. (2019b). A conversation about Christianity with Alain Jugnon, Jean-Luc Nancy and Bernard Stiegler. In *The age of disruption: Technology and madness in computational capitalism* (pp. 315-329). Polity Press.
Stiegler, B. (2020). *Nanjing lectures: 2016-2019* (D. Ross, ed. & trans.). Humanities Press.
Strauss, L. (1978). *Thoughts on Machiavelli*. University of Chicago Press.
Strauss, L. (1996). Notes on the concept of the political. In C. Schmitt, *The concept of the political* (pp. 83-107). University of Chicago Press.
Strauss, L. (1997). *Spinoza's critique of religion*. University of Chicago Press.
Strauss, L. (2002). *The early writings (1921-1932)*. State University of New York Press.
Strauss, L. (2007a). The living issues of German postwar philosophy (1940). In H. Meier, *Leo Strauss and the theologico-political problem* (pp. 115-139). Cambridge University Press.
Strauss, L. (2007b). Reason and revelation (1948). In H. Meier, *Leo Strauss and the theologico-political problem* (pp. 141-180). Cambridge University Press.
Strauss, L. (2013a). Religious situation of the present (1930). In Yaffe, M. D., & Ruderman, R. S. (Eds.), *Reorientation: Leo Strauss in the 1930s* (pp. 225-235). Palgrave Macmillan.
Strauss, L. (2013b). The intellectual situation of the present (1932). In Yaffe, M. D., & Ruderman, R. S. (Eds.), *Reorientation: Leo Strauss in the 1930s* (pp. 237-253). Palgrave Macmillan.
Sutherland, P. (2019). Peter Sloterdijk and the 'security architecture of existence': Immunity, autochthony, and ontological nativism. *Theory, Culture and Society, 36*(7-8), 193-214.
Suuronen, V. (2021). Carl Schmitt as a theorist of the 1933 Nazi revolution: 'The difficult task of rethinking and recultivating traditional concepts.'" *Contemporary Political Theory, 20*, 341-363.

Szendy, P. (2016, August 14). Peter Szendy: Katechon. *Political Concepts*. Accessed March 25, 2021, from https://www.politicalconcepts.org/katechon-peter-szendy/#fn9.
Tarizzo, D. (2012). What is a political subject? *Politica Comun*, 1. https://doi.org/10.3998/pc.12322227.0001.001.
Tarizzo, D. (2018). Europe, neoliberalism, and the retreat of political philosophy. *Griffith Law Review, 27*(4), 439–452.
Taubes, J. (2003). *The political theology of Paul*. Stanford University Press.
Thornton, H. (2002). Cain, Abel and Thomas Hobbes. *History of Political Thought, 23*(4), 611–633.
Tolmie, D. F. (Ed.). (2010). *Philemon in perspective: Interpreting a Pauline letter*. De Gruyter.
Tolmie, D. F. (2017). "A beloved brother in the Lord": On the reception of Christology and ethics in Philemon 15–16 In Tolmie, D. F., & Venter, R. (Eds.), *Making sense of Jesus: Experiences, interpretations and identities* (pp. 66–83). Sun Press.
Treiber, H. (2020). *Reading Max Weber's sociology of law*. Oxford University Press.
Ulmen, G. (1985). The sociology of the state: Carl Schmitt and Max Weber. *State, Culture and Society, 1*(2), 3–57.
Urbinati, N. (2019). *Me the people: How populism transforms democracy*. Harvard University Press.
Vandenbloom, L. (2020). The faith of the Black Lives Matter movement. *Religion Unplugged*. Accessed March 11, 2021, from https://religionunplugged.com/news/2020/7/10/the-faith-of-the-black-lives-matter-movement.
Vargas, J. P. A. (2021). Populism, acclamation, and democracy: The politics of glory in the populist era. *Constellations*, 1–15. https://doi.org/10.1111/1467-8675.12581.
Vattimo, G. (1999). *Belief*. Polity Press.
Vattimo, G. (2002). *After Christianity* (L. D'Isanto, trans.). Columbia University Press.
Vattimo, G. (2007). Towards a nonreligious Christianity. In Caputo, J. D., & Vattimo, G., *After the Death of God* (J. W. Robbins, ed.; pp. 27–47). Columbia University Press.
Vidal, F. (2007). Miracles, science, and testimony in post-tridentine saint-making. *Science in Context, 20*(3), 481–508.
Vinx, L. (2015). *Guardian of the constitution: Hans Kelsen and Carl Schmitt on the Limits of Constitutional Law*. Cambridge University Press.
Vinx, L., & Zeitlin, S. G. (2021). *Carl Schmitt's early legal theoretical writings: Statute and judgment and the value of the state and the significance of the individual*. Cambridge University Press.

Virno, P. (2008). *The multitude: Between innovation and negation* (I. Bertoletti, J. Cascaito, & A. Cason, trans.). Semiotext(e).

Voegelin, E. (2000). *Modernity without restraint: The collected works of Eric Voegelin, volume 5* (M. Henningsen, ed.). University of Missouri Press.

Vorenberg, M. (2004). *Final freedom: The Civil War, the abolition of slavery, and the Thirteenth Amendment*. Cambridge University Press.

Wacker, B. (1996). Vor einigen Jahren kam einmal ein Professor aus Bonn . . . : Der Briefwechsel Carl Schmitt. In Wacker, B. (Ed.), *Dionysius DADA Areopagita: Hugo Ball und die Kritik der Moderne* (pp. 207–239). Ferdinand Schöningh.

Weber, M. (1998). Preliminary report on a proposed survey for a sociology of the press. *History of the Human Sciences, 11*(2), 111–120.

Wessels, G. F. (2010). The Letter to Philemon in the context of slavery in early Christianity. In Tolmie, D. F. (Ed.), *Philemon in perspective: Interpreting a Pauline letter* (pp. 143–168). De Gruyter.

White, L. (1967). The historical roots of our ecological crisis. *Science, 155*(3767), 1203–1207.

Wiedemann, E. (2020/21). La réalisation optimale de l'idéal démocratique par l'extension du marché selon Milton Friedman. *Consecutio Rerum, 9*(1), 69–96. http://www.consecutio.org/wp-content/uploads/2021/11/CR9.

Williams, D. K. (2012a). "No longer as a slave": Reading the interpretation history of Paul's Epistle to Philemon. In Johnson, M. V., Noel, J. A., & Williams, D. K. (Eds.), *Onesimus our brother: Reading religion, race and culture in Philemon* (pp. 11–45). Fortress Press.

Williams, D. K. (2012b). African American approaches: Rehumanizing the reader against racism and reading through experience. In Marchal, J. A. (Ed.), *Studying Paul's letters: Contemporary perspectives and methods* (pp. 155–172). Fortress Press.

Wolter, M. (2010). The Letter to Philemon as ethical counterpart of Paul's doctrine of justification. In Tolmie, D. F. (Ed.), *Philemon in perspective: Interpreting a Pauline letter* (pp. 169–180). De Gruyter.

Yelle, R. A. (2019). *Sovereignty and the sacred: Secularism and the political economy of religion*. University of Chicago Press.

Zarka, Y.-C. (2005). *Un détail nazi dans la pensée de Carl Schmitt: La justification des lois de Nuremberg du 15 Septembre 1935*. Suivis de deux textes de Carl Schmitt. PUF.

Zeitlin, S. G. (2020). Indirection and the rhetoric of tyranny: Carl Schmitt's *The Tyranny of Values* 1960-1967. *Modern Intellectual History, 18*(2). https://doi.org/10.1017/S1479244319000398.

Index

Agamben, Giorgio, 2, 8, 12, 14, 17–18, 24, 85, 147, 172–175, 192n5, 194n5, 195n10, n12, 203n7, 206n23, 209n6
Agenda for Sustainable Development Goals 2030, 186
anarchism, 9, 14, 157, 173, 191n4, 193n2, 204n9, 209n5; Schmitt's engagement with, 7, 26–28, 48, 83, 157, 171
Anders, Günther, 176
animals, 12, 80, 84–88, 198n4, 198–199n6; human/non-human binary, 84–87, 199n8
anomie, 15, 169–171, 173–175
Anthropocene, the, 12, 53, 148, 156, 182, 188–189, 197n2, 199n7; and political theology, 4–5, *see* Chapter 4, 75–95 *passim*, 162–163, 175
anthropocentrism, 5, 12, 76–78, 81–86, 89–90, 177, 189, 198n4, 199n6
Antichrist, 14, 163–164, 169–171, 173–174
Apocalypse, 8, 90–91, 149, 162–163, 165, 168, 208n1
Article 48 of Weimar Constitution, 22, 24, 130, 205n21
Augustine, Saint, 180, 209n8
autoimmunity, 8, 20, 174n1, 207n8

Bakunin, Mikhail, 7, 26–28, 38–39, 157, 192n5, 208n18; *see also* Anarchism
Balibar, Étienne, 11, 58, 71, 181, 197n30
Ball, Hugo, 7, 10–11, 37–44, 49–50, 192n3, 192n4, 192n5, 193n7, 193n9
Barth, Karl, 4
Benjamin, Walter, 9, 19, 24, 156–157, 172–173, 208n17
biopolitics, 18, 53
Black Lives Matter, 148, 197n27; *see also* New protest movements
Bloch, Ernst, 14, 155–157
Blumenberg, Hans, 3, 77–78, 103, 192n8
Böckenförde, Ernst-Wolfgang, and the German Federal Republic, 117; critique of Catholicism, 118–120; Böckenförde-Diktum, 13, 120–123, 133–137; ethical state, 123–127; civil religion, 127–128; state of exception, 128–131
Bolsonaro, Jair, 88, 141, 188, 207n7
Bonald, de Louis, 24
Book of Revelations, 60, 168, 208n1
Brexit, 6
Buber, Martin, 9, 158
Burke, Edmund, 23

Cacciari, Massimo

Cain and Abel, 66, 83–84, 196n18
care, ethics of, 5, 15, 168, 175–179, 183, 189; *see also* Pulcini, Elena
Christian eschatology, 75, 149–151, 153, 155–157, 163–164, 169, 171–174, 176
Christian political theology, and Jewish political theology, 9, 156; and Islamic political theology, 9
Cimatti, Felice, 85–87, 199n7, n9, n11, climate change, 78, 80–81, 90–92, 94, 164–165, 180, 185, 197; *see also* Anthropocene
Cohen, Hermann, 9
community, political, 22, 40, 68, 81–83, 87–88, 93, 106, 139, 140, 143, 175–176; Christian, 58, 62–64, 66, 75, 135, 181, 194n5, 195n12, 196n15; mystical, 157–158; communitarianism, 4, 165, 176, 181
conservatism, 24, 29, 120, 142, 150, 189; religious, 3, 29, 140, 188; revolutionary, 10, 22–23, 26, 27, 32, 164, 175, 188
conspiracy theories, 2, 17, 139–140, 167, 169, 193, 207n5
constituting power, 24, 30–32, 147, 173; and destituting power, 147
cosmopolitanism, 5, 9, 15, 83, 88, 92, 141l and Christian theology, 152–153, 179–181; cosmpolitics, 94, 181–183
COVID-19 pandemic, 12, 50, 78, 80–81, 138–139, 143, 148–149, 162, 167–168, 185, 188; states' response to, 2, 18–19, 50
culture wars, 28–29, 31, 187

Däubler, Theodor, 99, 200n1
Deleuze, Gilles and Guattari, Felix, 12, 86, 93, 203n26

dictatorship, 24, 27, 30, 32, 39–43, 145, 193n8
Donoso Cortés, Juan, 26–27, 39–40, 42, 48

ecological entanglement, 6, 12, 78–79, 84, 88, 93–94, 177, 179, 182–183, 198n4; *see also* Keller, Catherine
end of times, 90, 149, 163–164, 167–171
Esposito, Roberto, 11, 38, 54–55, 66–68, 196n19, 196n22, 202n20
Extinction Rebellion XR, 148–149, 197n27; *see also* New protest movements

Frankfurt School, 151
fraternity, 11, 53, 66–72, 75, 192n2, 194n3, 194n20, 194n21
French Revolution, 24, 67, 118, 121
Freudian theory, 66–67, 69, 196n19
friend/enemy opposition, 10–11, 13–14, 21–22, 33–34, 45, 47, 50, 70–72, 75, 82, 86, 91, 93, 101, 103, 105–106, 110, 118, 124, 134, 143, 183

Gaia, 78, 89–92
Garden of Eden, 83–84
Global Financial Crisis (2008), 187
globalization, 6, 92, 109, 141, 143, 162, 165, 176, 178, 180–182, 185–187, 204n14, 206n3
Gregory of Nyssa, 93

Habermas, Jürgen, 3, 33–34, 125, 137, 192n7, 204n10
Haraway, Donna, 198n4
Hayek, Friedrich, 53, 193n19; *see also* neoliberalism
Heidegger, Martin, 104–106

Heller, Hermann, 124, 204n8
Hobbes, Thomas, 2, 11, 22, 26, 31, 40, 45–46, 48–49, 59, 61, 66–67, 81, 101, 133–134, 164, 170, 191n3, 193n14, 196n18, 198n6

identity politics, 14, 32–33, 87–88, 144, 176–177
immigration, 110–111, 141, 143, 176, 185, 207n5
Indignados, 146
Intergovernmental Panel on Climate Change (IPCC 2021), 80

John of Patmos, 165; *see also* Book of Revelations
Jonas, Hans, 177
Judaism, 9, 14, 44, 61, 152, 156–158, 191n4
Judeo-Christian tradition, 12, 76, 80, 84, 89, 155
Justice, 37–38, 75, 83, 92, 119, 138–140, 151, 153, 157, 161, 163, 177–179, 182–183, 189, 192n2, 198n3; racial, 137, 148; ecological, 14, 84, 137, 148, 151–152, 158, 161; neoliberalism's occlusion of, 37, 50–53

katechon, 3, 14–15, 57, 102, 159, 161–176, 188, 192n2, 194n2, 194n3, 195n9, 200n8, 209n4
Keller, Catherine, 6, 12, 92–94, 179, 208n1
Kelsen, Hans, 25, 58, 191n2
Kingdom of God, 8, 84, 151, 155, 163, 172, 189

Landauer, Gustav, 14, 157–158, 204n9
Latour, Bruno, 12, 89–92

League of Nations, 82
Letter to Philemon, 11, 57–58, 61–66, 70, 72, 192n2, 194n3, 194n5, 195n11, 195n12, 196n15, 196n17
liberal democracy, crisis of legitimacy, 1–5, 7, 9, 14, 1, 34–35, 137, 161, 166, 186
liberalism, 37, 50, 126, 142, 152; Schmitt's critique of, 4, 11, 13, 26–29, 31, 39, 44–50, 53, 60, 71–72, 77, 118, 125, 144, 157, 171, 193n13, 195n8, 197n29
liberation theology, 8, 149, 151–152, 155, 207n11
lockdowns, 2, 17, 139
Löwith, Karl, 155

Maistre, de Joseph, 23, 39–40, 42
Marxism, 155–157, 207n11
Meister Eckhart, 157
messianism, 8, 14, 138, 142, 149, 151, 155–158, 163, 166–167, 172–176, 189, 194n5, 195n12, 203n7
Metz, Johann Baptist, 14, 149–151, 153, 156, 179, 208n14
miracles, 3, 7, 26, 40, 58–61, 75, 195n6, 195n7
Modi, Narendra, 88
Moltmann, Jürgen, 4, 7–8, 14, 149–153, 155, 179, 208n15
Mouffe, Chantal, 5, 33–34
Mühlmann, Heiner, 107–108, 111, 201n16
Müller, Adam, 24

Nancy, Jean-Luc, 58, 66, 68–69, 71, 178, 196n20, 196n21, 196n22, 196n23, 196n24, 196n25, 196n26
nation state, 8, 81–83, 91–92, 110–111, 153, 162, 166–167, 175–176, 186, 188

nationalism, 29, 33, 35, 67, 90, 137, 140, 143, 154, 206n3
National socialism, 1–2, 20, 22, 34, 117–119, 139, 150, 162, 203n3
neoliberalism, 2, 4, 14, 51–53, 81, 93, 139, 158, 165–166, 174, 187–189, 193n18, 193n19, 194n20; and liberalism, 11, 31, 37, 50–51
new protest movements, 13–14, 137–138, 146–149, 152, 155, 158, 161, 182, 189, 197n27
Nicholas of Cusa, 93
nihilism, 2, 10, 14, 20, 22, 90, 113, 150, 161, 167–168, 171, 174, 178

Occupy Wall Street, 146
Onesimus, 11, 58, 62–66, 75, 194n5, 196n15
Órban, Viktor, 23, 141–142, 188

Paris Climate Agreement 2015, 81, 186
Paul, Saint, 11, 14, 57–58, 60–66, 68, 70, 79, 102, 159, 163–164, 168–170, 172–173, 180, 192n2, 194n3, 195n9, 195n11, 195n12, 195n14, 196n15, 196n17, 196n18, 200n8, 209n7
Peterson, Erik, 3, 9, 44, 102, 120, 171, 191n3, 193n4, 208n12, 209n8
political romanticism, 23, 38–39, 43, 99, 116
political religion, 139–140, 152; see also Voegelin, Eric
populism, 2, 4, 6, 13–14, 23, 29–30, 32–35, 50, 87–88, 90–92, 137–138, 146–149, 154–155, 158, 161, 166, 168, 175–176, 186, 188, 192n5, 206n3, 206n4, 207n9; and political theology, 140–146
Porto Alegre summit, 182
postcolonialism, 62
post-humanism, 89, 104

post-industrial society, 138–139, 202n24
post-truth, 2, 91, 139, 167; see also conspiracy theories
process theology, 6, 93–94; see also Whitehead, A. N.
Protestant Reformation, 41, 121, 169
Proudhon, Pierre-Joseph, 26, 83, 157, 180, 200n1, 202n18
Pulcini, Elena, 176–179
Putin, Vladimir, 141

revolution, 1–2, 8, 20, 24, 26, 28, 30, 67, 118, 147, 155–157, 161–163, 171, 173; and counter-revolution, 1–2, 14, 20, 22–24, 27–28, 164, 188
rights, 11, 15, 34, 67, 82–83, 121, 138, 142, 148–149, 152–153, 166, 178, 181–182, 186, 189, 200n4, 209n3; non-human/ecological, 88, 180, 182, 199n10
Roman Catholicism, 3, 5, 7, 9–10, 28, 39–43, 49, 100, 150, 171, 188
Roman Empire, 8, 11, 58, 61–63, 163, 170, 172, 209n4
Roman law, 58, 61–62
Rosenzweig, Franz, 9
Rousseau, Jean-Jacques, 32, 127–128, 204n16, 205n17, 205n18, 205n19, 207n9

Schmitt, Carl, oeuvre, 6–7; legacy and reception, 1–7; and political theology, 7–9; and National Socialism, 1–2, 22, 39, 119, 203n3
Second Coming of Christ, 14, 163, 169, 175
Second Letter to the Corinthians, 60, 195n12
Second Letter to the Thessalonians, 57, 168–169; see also *Katechon*
Second Vatican Council, 29, 118

secularism, 1, 3-4, 10, 20-21, 25-26, 28-29, 34-35, 42-43, 58, 77-78, 89-91, 120-123, 125-130, 134-135, 139, 142, 150-153, 155-156, 169, 179, 183, 192n8; post-secularism, 14, 137-138, 146-149, 181, 189
Silicon Valley Big Tech, 166-167
slavery, 4, 11, 58, 62-66, 148, 194n5, 195n12, 195n13, 196n16
Sloterdijk, Peter, 13, 98, 103-111, 201n11, 201n12, 201n13, 201n14, 201n16, 201n16, 201n17, 202n18, 202n19, 202n20
sovereign state of exception, 1-3, 8, 10, 13, 17-20, 22-26, 42, 50, 58, 75, 81, 93, 106-107, 118, 128, 130-134, 147, 150, 156-157, 171-172, 174, 188, 192n8, 198n6, 205n21, 205n22, 206n24
Steigler, Bernard, 13, 98, 111-116, 139, 202n21, 202n22, 202n24, 202n25, 203n26, 208n8
Strauss, Leo, 7, 9-11, 37, 44-50, 193n12, 193n14, 193n15, 193n17

Taubes, Jacob, 7-9, 171, 173, 196n18
technology, 13, 97, 104-111, 112-114, 189, 208n3; Schmitt's critique of, 2, 6-7, 12, 20-22, 35, 76-77, 97-102, 111, 115-116, 171, 202n23; biotechnology, 154, 165, 202n25, 208n15; techno-feudalism, 166-167
Tertullian, 164, 170
Thiel, Peter, 167
Trump, Donald, 6, 23, 88, 140-141, 188, 206n2, 207n6, 207n7

Ukraine war, 162, 166, 185, 191n2
UN Human Rights Convention, 186
Universal Declaration for the Rights of Mother Earth (2012), 88
Universalism, 70-72, 109-110, 152-154, 180-181, 197n27, 197n30, 209n7

Voegelin, Eric, 139-140

war on terror, 1, 32
Weber, Max, 26, 99-100, 200n2, 200n3, 200n4
Weimar Constitution, 1-2, 22, 24, 100, 119, 191n2, 200n5, 205n21
Weimar Republic, 10, 13, 19-20, 25, 31, 101, 103, 118, 130, 144
Whitehead, Alfred North, 6, 93

www.ingramcontent.com/pod-product-compliance
Lightning Source LLC
Chambersburg PA
CBHW020650230426
43665CB00008B/381